Witchcraft at Salem

Witchcraft
at
Salem

CHADWICK HANSEN

GEORGE BRAZILLER

NEW YORK

He who believes in the Devil, already belongs to him.

THOMAS MANN, *Doctor Faustus*

FOR BETTY

Preface

The purpose of this book is to try to set straight the record of the witchcraft phenomena at Salem, Massachusetts, in the year 1692, about which much has been written and much misunderstood. The more I studied the documents of what actually took place in the community, and what was actually said and written by the participants, the more I found myself in opposition to the traditional interpretation of these events. It seemed to me that a serious reconsideration of them was in order. But I could see no point in employing the common revisionist technique of quarreling with my predecessors item by item and person by person, for to do so would be to bury the account of what did happen in an immense and tedious analysis of what did not. What was needed was a fresh and objective review of the entire matter.

The traditional interpretation of what happened at Salem is as much the product of casual journalism and imaginative literature as it is of historical scholarship. It might be summarized as follows: (1) no witchcraft was practiced in Massachusetts; (2) the behavior of the "afflicted" persons, including their convulsive fits, was fraudulent and designed chiefly to call attention to themselves; (3) the afflicted persons were inspired, stimulated, and encouraged by the clergy (especially Cotton Mather), who used the fear of witchcraft as a means of bolstering their flagging power in the community; (4) the clergy whipped the general populace into a state of "mass hysteria" with their sermons and writings on witchcraft; (5) the only significant opposition to the proceedings at Salem came from the merchant class, specifically from Thomas Brattle and

Robert Calef; and (6) the executions were unique in Western civilization, and therefore monstrous, and attributable to some narrowness or fanaticism or repressiveness peculiar to Puritans.

Yet the facts are quite contrary to these common assumptions. To begin with, witchcraft actually did exist and was widely practiced in seventeenth-century New England, as it was in Europe at that time (and still is, for that matter, among the unlearned majority of mankind). It worked then as it works now in witchcraft societies like those of the West Indies, through psychogenic rather than occult means, commonly producing hysterical symptoms as a result of the victim's fear, and sometimes, when fear was succeeded by a profound sense of hopelessness, even producing death.

The behavior of the afflicted persons was not fraudulent but pathological. They were hysterics, and in the clinical rather than the popular sense of that term. These people were not merely overexcited; they were mentally ill. Furthermore, they were ill long before any clergyman got to them.

The general populace did reach that state of public excitement inaccurately called "mass hysteria," but this was due to the popular fear of witchcraft rather than to the preachings of the clergy. The public excitement continued well after the leadership, both clerical and secular, had called a halt to the witchcraft proceedings. In fact the clergy were, from beginning to end, the chief opponents to the events at Salem. In particular, Cotton Mather was anything but the wild-eyed fanatic of tradition. Throughout most of the proceedings he was a model of restraint and caution, and at one point he went further than any of his colleagues dared go in proposing a method to protect the innocent.

The writings of Brattle and Calef came too late to have any significant influence on the course of events in Massachusetts.

Finally, the executions at Salem were by no means unique. Belief in witchcraft was quite as common among seventeenth-century Anglicans, Quakers, Lutherans, and Catholics as it was among Puritans. Executions for witchcraft reached their height in Western civilization during the seventeenth century and continued in Europe until the end of the following century, more than a hundred years after the outbreak at Salem.

Thomas Hutchinson was the first historian to conclude that the events at Salem had been nothing but "fraud and imposture." Yet he also recorded that at the time his history was published—1750—there were "a great number of persons" who thought the afflicted girls had "been under bodily disorders which affected their imaginations," and some, "perhaps but few," who believed them to have been possessed. Hutchinson was aware that there was nothing unusual about outbreaks of witchcraft in the seventeenth century, and aware as well of the force of popular credulity; his account is much more balanced than those of most of his successors.

Very nearly the least balanced of those successors was the Reverend Charles Wentworth Upham, who published his *Lectures on Witchcraft* in 1831, and followed this with his two-volume *Salem Witchcraft*, which has remained the standard history, in 1867. Upham had been a minister of Salem and then its mayor. He was as interested in genealogy and local history as in witchcraft, and therefore he outlined in considerable detail the village quarrels he thought to be one cause of the events. (He did this as he seems to have done everything, with much inaccuracy; the history of petty malice in Essex County remains to be written.) In his rambling tomes—so nearly incoherent that they could not be divided into chapters—Upham suggested a great many other causes for the witchcraft, many of them conflicting. But the overall impression he leaves is that the entire affair was a monstrous conspiracy, in which the ministers and magistrates took advantage of the fraudulent behavior of the afflicted girls to exercise a mindless and irresponsible power at the expense of the suffering community. His particular villain was Cotton Mather. Taking his cue from Robert Calef, he represented Mather as the man who "got up" Salem witchcraft.

W. F. Poole challenged Upham's view in a long article in the

North American Review (April, 1869). Some of Poole's arguments were cogent enough, but unfortunately his strongest appeals were to ancestral piety and clerical solidarity—he was shocked that Upham had attacked a fellow-clergyman. Therefore it was relatively easy for Upham to demolish Poole in a rebuttal published in *The Historical Magazine* (September, 1869). In the process he gave an abundant display of the paranoia that made a conspiratorial theory of history so attractive to him. Yet it was the consensus of the historical profession that he had won the argument, and George Bancroft adopted the conspiratorial thesis in his monumental *History of the United States of America.*

According to John Fiske, Bancroft's account was nothing but secondhand Upham "embellished with cheap rhetoric." This is not entirely fair, since Bancroft did bring narrative coherence to Upham's view, and this was no mean achievement. But he also introduced a series of errors of his own invention and simplified the issues in the interest of a melodramatic style that fully deserves Fiske's criticism. Since Upham was virtually unreadable Bancroft's account became the main, and often the only, source for innumerable lesser histories, including almost all school histories. His influence extended far beyond the schoolbooks; Lecky's account of the Salem trials is based on Bancroft, and he is also the model for such twentieth-century anti-Puritan historians as Beard, Parrington, and James Truslow Adams. The central line of erroneous interpretation, then, descends from Robert Calef to Upham to Bancroft, and from Bancroft through innumerable channels to the current popular view.

Many writers have taken exception to one point or another in the traditional interpretation. The point raised most often has been that witchcraft trials were not at all unusual in the seventeenth century; that they were in fact typical of Western civilization at that time. George Lyman Kittredge has put it best:

The Salem outbreak was not due to Puritanism; it is not assignable to any peculiar temper on the part of our New England ancestors; it is no sign of exceptional bigotry or abnormal superstition. Our forefathers believed in witchcraft, not because they were Puritans, not because they were Colonials, not because they were New Englanders,—but because they were men of their time. They shared the feelings and beliefs of the best hearts and wisest heads of the seventeenth century. What more can be asked of them?[1]

And he added that

it is hard to satisfy modern writers on witchcraft, who insist on censuring the sixteenth and seventeenth century on a basis of modern rationalism. It is quite certain that if some of those who now sit in judgment on the witch-prosecutors had been witch judges, no defendant would ever have escaped.[2]

The same issue has been raised, with varying degrees of incisiveness, by John Fiske, Edward Eggleston, W. F. Poole, Kenneth B. Murdock, Samuel Eliot Morison, and many others, including Perry Miller,[3] who protested that on this point further refutation had become a bore. But boring or not, the refutation has not taken hold. The common scholar as well as the common man has continued to believe that there was something peculiarly puritanical about the Salem trials.

A second exception has been that Cotton Mather was not, as Calef put it, "very forward" in carrying on witchcraft examinations, that in fact he counseled moderation throughout the trials. W. F. Poole saw this. So, among others, did Longfellow, Barrett Wendell, Samuel Eliot Morison, and Marion L. Starkey.[4] But none of them seems to have recognized how very far the younger Mather went in attempting to protect the innocent, nor how thoroughly Calef lied about Mather's treatment of Margaret Rule. Starkey, for one, accepts Calef's lies at face value and consequently makes Mather out to be little better than a fool.

A third departure from the traditional interpretation has been to call the behavior of the afflicted persons hysterical. George M. Beard was the first to do so, and he has been followed by John Fiske, Winfield S. Nevins, Perry Miller, and Marion L. Starkey,[5] among others. Yet no one who has used the word "hysterical" seems to have fully realized its implications. The difficulty lies in the fact that the word has different meanings in common usage from those it has in medical usage. In the former it means little more than a state of excitement in which the subject may temporarily lose self-control. The afflicted persons at Salem were in a far worse state than that. Their condition was pathological, and much more serious than has previously been supposed. Marion L. Starkey makes a diagnosis of hysteria the very basis of *The Devil in Massachusetts*. Yet because she confuses the popular and the medical meanings of the term she regards the Salem girls' behavior as more fraudulent than pathological, and in the long run her interpretation differs only in detail from that of Upham. In her case and in others this popular usage has led finally to little more than inaccurate talk about "mass hysteria."

Finally, and most significantly, a few persons have recognized that image magic was actually employed in Massachusetts, and at least two have wondered whether there might not have been something behind the charges of witchcraft after all. Poole tells us that Longfellow examined some of the seventeenth-century narratives before composing his play on the Salem trials, *Giles Corey of the Salem Farms*. Longfellow was learned enough to recognize that Cotton Mather's suspicions had been aroused by concrete evidence of image magic. He also recognized that Mather had counseled judicial caution. That was as far as he got, but it was much farther than most. *Giles Corey* is a bad play, but it is much better history than most of the historians have written. Barrett Wendell also knew there had been image magic at Salem and was startled to discover that nineteenth-century spiritualists were believers in the possibility of accomplishing harm through such means. He went so far as to compare the Salem trial evidence to his own experiences with spiritualism; this comparison is the central substance of his article, "Were the Salem Witches Guiltless?"[6] and of his handling of witchcraft in his biography of Cotton Mather. But spiritualism was a blind alley, and Wendell never got further than wondering whether there might not have been something to the charges after all.

David R. Proper, formerly librarian of Essex Institute, tells me that Kittredge suspected there might have been witchcraft practiced at Salem. However, he did not pursue his suspicions; at least I have not been able to discover any further evidence that would lead me to believe otherwise. Finally, the late dean of twentieth-century New England studies, Perry Miller, knew there had been image magic in the Glover case of 1688 at Boston, yet he was unable to take seriously a practice he found so contemptible.[7] But it has to be taken seriously. One cannot fully understand any aspect of the events at Salem without a recognition of the genuine power of witchcraft in a society that believes in it. The failure to appreciate this fact has vitiated all previous accounts of witchcraft at Salem.

Since previous historians have been of relatively minor use to me I have depended very heavily upon both trial documents and contemporary narratives. At first I hoped to preserve the spelling and punctuation of the originals, but some of the trial documents employ spelling and punctuation so very deviant as to be incomprehensible to the literate nonspecialist. Therefore I have modernized the texts of the trial documents and, for the sake of consistency, the contemporary narratives as well. I have not, of course, modernized the diction, but where a word or a phrase seemed to me to present unusual difficulties to the common reader I have offered an explanation in brackets. It is true that in the process of modernization much of the rhetorical quality of a writer like Cotton Mather is lost, but perhaps in the present case the gain in clarity will be sufficient compensation.

Because I have depended so heavily on trial documents and because the majority of them are dated, I have not modernized dates, preserving the Old Style in order to simplify the task of anyone who wishes to consult the originals. I have, however, begun the year at January 1 because the documents generally do offer that alternative (e.g., 1691/2).

Like others working in this period I am deeply indebted to the American Antiquarian Society microprint edition of works in Evans' *American Bibliography* and to the University Microfilms edition of works in the *Short-Title Catalogue.* I am also particularly indebted to the staff of the Essex County Court House for permission to use the WPA transcript of witchcraft documents and to the staffs of the Essex County Court House, the Essex Institute, the Massachusetts Historical Society, and the New York Public Library for permission to check the transcript with original documents in their possession. For access to other materials I wish to thank the staffs of the Massachusetts Historical Society (especially Malcolm Freiberg, Editor of Publications), the Essex Institute (especially David R. Proper, former librarian), the American Antiquarian Society (especially James E. Mooney, Editor), the New York Public Library, the Library of Congress, and the libraries of Columbia University, Cornell University, Harvard University, Haverford College, the University of Pennsylvania, the Philadelphia College of Physicians, and the Pennsylvania State University (especially Charles W. Mann, Jr., Chief of Special Collections).

I also wish to thank the Pennsylvania State University for providing the sabbatical leave during which most of my manuscript was written, its Central Fund for Research for providing travel grants and a grant for photographs, its English Department for providing research assistants, and the assistants themselves: Terry Howard-Wallace and Ben Fiester.

My first attempt at formulating my early findings appeared under the title "Salem Witchcraft and DeForest's *Witching Times*" in *Essex Institute Historical Collections,*[8] and I thank David B. Little, Director and Editor, for permission to reprint portions of that article here.

A number of my colleagues have offered suggestions at various stages of my project—on talks which I gave on the subject as well as on portions of the manuscript. For such suggestions I am grateful to Professors Philip Young, Alan Trachtenberg, Harrison T. Meserole, and to Professor Alan Heimert of Harvard University.

I wish to thank my editor, Mr. Edwin Seaver, not only for

his suggestions concerning the manuscript, but also for his consistently cooperative attitude, which has made revision a pleasure rather than a chore.

Finally, I am much indebted to my family, and most particularly to my wife, who has been helpful in very many ways. Not the least of these was her happy recognition that there were no ulterior motives in my dedicating a book on witchcraft to her.

C. H.

Contents

1

$\Leftrightarrow\!\!\Leftrightarrow\!\!\Leftrightarrow\!\!\Leftrightarrow\!\!\Leftrightarrow$

Witchcraft

Early in the year 1692 several girls of Salem Village (now Danvers), Massachusetts, began to sicken and display alarming symptoms. The most disturbing and most frequent of these symptoms was convulsive fits: fits so grotesque and so violent that eyewitnesses agreed the girls could not possibly be acting. "Their motions in their fits," wrote the Reverend Deodat Lawson, "are preternatural, both as to the manner, which is so strange as a well person could not screw their body into; and as to the violence also it is preternatural, being much beyond the ordinary force of the same person when they are in their right mind."[1] The Reverend John Hale of Beverly confirmed Lawson's description. "Their arms, necks, and backs," he wrote, "were turned this way and that way, and returned back again, so as it was impossible for them to do of themselves, and beyond the power of any epileptic fits, or natural disease to effect."[2]

There were other symptoms almost equally alarming: temporary loss of hearing, speech, and sight; loss of memory, so that some of the girls could not recall what had happened to them in their fits; a choking sensation in the throat; loss of appetite. Later there were terrifying hallucinations; they saw specters who tormented them in a variety of ingenious and cruel ways. They felt themselves pinched and bitten, and often there were actual marks upon the skin.

These symptoms are readily recognizable. The most cursory examination of the classic studies of hysteria—of Charcot, of Janet, of Breuer and Freud—will demonstrate that the afflicted girls of Salem were hysterical in the scientific sense of that term.[3] It has, of course, been customary to call these girls hysterical, but only in the loosest and most popular sense of the word. Thus the same historians who have called them hysterical have also called them liars, although the terms are mutually exclusive so far as conscious motivation is concerned. With minor exceptions the girls' behavior belongs to the history of pathology rather than the history of fraud.

In any case, their behavior was both conspicuous and distressing. Two of them, Elizabeth Parris and Abigail Williams, were the daughter and niece of the Reverend Samuel Parris of Salem Village, and the Reverend Mr. Parris treated their affliction with those universal remedies of seventeenth-century Massachusetts, prayer and fasting. But he also did what you or I would do if our children began behaving in that fashion: he took them to the doctor—to a series of doctors, in fact—and he persuaded other parents and guardians to do the same. For some time the physicians were puzzled, but eventually one of them—tradition says it was Dr. William Griggs of Salem Village—produced a diagnosis. "The evil hand," he announced, "is upon them"; the girls were victims of malefic witchcraft.

The diagnosis was in no way unusual. The overwhelming majority of seventeenth-century physicians, like other learned men, believed in witchcraft and considered it the cause of some diseases. An instructive parallel to Doctor Griggs's opinion is that of Sir Thomas Browne, the celebrated author of *Religio Medici*, who was called as expert witness by an English witchcraft court convened at Bury St. Edmunds in 1664. He gave as his opinion:

that these swooning fits were natural, and nothing else but what they call the mother, but only heightened to a great excess by the subtlety of the Devil, co-operating with the malice of these which we term witches, at whose instance he doth these villainies.[4]

"The mother" was the common abbreviation for "the suffocation of the mother," one of the seventeenth-century English terms for hysteria; it referred to the choking sensation in the throat that was one of the commoner symptoms. Thus, Sir Thomas Browne was entirely correct in his indentification of the illness, and it is quite possible that Dr. Griggs, too, was right in whatever identification he made of the Salem symptoms.

What is more surprising is that Dr. Griggs was probably also correct in his identification of the cause. It does seem to have been witchcraft that was responsible for the girls' afflictions.

Witchcraft is not easy to define, because it is not, like the major formal religions, a coherent body of belief. But in Western civilization since prehistoric times there has been a loosely grouped body of magical lore—charms, spells, and so forth—having to do primarily with fertility and infertility, and with health and sickness, as well as a series of more marginal concerns, including the foretelling of the future. Such lore has obvious, if tenuous, connections with pre-Christian fertility worship, whose tutelary deity was a fertility god. Probably the commonest of such gods has been the deified sun, but the next most common was the deified herd animal, the cow, or, more often (because of his reputation for lechery) the goat. Half human and half bestial, with horns and cloven hooves, he appeared as Dionysus or Bacchus, the chief fertility god of the classical world, and was also to be found in the pantheons of northern Europe.[5] Apparently the early Christians thought him the most abominable of all the pagan deities; they gave his attributes, his horns and cloven hooves, to the Devil, adding to these the wings of the fallen angel.

That he was once an extraordinarily powerful god cannot be doubted; there are instances of his survival in pre-Christian form as late as the twentieth century. A traveler in southern Ireland during the thirties reported seeing villagers dance in a ring around a goat whose horns and hooves had been painted gold. They informed him that on the coming Sunday they would roast and eat it, because "they had done it always."[6] I myself have seen one survival of the horned god: the Austrian Krampus. He has now degenerated into a bogeyman for children. Black and furry, with horns and a contorted face, he is the companion of St. Nicholas, and attends to bad children while St. Nicholas attends the good. But Krampus' chief attribute is evidence that he is not really a children's deity. He carries a bundle of dried twigs, and the belief is that if he strikes you with them you will be sterile for a year—a punishment scarcely appropriate to naughty toddlers. Krampus is an Alpine inversion of the fertility god. He appears in December because that is the month of the winter solstice, when nature is most barren. In Styria, he is baked in bread and eaten—further evidence of his previous divinity. (Eating figures made of candy has little importance, but bread is the staff of life, and therefore the most common symbol for the body of a god, as in the Christian communion.)

The horned god's power may also be seen in the fact that medieval and renaissance artists frequently forgot to give him his Christian attribute, the fallen angel's wings, but never forgot his horns, the attribute that made him a fertility god. This is true not only of provincial works of art but also of those created for the centers of Western civilization. In the dome of the Baptistery at Florence, for example, is a mosaic "Last Judgment," and at the center of its Hell sits a Devil who is wingless but conspicuously horned. The same is true of the Devil in Giotto's "Last Judgment" in the Arena Chapel in Padua.

If the tutelary deity of witchcraft was the deified herd animal, this does not mean that everyone who has used a charm was a formal worshipper of Satan. Most of the tales of witches' Sabbaths strike one as either hallucinations or fictions. Nevertheless, not much more than two centuries ago everyone who used a charm believed he was making an appeal to dangerous occult forces, and at possible peril to his soul. But the degree of peril was relative, and proportionate to the degree of witchcraft which, like murder, comes in three degrees.

The first is the practice of white magic—charms or spells used for benevolent purposes. Carrying a rabbit's foot (the rabbit, like the goat, is notorious for its fertility) is white magic. So is nailing a horseshoe over the door (the open end must be upward, so the shape will suggest the horns of the herd animal). Since the intention was innocent, the practice of white magic was seldom a cause for official concern. It was, of course, an appeal to occult forces that were specifically non-Christian, and as such it could, and sometimes did, draw a stern verbal rebuke from the clergy. But that was all.

The second degree of witchcraft is black magic—magic used maliciously—and in the seventeenth century black magic was very serious indeed; it was an appeal to the Prince of Evil in order to accomplish evil.

The third degree is pact, where the witch is no longer merely invoking the Devil's aid through her charms and spells, but actually believes she has made a contract to serve him.

The popular view, and indeed the view of most historians, is that no actual witchcraft was practiced in New England. But this view is mistaken. It can be demonstrated that all three degrees of witchcraft were practiced there during the latter seventeenth century: white magic commonly; black magic not uncommonly, and pact on at least one occasion.

Before turning to the record, let us first consider why witchcraft was so serious a matter in the seventeenth century; why it was so widely practiced and believed in; and why in some instances the witch actually did succeed in harming her victim.

The penalties for witchcraft were relatively light in the early years of Christian history. In the seventh century Theodore, Archbishop of Canterbury, in his *Liber Poenitentialis,* considered the penance appropriate to a person who has been imitating "a stag or a bull; that is, making himself into a wild animal and dressing in the skin of a herd animal, and putting on the heads of beasts." To "those who in such wise transform themselves into the appearance of a wild animal" he assigned "penance for three years because this is devilish."[7] At this time paganism was still so widespread and Christianity so new that, according to the Venerable Bede, King Redwald of East Anglia "had in the same temple an altar to sacrifice to Christ and another to offer victims to demons."[8]

Elements of paganism remained strong throughout the

Middle Ages, inside the church as well as out. In 1282 the priest of Inverkeithing led a fertility dance around the churchyard.[9] And Giraldus Cambrensis (ca.1146–ca.1220) reported, "though I say it with tears," that there were priests who celebrate "masses over images of wax, to curse someone."[10] The remedy for such an appalling situation, Giraldus thought, was to ordain fewer priests and take more care in their selection. His advice, of course, was not followed, and members of the clergy continued to practice the black arts as late as the eighteenth century.

Toward the end of the Middle Ages and the beginning of the Renaissance both church and state began to take witchcraft more seriously. The crucial century was the fifteenth, which saw a number of important trials, including those of Joan of Arc, Gilles de Rais, and the Duchess of Gloucester. At the end of this century, in 1490, *Malleus Maleficarum* (*The Hammer of Witches*) was published. The authors were James Sprenger and Henry Kramer, two German Dominicans, and their book was published with the Papal Bull by which Innocent VIII gave them jurisdiction as Inquisitors for the Germanic countries. *Malleus* gave a thorough definition of witchcraft, with rules on how to investigate, try, and judge cases of witchcraft. It remained an important work for more than two hundred years; Increase Mather knew it and referred to it.

The publication of *Malleus Maleficarum* gives us a convenient date for the opening of that general war against the Devil which occupied all Christendom during the sixteenth and seventeenth centuries. The full horror of that warfare will never be known in all of its details. Even the statistics of convicted witches who were executed vary widely from one authority to another. But it is clear that the battle reached its height during the first half of the seventeenth century, when, for example, approximately nine hundred witches were burned in the single city of Bamberg, and approximately five thousand in the single province of Alsace.

It is at first thought surprising that witchcraft executions should have reached their height during the seventeenth century, which was, as we have all been taught, the century that produced most of the seminal ideas of modern science. Whitehead called it "the century of genius," and with good reason. In English science alone it was the time of Bacon, who first saw the possibilities of an inductive scientific method; of Robert Boyle, who in *The Skeptical Chemist* replaced the four Aristotelian elements (earth, air, fire, and water) with the modern definition of an element as a chemically irreducible substance, and thus made modern chemistry possible; of Newton, who laid the mathematical and mechanical foundations of classical physics. The difficulty is that we tend to remember these men only for those ideas we still value, forgetting the other contents of their minds.

We forget that Bacon believed you could cure warts by rubbing them with a rind of bacon and hanging it out of a window that faced south, and that witchcraft may take place "by a tacit operation of malign spirits."[11] We forget that Boyle believed in an astonishing and repulsive variety of medicaments, including stewed earthworms, a worsted stocking that has long been worn next to the flesh, and human urine. The latter substance, taken both internally and externally, was one of the favorite items in his pharmacopoeia; it would, he thought, "require rather a whole book than a part of an essay, to enumerate and insist on" its "medical virtues."[12] It was Boyle who proposed that English miners be interviewed as to whether they "meet with any subterraneous demons; and if they do, in what shape and manner they appear; what they portend, and what they do."[13] And Newton, the greatest scientist of his age, spent more of his time on the occult than he did in the study of physics. He explicated, for example, apocalyptic passages in the Bible, and interpreted the measurements of Solomon's temple, hoping in both cases that a mystic reading of the scriptures would lead him to the inmost secrets of the universe.

We should remember also that the seventeenth century firmly believed in a dualistic universe: in a material or visible world, and a spiritual or invisible world as well. Heaven was still a concrete reality, as were the Angels who inhabited it; so was Hell and its Devils. As John Locke argued in his *Essay Concerning Human Understanding*:

if this notion of immaterial spirit may have, perhaps, some difficulties in it not easily to be explained, we have therefore no more reason to deny or doubt the existence of such spirits, than we have to deny or doubt the existence of body; because the notion of body is cumbered with some difficulties very hard, and perhaps impossible to be explained or understood by us.[14]

Like other learned men of his time, Locke not only believed in a world of spirits, but that spirits can appear in this material world: "that Spirits can assume to themselves bodies of different bulk, figure, and conformation of parts."[15] To be sure, Locke warned that "universal certainty" concerning the world of spirits was beyond us; we could know it, he thought, only as it impinges on our senses. But that, of course, is precisely what was thought to happen in witchcraft.

And Locke is typical. Scientists, philosophers, lawyers, physicians, the learned community in general believed firmly in the existence of an invisible world, and in the capacity of the inhabitants of that world to intrude on this one. There were, of course, some exceptions: a few materialists—Sadducees, the pious called them, after the ancient Jewish sect who doubted the existence of spirits. The arch-materialist was Thomas Hobbes. "The universe," he wrote,

that is, the whole mass of things that are, is corporeal, that is to say, body, and hath the dimensions of magnitude, namely length, breadth, and depth; also, every part of body is likewise body, and hath the like dimensions, and consequently every part of the universe is body, and that which is not body is no part of the universe: and because the universe is all, that which is no part of it is nothing, and consequently nowhere.[16]

Hobbes's statement that spirit is "nowhere" is as uncompromising a statement of materialism as we have ever had; one would expect such a man to be skeptical of witchcraft. A man who did not believe in an invisible world would scarcely give credence to what Cotton Mather called "the wonders of the invisible world."

Hobbes was a skeptic, but his skepticism was rather different in character from that of the nineteenth or twentieth century. "As for witches," he wrote in his *Leviathan*, "I think not that their witchcraft is any real power; but yet that they are justly punished, for the false belief they have that they can do such mischief, joined with their purpose to do it if they can; their trade being nearer to a new religion than to a craft or science."[17] (The last clause is remarkably perceptive, although it was, of course, survivals of old religion rather than anything new that were to be found in witchcraft.)

If you had been sticking pins in your neighbor's image or casting spells on his cow, you would not have wanted Thomas Hobbes to be your judge. He would not have believed in your occult powers, but he would have hanged you anyway, for your heresy and for your malice. What is of immediate interest to us, however, is not Hobbes' ferociousness, but the degree of his skepticism. He was convinced that witchcraft did not work, but it did not occur to him for one moment to doubt that people practiced it. In fact, nobody in the seventeenth century or before doubted the existence of witchcraft as a common practice; skepticism extended only to the questions of whether it worked, and if so whether by spiritual or natural means, and if those who practiced it should be held legally accountable.

Skepticism on these grounds was not common, but neither was it rare. Reginald Scot, whose *The Discovery of Witchcraft* (1584) was the best Elizabethan attack on the belief in witchcraft, argued that it did not usually work, and that fraud was the real crime of which the witch was guilty: "cozening witches" should, he thought, be tried on that charge. Scot also believed, and so did many others, that the methods used to investigate witchcraft cases were so uncertain that they should not be made the grounds for capital punishment. Thomas Ady repeated Scot's arguments (with full and open acknowledgment of their source) in his *A Candle in the Dark* (1655). Variations on them were produced by John Wagstaffe in his

The Question of Witchcraft Debated (1669) and by John Webster in his *The Displaying of Supposed Witchcraft* (1677). The limited skepticism represented by Ady, Wagstaffe, and Webster was increasing sharply in the latter seventeenth century. There were also a few who believed, with Montaigne, that witches were insane—candidates for the asylum rather than the courtroom.

It should be emphasized that all of the learned, whether believers or skeptics in principle, were skeptical of the majority of witchcraft cases that came to their attention, because they were all too well aware of the abysmal depth and infinite extent of popular credulity. Every accident, every sudden or unusual illness of man or of beast, every inexplicable or menacing circumstance of any sort was apt to raise the cry of witchcraft among the common people. The learned knew this, and were disposed to approach the individual case with skepticism. We should beware, however, of making a general principle of this statistical skepticism. In 1711 Bishop Berkeley, the philosopher, wrote to a friend that "I do not believe one in a thousand of these stories to be true." But, he added, "neither on the other hand do I see sufficient grounds to conclude peremptorily against plain matter of fact well attested."[18] He enclosed with his letter one such instance of "plain matter of fact"; an account of an Irish case which Berkeley firmly believed to be an instance of malefic witchcraft. The "plain matter of fact" is no more convincing—indeed is less convincing—than the facts produced in Massachusetts.

We must bear in mind that in a society which believes in witchcraft, it works. If you believe in witchcraft and you discover that someone has been melting your wax image over a slow fire or muttering charms over your nail-parings, the probability is that you will get extremely sick. To be sure, your symptoms will be psychosomatic rather than organic. But the fact that they are obviously not organic will make them only more terrible, since they will seem the result of malefic and demonic power. So it was in seventeenth-century Europe, and so it was in seventeenth-century Massachusetts.

The hideous convulsive fits were thought to be the result of witches and demons wrenching the bodies of their victims into tortuous postures. The loss of hearing, speech, sight, appetite, and memory were deprivations caused by Satan himself. The contraction of the throat—the *globus hystericus*—was seen as an attempt by demons to make the victim swallow occult poisons. And when she swallowed rapidly and her belly swelled (what is actually involved here is a kind of accelerated ulcer formation), it was thought the demons had succeeded. When blisters appeared upon the skin (many skin diseases are functional rather than organic), they were thought to have been raised by brimstone out of Hell. Many of these symptoms, including the skin lesions, would pass fairly rapidly. Cotton Mather, who was a Fellow of the Royal Society, a former medical student, and a thorough and careful observer, remarked more than once on the surprising rapidity with which "witch-wounds" healed. But other symptoms would persist. And a new fit would bring a repetition of the old afflictions, or new ones equally alarming.

The cause of these hysterical symptoms, of course, was not witchcraft itself but the victim's fear of it, and that is why so many innocent persons were executed. It is impossible now, and was in many instances impossible then, to tell how many of the persons executed for witchcraft were actually guilty of practicing it. It is surely no exaggeration to say that the majority, even the vast majority, were innocent victims of hysterical fears. But we should again be wary of converting a statistical truth into a general principle. While it is clearly true that the majority of persons executed for witchcraft were innocent, it is equally true that some of them, in Massachusetts and elsewhere, were guilty.

2

Witchcraft in New England

Contrary to popular opinion, New England's record in regard to witchcraft is surprisingly good, as Governor Thomas Hutchinson pointed out in 1750: "more having been put to death in a single county in England, in a short space of time, than have suffered in all New England from the first settlement until the present time."[1] Through most of the seventeenth century the record is really astonishing. While Europe hanged and burned literally thousands, executions in New England were few and far between. (Witches were burned on the Continent and in Scotland, where witchcraft was a heresy, but hanged in England and in New England, where it was a felony. Burning seems not to have been motivated by the wish to inflict a particularly painful death; Scottish witches, for instance, were first garroted by the executioner, who then proceeded to burn the corpse and scatter its ashes. Most probably, burning was an attempt to prevent the resurrection of the body.)

There were a few New England cases of witchcraft before 1692, and it is worth looking at four of these for the light they throw upon the Salem trials.

The first is that of Mrs. Anne Hibbins. Her husband, who died in 1654, had been a man of importance: a Boston merchant, a Colonial Agent, and for several years one of the Assistants. Tradition has it that she was a sister of Governor Bellingham. She was apparently quarrelsome—quarrelsome enough so that her church censured her for it—and one quarrel was her undoing. She seems to have come upon two of her neighbors talking, to have told them she knew they were talking about her, and then to have reconstructed their conversation with enough fidelity to convince them she was possessed of "preternatural" knowledge. She was brought to trial in 1655, and the jury brought her in guilty. But the presiding magistrates refused to accept the verdict, apparently believing her innocent, and their refusal automatically threw the case into the General Court. There again she was found guilty; the governor pronounced the required sentence of death; and in 1656 she was executed. We have seen that some of the magistrates were not satisfied of her guilt, and apparently the same was true of some of the clergy. A surviving letter tells us that the Reverend John Norton "once said at his own table" before the Reverend John Wilson and others that Mistress Hibbins

was hanged for a witch only for having more wit than her neighbors. It was his very expression; she having, as he explained it, unhappily guessed that two of her persecutors, whom she saw talking in the street, were talking of her,—which cost her her life, notwithstanding all he could do to the contrary, as he himself told us.[2]

The Hibbins case shows how slender and how circumstantial were the grounds necessary to bring an accusation of witchcraft against anyone with a reputation for malice. It also shows that the popular elements in society (the jury, and the people's representatives in the General Court) were far more ready to believe in witchcraft than the leaders of society (the magistrates and ministers). This latter conclusion is reinforced by the fact that before 1692 there were far more acquittals than convictions in New England; there were more people willing to charge their neighbors with witchcraft than magistrates willing to convict them.

A case which took place in Hartford, Connecticut, in 1662 is known in rather more detail than that of Mrs. Hibbins. Anne Cole, "a person esteemed pious," was taken with "strange fits." As with the Salem girls, the fits were both violent and public.

Extremely violent bodily motions she many times had, even to the hazard of her life in the apprehensions of those that saw them. And very often great disturbance was given in the public worship of God by her and two other women who had also strange fits. Once in especial, on a day of prayer kept on that account, the motion and noise of the afflicted was so terrible that a godly person fainted under the appearance of it.[3]

In some of her fits strange voices came from her, voices that were clearly not her own. Such voices are now known to be a consequence of multiple personality, which is the extreme form of the hysterical fugue. But the seventeenth-century observers of Anne Cole judged them to be the voices of demons who had entered into her, and that judgment was sensible enough in view of the fact that the voices seemed to be plotting ways in which Anne Cole might be further afflicted. Eventually, seeming to realize that they were being overheard, one of the voices announced, " 'Let us confound her language, [that] she may tell no more tales.' " For some time nothing came from her but "unintelligible mutterings"; then the conversation resumed, but in a Dutch accent, and this time names were mentioned, names of the witches who were responsible for these afflictions.

When Anne Cole was out of her fits she "knew nothing of those things that were spoken by her" during them, but she was understandably distressed to find she had been speaking things which, to the best of her knowledge, had never been in her mind; it was a "matter of great affliction to her." It must have been afflicting to the local magistrates as well; they now had accusations of witchcraft against several persons, but the source of those accusations was not Anne Cole; it was a committee of demons who had infested her. The magistrates investigated further, and imprisoned some (and perhaps all) of the accused on suspicion of witchcraft. One of these, a "lewd, ignorant, considerably aged woman" named Rebecca Greensmith sent for the two clergymen who had taken down in writing the demonic conversation issuing from the mouth of Anne Cole. She had the transcript read to her, and then "forthwith and freely confessed those things to be true," confirming the statement of the voices "that she (and other persons named in the discourse) had familiarity with the Devil." She confessed to a number of other things as well, including "that the Devil had frequent use of her body with much seeming (but indeed horrible, hellish) delight to her."

Reports of copulation with demons (including the un-
pleasantness of the experience) are common in the literature of
Continental witchcraft, but this is one of the few known cases
in New England. What is involved is apparently an erotic fit in
which the woman actually goes through the motions of copulation and achieves an orgasm; similar fits have been observed in
mental patients in the twentieth century.[1] Thus it appears that
in the case of Anne Cole the confessor as well as the afflicted
person was an hysteric. This is a pattern we shall see again at
Salem.

Rebecca Greensmith was hanged in 1663. So was her
husband Nathaniel, although we do not know the grounds for
his conviction; according to Increase Mather[5] he did not confess. "Most" of the other persons accused by the demonic
voices "made their escape into another part of the country."
What happened to the others we do not know, but they were
apparently not executed. And since at least one of those who
made her escape had at first been imprisoned on suspicion of
witchcraft (Judith Varlet, a relative of Governor Peter Stuy-
vesant of New York), it can be assumed that the authorities were reluctant to press the matter further. The evidence
they had was, after all, highly suspect, coming from demonic
voices on the one hand and a confessed witch on the other. In
any event, after the "execution of some and escape of others"
Anne Cole's fits ceased, and did not return. Twenty years later,
in 1682, the Reverend John Whiting reported that "she yet
remains maintaining her integrity." This, together with what
the voices said, suggests that Anne Cole's fits probably were
caused by her fear of witchcraft and cured by the removal of
that fear.

The next two cases are remarkable for a number of reasons,
one of them being the exemplary thoroughness with which the
symptoms of the afflicted persons are described, which makes it
possible to say without question that these were pathological
cases of hysteria.

The first took place in Groton, Massachusetts, in 1671–1672

and was recorded by the Reverend Samuel Willard, then minister of Groton (during the Salem trials he was a member of the Boston clergy). On October 30, 1671, Elizabeth Knapp began to behave strangely:

In the evening, a little before she went to bed, sitting by the fire she cried out, "Oh! My legs!" and clapped her hand on them; immediately, "Oh! My breast!" and removed her hands thither; and forthwith, "Oh! I am strangled!" and put her hands on her throat.[6]

The similarity to Janet's twentieth-century description of the onset of a typical hysterical fit is unmistakable; it starts, he writes,

with a pain or a strange sensation situated at such or such a point of the body. . . . [It] often begins in the lower part of the abdomen [and] seems to ascend and to spread to other organs. For instance, it very often spreads to the epigastrium, to the breasts, then to the throat. There it assumes rather an interesting form, which was for a very long time considered as quite characteristic of hysteria. The patient has the sensation of too big an object, as it were, a ball, rising in her throat and choking her.[7]

The choking sensation we shall find over and over again; it is the *bolus hystericus* and is related to the "lump in the throat" felt by normal people in moments of extreme stress. The normal person, like the hysteric, tries to relieve it by swallowing; this is why the comic-strip artist has his characters say "Gulp" when they are in trouble.

The choking sensation in the throat was followed by "fits in which she was violent in bodily motions, leapings, strainings and strange agitations, scarce to be held in bound by the strength of three or four; violent also in roarings and screamings." The fits continued until January 15, 1672, the date of Willard's writing. Several of the details he recorded are worth noting. On November 15 "her tongue was for many hours together drawn into a semicircle up to the roof of her mouth, and not to be removed, for some tried with the fingers to do it." On December 17 her tongue was drawn "out of her mouth most frightfully, to an extraordinary length and greatness." Devils appeared to her, and witches; "Oh," she cried to one of them, "you are a rogue." On November 29 she had a particularly grotesque hallucination, when she believed a witch in the shape of a dog with a woman's head was strangling her. The hallucinations and the woman's sufferings were terrifyingly convincing; Willard noted that when she thought the witch was strangling her "she did oftentimes seem to our apprehension as if she would forthwith be strangled."

Elizabeth Knapp's case is strikingly similar to that of Ler—, one of the best-known cases of J.-M. Charcot, the nineteenth-century psychologist. Her fits, he wrote,

are characterised in the first stage by epileptiform and tetaniform convulsions; after this come great gesticulations of a voluntary character, in which the patient, assuming the most frightful postures, reminds one of the attitudes which history assigns to the demoniacs. . . . At this stage of the attack, she is a prey to delirium, and raves evidently of the events which seem to have determined her first seizures. She hurls furious invectives against imaginary individuals, crying out, "villains! robbers! brigands! fire! fire! O, the dogs! I'm bitten!"—Reminiscences, doubtless, of the emotions experienced in her youth.[8]

When the convulsive portion of Ler—'s attack was over other symptoms usually followed, including "hallucination of vision; the patient beholds horrible animals, skeletons, and specters" and "lastly, a more or less marked permanent contracture of the tongue." Charcot drew this contracture of the tongue; it is quite appalling. Willard was not exaggerating in calling it frightful. (See plate 3.)

Elizabeth Knapp displayed still other symptoms that are identifiably hysterical, including loss of speech on some occasions, and on others speaking in voices other than her own; once "she barked like a dog, and bleated like a calf." Willard noted that her fits did not seem to do her any permanent physical damage:

She hath no ways wasted in body or strength by all these fits, though so dreadful, but gathered flesh exceedingly, and hath her natural strength when her fits are off, for the most part.

This is typical; as Janet remarks, the "hysteric patient, after howling for several hours, feels rather comfortable; she experiences, as it were, a relaxation, and declares she is much better than before the fit."[9] This ability of the hysteric to function normally when she is out of her fits has often raised the question of whether they are genuine. Willard thought they must be, if only for their violence: "such a strength is beyond the force of dissimulation." (It should be noted that hysterics are not always well in the intervals between their fits. Some, for instance, lose their appetites and starve themselves. It is probably such cases who are referred to in the statute of James I against witchcraft as being "wasted, consumed, pined."[10])

On November 1 Elizabeth Knapp named one of her neighbors as the probable cause of her afflictions. The accused woman was sent for, and entered the house while the afflicted girl was in a fit. Her eyes were closed, as they usually were in her fits, yet she could distinguish this neighbor's touch from all others, "though no voice was uttered." That would have been quite enough to convict the neighbor in many witchcraft cases. But fortunately she was permitted to pray with the afflicted girl, and at the conclusion Miss Knapp "confessed that she believed Satan had deluded her." Willard was happy that "God was pleased to vindicate the case and justify the innocent," and reported that Miss Knapp never again complained of any "apparition or disturbance from this neighbor." Instead, she turned to accusing the Devil, who had, she said, been offering her a covenant for several years, a covenant she had frequently been tempted to sign. About a month later she accused another person of witchcraft, this time during a period of hallucinations. Her father brought the woman to the house, and Willard, who had been asked to be present, noted that her fit became particularly violent when this woman entered. But, Willard wrote, "we made nothing of it" since her fits had been as violent on other occasions. Instead they inquired carefully into the matter and found "two evident and clear mistakes" in the accusation. This was enough to exonerate the second accused woman.

Elizabeth Knapp was still having fits when Willard wrote about her, and all he could be certain of was that "she is an object of pity." He did not think she was bewitched, but he did believe she was possessed (that is, that Devils had entered into her). This remained his opinion (and that of most others) when the case was remembered in 1692. He also believed that the girl's terrible afflictions provided an occasion for the community to examine its collective conscience. Therefore he admonished his congregation in a sermon, "Let us all examine by this Providence [i.e., this event] what sins they have been, that have given Satan so much footing in this poor place."[11]

Before proceeding to the fourth and most important example, it should be noted that the convulsive fits which played so prominent a part in most witchcraft cases, and continued to be one of the most common symptoms of hysteria through the early years of the twentieth century, have now become relatively rare in Western civilization.

D. W. Abse reports fits occurred in only six out of one hundred and sixty-one cases of hysteria treated at a British military hospital during World War II, but that they were the most common symptom among Indian Army hysterics treated at Delhi during the same period.[12] There are a number of possible explanations for this curious fact. Hysterics are notoriously suggestible, so the change may be ascribable to nothing more than the refusal of our culture to give the hysterical fit the respectful and awed attention it used to command. In any case, it seems clear that abnormal behavior varies with time and place just as normal behavior does. But since this particular variation occurred so recently, and after the classic studies of hysteria had been completed, it is possible to identify the seventeenth-century Massachusetts fits for what they were.

And it was with fits that our fourth case begins. In Boston, in midsummer of the year 1688, four previously well-behaved children of a "sober and pious" mason, John Goodwin, began to have "strange fits, beyond those that attend an epilepsy, or a catalepsy."[13] The words are those of Cotton Mather. Mather was a medical student before he was a minister, and a far more careful observer than he has been given credit for. He spent a great deal of his time with the Goodwin children and he has left us a thorough account of their symptoms in his *Memorable Providences:*

Sometimes they would be deaf, sometimes dumb, and sometimes blind, and often all this at once. One while their tongues would be drawn down their throats; another while they would be pulled out upon their chins to a prodigious length. They would have their mouths opened unto such a wideness that their jaws went out of joint, and anon they would clap together again with a force like that of a strong spring-lock. The same would happen to their shoulder-blades, and their elbows, and hand-wrists, and several of their joints. They would at times lie in a benumbed condition and be drawn together as those that are tied neck and heels [this was one of the few tortures permitted under seventeenth-century English law; neck and heels were chained together so that the body was bent into an exaggerated and painful foetal posture], and presently be stretched out, yea, drawn backwards to such an extent that it was feared the very skin of their bellies would have cracked [this is the *arc de cercle* of the nineteenth-century French psychiatrists]. They would make most piteous outcries that they were cut with knives, and struck with blows that they could not bear. Their necks would be broken so that their neck-bone would seem dissolved unto them that felt after it, and yet on the sudden it would become again so stiff that there was no stirring of their heads. Yea, their heads would be twisted almost round,[14] and if main force at any time obstructed a dangerous motion which they seemed to be upon, they would roar exceedingly. Thus they lay some weeks most pitiful spectacles. . . .

Again the symptoms are those of the hysteric: the convulsive movements, the distorted postures, the loss of hearing, speech, sight, and so forth. The fits had started immediately after one of the children had quarreled with an Irish washerwoman, whose mother, Goodwife Glover, "a scandalous old woman" whose late husband had complained about the neighborhood "that she was undoubtedly a witch," had "bestowed very bad language upon the girl."

The neighbors advised the family to try white magic, but the pious father, John Goodwin, refused to traffic with the occult. He consulted first with "skillful physicians," particularly with Dr. Thomas Oakes, who gave his opinion that "nothing but an hellish witchcraft" could be the cause of the children's afflictions. Next he turned to the Boston clergy, who held a day of prayer at the Goodwin house, after which one of the four children was permanently cured. And finally he entered a complaint against Goodwife Glover with the magistrates. When they examined her she "gave such a wretched account of herself" that they committed her to jail under indictment for witchcraft.

Cotton Mather gives a concise account of her trial:

It was long before she could with any direct answers plead unto her indictment, and when she did plead it was with confession rather than denial of her guilt. Order was given to search the old woman's house, from whence there were brought into the court several small images, or puppets, or babies, made of rags and stuffed with goat's hair and other such ingredients. When these were produced the vile woman acknowledged that her way to torment the objects of her malice was by wetting of her finger with her spittle and stroking of those little images. The abused children were then present, and the woman still kept stooping and shrinking as one that was almost pressed to death with a mighty weight upon her. But one of the images being brought unto her, immediately she started up after an odd manner and took it into her hand. But she had no sooner taken it than one of the children fell into sad fits before the whole assembly. This the judges had their just apprehensions at, and carefully causing the repetition of the experiment found again the same event of it. They asked her whether she had any to stand by her [i.e., as character witnesses]. She replied, she had, and looking very pertly in the air she added, "No, He's gone." And then she confessed that she had one who was her Prince, with whom she maintained I know not what communion. For which cause, the night after, she was heard expostulating with a Devil for his thus deserting her, telling Him that because He had served her so basely and falsely she had confessed all. However, to make all clear the court appointed five or six physicians one evening to examine her very strictly, whether she were not crazed in her intellectuals and had not procured to herself by folly and madness the reputation of a witch. Diverse hours did they spend with her, and in all that while no discourse came from her but what was pertinent and agreeable. Particularly, when they asked her what she thought would become of her soul, she replied, "You ask me a very solemn question, and I cannot well tell what to say to it." She owned herself a Roman Catholic and could recite her Pater Noster very readily, but there was one clause or two always too hard for her, whereof she said she could not repeat it if she might have all the world. In the upshot the doctors returned her *compos mentis,* and sentence of death was passed upon her.

There has never been a more clear-cut case of witchcraft. Image magic is the commonest form of black magic. The impulse behind it survives even when the belief in magic is gone (as any one knows who has torn up the photograph of a person with whom they were angry. College students are obeying the same impulse when they hang or burn someone in effigy, and it is worth noticing that hanging and burning were the means of executing witches. Nobody is ever shot, or stabbed or garroted in effigy.) The dolls were stuffed with goat's hair because it is the goat who is deified in Satan's horns and cloven hooves. Spittle was applied to them because spittle was believed to have occult power, a belief that still survives in the idea of spitting on one's hands before undertaking a particularly arduous task.

To determine whether or not the plea should be insanity, the defendant was examined by a committee of physicians, who agreed that she was sane. Plainly Goodwife Glover believed that she had made a pact with Satan. When she was asked who would stand by her, she attempted to call on Him, and she was overheard at night, in her cell, berating Him for having abandoned her. But what is most important is that her witchcraft plainly worked, and in no indiscriminate fashion. When she tormented one of her dolls, one of the Goodwin children "fell into sad fits." When it is remembered that in a society which believes in witchcraft the violent hysterical symptoms to which the Goodwin children were subject not infrequently terminate in death,[15] it cannot be said that the Boston court acted either harshly or unjustly. Indeed, when one considers the ferocity of seventeenth-century English law, simple hanging seems almost a lenient sentence.

Cotton Mather visited Goodwife Glover twice in jail after she had been condemned, and made a serious effort to convert her. Her Prince, he told her, had cheated her, to which she answered, " 'If it be so, I am sorry for that!' " He "set before her the necessity and equity of her breaking her covenant with Hell, and giving herself to the Lord Jesus Christ by an everlasting covenant." She answered that he "spoke a very reasonable thing, but she could not do it." He asked if he might pray for her, to which she answered that "If prayer would do her any good, she could pray for herself." He asked again for her permission to pray, and she replied that she could not give it unless her "spirits" would give her leave—"spirits," or "angels," or "saints"; she spoke only in Irish, the language she had also used at the trial, and the translator told Mather that the Irish word would bear any of those translations. He prayed for her anyway, and when he was through she thanked him for it. But, he wrote, "I was no sooner out of her sight than she took a stone, a long and slender stone, and with her finger and spittle fell to tormenting it; though whom or what she meant, I had the mercy never to understand."

During these visits Mather also asked her "many" questions about her witchcraft. On one occasion she replied that she "would fain give . . . a full answer" but her spirits would not give her leave. She told him that she used to go to meetings where her "Prince," who was the Devil, was present along with four other persons, whom she named, including one "whom it might have been thought natural affection would have advised the concealing of"—presumably her daughter.

When she was on her way to the gallows she announced that the children's afflictions would not cease at her death, because others had a hand in the witchcraft as well as she. The afflictions did continue, but Mather kept the names the witch had mentioned to himself, presumably on the grounds that one should not accept the testimony against others of a confessed witch. After all, the Devil was, as Mather often called him, "the Prince of Lies," and this woman had been his worshipper.

The children's fits continued more violently than ever, except that the boy could be given sporadic relief by striking at the specters which he saw. The theory was that if you could hit the specter you could injure the witch, and on one occasion it was reported "that a wound was this way given to an obnoxious woman in the town." Again Mather refused to make the name public, "for we should be tender in such relations, lest we wrong the reputation of the innocent by stories not enough inquired into."

Eventually Mather took the eldest Goodwin girl into his own home, partly in an attempt to cure her through prayer and fasting, and "also that I might have a full opportunity to observe the extraordinary circumstances of the children, and that I might be furnished with evidence and argument as a critical eye-witness to confute the sadducism of this debauched age." He was always the scholar; he recognized that this was a classic case and had already determined on publishing an account of it in an attempt to convert materialists to the belief in an invisible world.

The girl provided a thorough display of symptoms. Most of them we have noticed before, but there were others as well. Her belly would swell "like a drum, and sometimes with croaking noises in it"; on one such occasion Mather was praying for "mercy on a daughter vexed with a Devil," and "there came a big, but low voice from her, saying, 'There's two or three of them' (or us!)." One of her more grotesque hallucinations was riding on a spectral horse. She would go through the motions of riding, and at the conclusion of one such spell she announced that she had been to a witch meeting, and had learned who was the cause of her affliction. There were three of them, she said. She named them, and announced that " 'if they were out of the way, I should be well.' " But Mather made no move to put them "out of the way." After all, this was a girl through whom

Devils were speaking, and so once more he kept the names of the accused to himself.

The girl was able to get relief from her afflictions in Mather's study. She believed, to his mixed embarrassment and pleasure, that God would not permit her Devils to enter there. One of her more curious symptoms was "flying"; "she would be carried hither and thither, though not long from the ground, yet so long as to exceed the ordinary power of nature in our opinion of it." There is probably nothing more to this "flying" than the violence of motion we have seen in the fits throughout. Yet it may not be so simple; levitation was reported on another occasion when the record is less easy to explain, and we shall return to the problem in dealing with that occasion.

A persistent symptom was her inability to pray, or to hear prayers said on her behalf, or to read Puritan religious works. "A popish book . . . she could endure very well," and she was able to read "whole pages" of "a Quaker's book," although she could not read the words "God" or "Christ" but skipped over them. "When we urged her to tell what the word was that she missed, she'd say, 'I must not speak it; they say I must not, you know what it is, it's G and O and D.'" She could not read the Bible, and if someone else read it, even silently, "she would be cast into very terrible agonies." Puritan catechisms had the same effect; the Assembly's Catechism or Mather's grandfather John Cotton's catechism for children, *Milk for Babes*, "would bring hideous convulsions on the child if she looked into them; though she had once learned them with all the love that could be."

American historians have made themselves merry over this particular symptom, suggesting that a Puritan catechism was enough to give anybody convulsions. But such suggestions only demonstrate the incapacity of these historians to understand a culture whose central concerns were religious. This girl had been piously raised in a pious society and believed herself afflicted by devils and witches; her inability to speak the name of God or to read the religious books her society believed in must have been a terrifying ordeal to her; her spelling God's name and reading Quaker and Catholic books were clearly substitutes. Breuer and Freud report an exactly parallel case in their *Studies in Hysteria:*

A very distressed young girl, while anxiously watching at a sick bed, fell into a dreamy state, had terrifying hallucinations, and her right arm, which was at the time hanging over the back of the chair, became numb. This resulted in a paralysis, contracture, and anesthesia of that arm. She wanted to pray, but could find no words [i.e., in her native language, German], but finally succeeded in uttering an English children's prayer. Later, on developing a very grave and most complicated hysteria, she spoke, wrote, and understood only English, whereas her native tongue was incomprehensible to her for a year and a half.[16]

Anyone who has had the common and terrifying dream in which one cannot speak or move will know something of how the elder Goodwin girl felt when she found she could not pray or read the Bible—but only something of it, since the dream lasts only for a moment and the girl's symptom lasted for months. It seems, in fact, to have been prayer that cured her —not her own, but that of Cotton Mather and other well-meaning members of the community who occasionally joined him. Then, according to Thomas Hutchinson, who published his *History of the Province of Massachusetts-Bay* in 1750:

The children returned to their ordinary behavior, lived to adult age, made profession of religion, and the affliction they had been under they publicly declared to be one motive to it. One of them I knew many years after. She had the character of a very sober virtuous woman, and never made any acknowledgment of fraud in this transaction.[17]

Hutchinson was a typical eighteenth-century rationalist, who thought all witchcraft a matter of fraud, so his testimony to the woman's later character is particularly valuable. In an early draft of his account of this case he tells us that she was one of his tenants, but unfortunately he does not tell us whether she was the child who had been under the care of Cotton Mather.[18]

The Glover case was classic. While it was still going on Joshua Moodey wrote to Increase Mather: "It is an example in all the parts of it, not to be paralleled."[19] Cotton Mather took the occasion to preach to his congregation a "Discourse on Witchcraft,"[20] in which a central concern was to demonstrate that prayer, faith, and a good life rather than charms were the proper "preservatives" against witchcraft. More important, however, was his use of the case as ammunition in the war of the pious against philosophical materialism.

Remember that persons skeptical of witchcraft did not doubt the practice of it, but only whether or not it worked, or worked through spiritual means. Thus the skeptic John Webster, in his *Displaying of Supposed Witchcraft*, was willing to concede that there were witches and devils who "have power to perform strange things."[21] But he spent his twelfth chapter on the question "whether they do not bring them to pass by mere natural means." What was at issue here was the reality of the spiritual world, the "invisible world" as Mather called it. The controversy over witchcraft, therefore, raised theological issues fundamental to the seventeenth-century Christian. "We shall come to have no Christ but a light within, and no Heaven but a frame of mind," said Mather, if the materialists—the Sadducees—should succeed in destroying the belief in an invisible world.

Whatever one's own belief, or lack of it, one has to admit that he was right. In the eighteenth and nineteenth centuries scientific materialism was to triumph, and the pious were to find that all the concreteness had left their religion, leaving nothing behind but a "light within" and a "frame of mind."

Conceive, then, of Mather's excitement. At a time which he recognized to be a crisis in the history of religious belief he had discovered a clear case of witchcraft which he thought could not possibly be explained on material grounds. He made it the central matter of his *Memorable Providences* (1689), a book which he hoped might once and for all confute materialism and reestablish Christianity on the firm foundation of a real and concrete spiritual world. The book met with considerable success. Richard Baxter, one of the most distinguished English Puritans, wrote a laudatory preface to the first London edition, and in Baxter's own *Certainty of the Worlds of Spirits* (1691) he spoke of it as the ultimate proof of the existence of a spiritual world. Any doubter, he said, "that will read . . . Mr. Cotton Mather's book of the witchcrafts in New England may see enough to silence any incredulity that pretendeth to be rational."[22]

The four cases we have reviewed confirm in detail what we have seen to be true in general. Accusations of witchcraft were continual among the common people, so continual that Cotton Mather took time in his "Discourse" to warn his congregation sharply against them:

Take heed that you do not wrongfully accuse any other person of this horrid and monstrous evil. . . . What more dirty reproach than that of witchcraft can there be? Yet it is most readily cast upon worthy persons when there is hardly a shadow of any reason for it. An ill look or a cross word will make a witch with many people who may on more ground be counted so themselves. There has been a fearful deal of injury done in this way in this town to the good name of the most credible persons in it. Persons of more goodness and esteem than any of their calumnious abusers have been defamed for witches about this country—a country full of lies.

But the charges of irresponsible accusers were checked by the responsibility of the community's leaders, the ministers and the magistrates. They had been reluctant to act in Mrs. Hibbins' case. At Groton, Willard's investigation had been so careful that two accusations of witchcraft were retracted and the case never brought to court, on the ground that it was possession rather than witchcraft. At Hartford a confessor and her husband had been hanged and at Boston a confessor, but in both instances, although more persons were accused, the individual case did not develop into a witch hunt.

There were other individual convictions, but they were outnumbered by the acquittals. For example, the records of the Court of Assistants[23] show that in 1662 Eunice Cole of

Hampton was found not guilty as indicted, although there was "just ground of vehement suspicion." In 1666 John Godfrey of Salem was discharged as not legally guilty, although there were again grounds for suspicion. (Godfrey seems to have been a thorough reprobate; at various times he was convicted of stealing, swearing, drunkenness, and suborning witnesses.) In 1673 Anna Edmunds was acquitted and her accusers ordered to pay charges. In 1675 Mary Parsons of Northampton was found not guilty, in 1681 Mary Hale of Boston, and in 1683 Mary Webster of Hadley. Also in 1683 James Fuller of Springfield, who had confessed but then retracted his confession, was found not guilty but was whipped and fined for "his wicked and pernicious willful lying and continuance in it until now, putting the country to so great a charge." In all the American colonies during the seventeenth century there were fewer than fifty executions for witchcraft, and excluding Salem there were fewer than thirty. This is a genuinely exemplary record, considerably superior to Europe for intelligence and restraint.

Before the Glover case a part of this restraint may have proceeded from the New Englander's conviction that he belonged to a chosen people. God, many thought, would not permit Satan to afflict the elect. The Devil might appear among "the wigwams of Indians, where the pagan Powaws often raise their masters in the shapes of bears and snakes and fires,"[24] but there would be few demonic terrors in the New Jerusalem.

This belief was shattered by the events of 1688. Goodwife Glover had demonstrated clearly that witchcraft did exist in Massachusetts, and witchcraft of the most serious and dangerous sort. The Devil was abroad in Zion, seeking whom he might devour.

3

❖❖❖❖❖❖

The Raising of the Devil

When the Devil broke forth again, at Salem Village in 1692, he was not immediately recognized. "When these calamities first began," wrote the Reverend Samuel Parris, "which was in my own family, the affliction was several weeks before such hellish operations as witchcraft were suspected."[1] The trouble, according to John Hale, could be traced back to experiments made with the occult.

I fear some young persons, through a vain curiosity to know their future condition, have tampered with the Devil's tools so far that hereby one door was opened to Satan to play those pranks, *Anno* 1692. I knew one of the afflicted persons who (as I was credibly informed) did try with an egg and a glass to find her future husband's calling [i.e., occupation], till there came up a coffin, that is, a specter in likeness of a coffin. And she was afterwards followed with diabolical molestation to her death, and so died a single person —a just warning to others to take heed of handling the Devil's weapons lest they get a wound thereby.

Another, I was called to pray with, being under sore fits and vexations of Satan. And upon examination I found that she had tried the same charm, and after her confession of it and manifestation of repentance for it, and our prayers to God for her, she was speedily released from those bonds of Satan.[2]

The egg and glass is a method of divining similar to crystal-gazing, the white of an egg poured into a glass being substituted for the fortuneteller's crystal ball. Little girls still play at divining their future husband's occupation, using a variety of methods including the old rhyme, "Rich man, poor man, beggar man, thief." It is quite innocent in the twentieth century, but it was anything but innocent for the two seventeenth-century girls who believed that they had conjured up a specter in the shape of a coffin. It is no wonder that they began to display hysterical symptoms, and that one of them was "followed with diabolical molestations to her death."

Hale does not name the children, but the one who was cured was most probably Elizabeth Parris, the minister's nine-year-old daughter. She disappeared from Salem Village late in March, when her father sent her to the household of Stephen Sewall in Salem Town, possibly because fits were known to be communicable and he wanted her removed from contact with those who were still having them. The other girl was probably Parris' eleven-year-old niece, Abigail Williams, although we have no way of being sure; there is very little information about the later lives of the afflicted girls. Tradition has it that they were assisted in their occult experiments by Tituba, a slave woman Parris had brought to New England from Barbados, where he had been a merchant before becoming a clergyman. Tituba, like her husband John, was a Carib Indian (*not* a Negro), and although the egg and glass is an English rather than an Indian method of divining she may well have been involved from the beginning. Certainly she would often have been charged with the care of the children, and certainly she was soon involved in another occult experiment.

In any case, the two girls were very sick. So were several of their friends who had also, presumably, been experimenting with the occult. Chief among these were Ann Putnam, Jr. (twelve years old), Mary Warren (twenty), Mercy Lewis (nineteen), Mary Walcott (sixteen), and Elizabeth Hubbard (seventeen). Parris took them to various doctors, but they grew steadily worse. When Doctor Griggs made his diagnosis of witchcraft Parris apparently did not at first accept it; he simply continued the prayer and fasting which he hoped would cure the girls.

If the minister was not anxious to believe the children were bewitched, the neighbors were. They began to ask the girls who was afflicting them, but at first they were unable to answer. It was then that Mary Sibley, the aunt of Mary Walcott, turned to white magic to break the witches' spell. On February 25 she went to the minister's Indian slaves, John and Tituba, and had them prepare a witch cake from a traditional English recipe, meal mixed with the children's urine. It was baked in the fire and then fed to the Parris dog, presumably on the theory that the animal was a familiar—a messenger assigned to a witch by the Devil.

The minister was appalled when he discovered, a month later, what had been done. Mary Sibley's witch cake was, as Parris put it, "a going to the Devil for help against the Devil." He lectured her privately about it and before the entire congregation called her "to deep humiliation for what she has done." She acknowledged her sinfulness in tears, but it was far too late. The witch cake had been baked, and by it, as Parris said, "the Devil hath been raised among us, and his rage is vehement and terrible; and, when he shall be silenced, the Lord only knows."[3] Because the witch cake worked—another instance of the efficacy of magic in a society which believes in it. Now the girls were able to name their afflicters: Tituba herself, and Sarah Good and Sarah Osburn—two old women of dubious reputation. When these names were known four "yeomen of Salem Village in the County of Essex"[4]—Joseph Hutchinson, Thomas Putnam, Edward Putnam, and Thomas Preston —appeared before their magistrates and swore out warrants for suspicion of witchcraft.

The warrants were issued on February 29, and on March 1 the three accused women were examined by two Salem magistrates who were to conduct the majority of the preliminary examinations: John Hathorne (whose great-great-grandson Nathaniel added a "w" to the family name) and Jonathan Corwin. The accused women did not make a very good showing.

Sarah Good behaved with all the malice and deceit one could expect of a witch. When she was asked who it was afflicted the children if she did not, she was quite willing to accuse her fellow-prisoner Sarah Osburn. Her husband, William, testified "he was afraid that she either was a witch or would be one very quickly." When Hathorne asked if he had any concrete evidence of her practicing witchcraft he replied that he had not; he thought her a witch for "her bad carriage to him." "Indeed," said he, "I may say with tears that she is an enemy to all good." Beside this unintentional pun he offered the information that he had seen a "strange tit or wart" on his wife's body, the implication being that this was a so-called "witch's tit" at which the Devil and his familiars sucked the blood of the witch. Her four-year-old daughter Dorcas also testified against her, announcing that her mother had familiars: "three birds, one black, one yellow and that these birds hurt the children and afflicted persons."[5]

John Hathorne asked most of the questions and established the judicial attitude that was to prevail throughout most of the examinations and the trials. Rather than adopting the stance of impartial investigator, as Willard had done at Groton in 1671, and Cotton Mather at Boston in 1688, he acted more like a prosecuting attorney than a magistrate, assuming the guilt of the person under examination and trying to force a confession with bullying questions:

"Sarah Good, what evil spirit have you familiarity with?"
"None."
"Have you made no contract with the Devil?"
"No."
"Why do you hurt these children?"
"I do not hurt them. I scorn it."
"Who do you employ, then, to do it?"
"I employ nobody."
"What creature do you employ, then?"
"No creature, but I am falsely accused."

Another precedent was set at this examination when Hathorne asked the children to look at Sarah Good and say whether she was one who afflicted them. They accused her to her face, "upon which they were all dreadfully tortured and tormented for a short space of time." When they recovered from their fits they charged her with causing them, saying that her specter had come and tormented them although her body remained "at a considerable distance from them." This was spectral evidence, that is, evidence concerning a specter or apparition of the accused, rather than her bodily person. It was eventually to become the central legal issue of the trials, but at the moment we need only see why it seemed initially so convincing to the examining magistrates. Here were girls afflicted with violent physical symptoms which had no known physical cause, but which a physician had attributed to witch-craft. There was a malicious old woman accused of causing them. When the sufferers accused her they were immediately thrown into convulsions. What could be more plausible than that the convulsions were inflicted as revenge for the accusa-tion? Yet such behavior was still unfamiliar enough in Salem so that one of the recorders noted that "none here sees the [spec-ters of the] witches but the afflicted and themselves."

Certainly Hathorne was convinced; when the children had recovered and repeated their accusation he turned to the woman.

"Sarah Good, do you not see now what you have done? Why do you not tell us the truth? Why do you thus torment these poor children?"

"I do not torment them."

"Who do you employ, then?"

"I employ nobody. I scorn it."

A part of Hathorne's bullying may have been a result of Sarah Good's evasiveness, a sample of which remains on record. She was known to go muttering away from people's houses, and when Hathorne asked her what she muttered she answered, "If I must tell, I will tell."

"Do tell us, then," said Hathorne.

"If I must tell, I will tell. It is the Commandments. I may say my Commandments, I hope."

"What Commandment is it?"

"If I must tell, I will tell. It is a psalm."

"What psalm?"

She hesitated. Then, "after a long time she muttered over some part of a psalm."

Almost any seventeenth-century person hearing such an exchange would infer, perhaps not without reason, that Sarah Good was lying—that what she actually muttered as she left her neighbors' houses were curses.

Certainly many of her neighbors thought her malicious, since they attributed to her a number of inexplicable events, including the death of a cow which perished in "a sudden, terrible and strange unusual manner."[6] Such testimony was common in witchcraft cases, and it has caused much unseemly hilarity among modern historians. Is it likely, they have asked, that His Satanic Majesty the Devil or any of his minions would stoop to concern themselves with the fate of a New England cow? The answer is that nothing is more likely. What else would a fertility god concern himself with but the health or sickness of crops, of animals, and of humans? From the standpoint of a society that still remembered who the Devil was, no testimony could be more relevant. As a matter of fact, the village witches who still exist in rural England are often expert in folk medicines, human and animal, as well as charms, and until recently many of them were midwives.[7]

Sarah Osburn also denied that she had hurt the children, but again they fell into fits. Hathorne asked her how this happened. Perhaps, she said, the Devil went about in her likeness doing harm, but she knew nothing about it.

Sarah Osburn was the first at Salem to assert the principle that the Devil can impersonate an innocent person. Whether he could or not was a matter of debate in the seventeenth century, but most Protestant authorities agreed with Goodwife Osburn that, as Hamlet put it, "the Devil hath power/ to assume a pleasing shape." However, the principle was not discussed at this hearing, since Sarah Osburn was as likely a suspect as Sarah Good, if for no other reason than her lying. Lying was still considered a serious sin in the seventeenth century, and a crime as well, legally punishable by the courts.

When Hathorne tried to find out how well Sarah Osburn knew Sarah Good she said she did not know her by name.

Then what did she call her when they met, Hathorne asked. For a while she made no answer, but at last said she called her "Sarah." The afflicted girls volunteered that Goodwife Osburn had said she was more likely to be bewitched than to be a witch, and when Hathorne asked the accused woman why she replied that "she was frighted one time in her sleep and either saw or dreamed that she saw a thing like an Indian, all black, which did prick her in her neck and pulled her by the back part of her head to the door of the house."[8] Hathorne asked if she had ever seen anything else, and she said no. But several of the audience volunteered that she had once said "she would never be tied to that lying spirit any more." Hathorne picked this up immediately, since it is the Devil who is Prince of Lies.

"What lying spirit is this? Hath the Devil ever deceived you and been false to you?"

"I do not know the Devil. I never did see him."

"What lying spirit was it then?"

"It was a voice that I thought I heard."

"What did it propound to you?"

"That I should go no more to meeting. But I said I would, and did go the next Sabbath day."

Hathorne asked if she had been tempted further, and she said no. Why then, he asked, hadn't she been at church? She had been sick, she said, and unable to go. But her husband and others contradicted her. "She had not been at meeting," they said, "this year and two months."

To understand why the matter of church attendance was considered so significant one must remember that the seventeenth century saw witchcraft as literal Devil worship, and therefore as a rival religion to Christianity. This is why the magistrates sometimes asked accused persons, as they asked Sarah Good, what God they served. And if the accused person avoided speaking the name of God (as Sarah Good did), they had reason to think it a suspicious circumstance.

The examinations of Sarah Good and Sarah Osburn afforded grounds for suspicion and for further examination.

But the major event of that first day of March was the examination of Tituba. It began like the others, but it changed
very quickly:

"Tituba, what evil spirit have you familiarity with?"
"None."
"Why do you hurt these children?"
"I do not hurt them."
"Who is it then?"
"The Devil, for aught I know."
"Did you never see the Devil?"
"The Devil," said Tituba, "came to me and bid me serve him."⁹

She went on, with a minimum of judicial prodding, to provide a detailed confession of witchcraft, the first of approximately fifty that were made during the Salem trials. The number and the character of these confessions we shall deal with
later, but for the present let us limit ourselves to what Tituba
had to say in her examinations of March first and second.

The Devil had come to her in the shape of a man—a tall
man in black, with white hair. Other times he had come in the
shape of an animal. He had told her he was God, that she must
believe in him and serve him six years, and he would give her
many fine things. He had shown her a book and she had made
a mark in it, a mark that was "red like blood." There were nine
marks in the book, and two of them had been made by Good
and Osburn. Goody Good had told Tituba she had made her
mark there, "but Goody Osburn would not tell; she was cross
to me." Sometimes the black man had brought four witches
with him—Good and Osburn and two women from Boston
whose names she did not know—and they had forced her to go
with them and afflict the children. She had gone "upon a stick
or pole and Good and Osburn behind me. We ride taking hold
of one another; don't know how we go, for I saw no trees nor
path but was presently there." Both Good and Osburn had
familiars. Sarah Good had a cat and a yellow bird, and the bird
sucked her "between the fore-finger and long-finger upon the
right hand." Sarah Osburn had a thing with "wings and two
legs and a head like a woman." The children had seen it on

February 29, after which it turned into a woman. She also had "a thing all over hairy, all the face hairy, and a long nose, and I don't know how to tell how the face looks." The thing had two legs "and is about two or three foot high, and goeth upright like a man, and last night it stood before the fire in Mr. Parris' hall."

At the end of Tituba's first examination the children were in fits, and Hathorne asked who afflicted them. Tituba said she saw the shape of Sarah Good tormenting them, and the girls confirmed it. The convulsions of Elizabeth Hubbard grew suddenly more violent, and Hathorne asked who afflicted her. "I am blind now," said Tituba. "I cannot see." Shortly afterward she had spells of losing her speech as well, and fell eventually into fits.

Tituba's confession is in general similar to witchcraft confessions from other times and places. Part of it may have been suggested to her. But not all. It is far too detailed and far too original in some of its details to have been merely the product of the magistrates' leading questions. Her concluding line, of course, suggests the experienced medium, and her loss of sight and loss of speech as well as her fits suggest the hysteric. The most likely conclusion is that her confession was the product both of experience with the occult and of hysterical hallucinations as vivid and as terrifying as those of the afflicted girls.

We do not know in detail how the community reacted to it. One would give much to have seen the expression on the Reverend Mr. Parris' face when he heard what had been warming itself only the night before at his domestic fire. One immediate reaction was the committing of the three accused women to jail. Sarah Osburn was to die there on the tenth of May. Tituba, like later confessors, was never brought to trial. She lay in jail until she was sold to pay the jailer's fees, her master refusing to pay them. Sarah Good was brought to trial, and we shall meet with her again.

Another reaction to Tituba's confession was to confirm the community in its fear of witchcraft, and particularly its fear of the three accused women. The night of March first William

Allen and John Hughes heard a strange noise; it continued, frightening them, but they approached and "saw a strange and unusual beast lying on the ground. . . . Going up to it, the said beast vanished away and in the said place started up two or three women and fled, . . . not after the manner of other women but swiftly vanished out of our sight, which women we took to be Sarah Good, Sarah Osburn and Tituba." The next night William Allen again had hallucinations: "Sarah Good visibly appeared to him in his chamber, said Allen being in bed, and brought an unusual light in with her. The said Sarah came and sat upon his foot. The said Allen went to kick at her, upon which she vanished and the light with her."[10] Notice that in this hallucination as in many others the hallucination stops as soon as the subject is able to move or speak.

But more important than the fear of witchcraft in general and of Tituba, Good, and Osburn in particular must have been the fear and wonder at Tituba's testimony about witches yet undiscovered. Who were the two witches from Boston? And who had made the nine marks in the Devil's book? Only two of those nine marks—Good's and Osburn's—were accounted for. Tituba's testimony was an open invitation to every trace of paranoia in the community, and many Salem citizens must have cast suspicious glances at a neighbor, wondering, Is she a witch? Is he a wizard? For the time being, however, they remained suspicions only; Tituba's testimony had opened the way for a witch hunt, but as yet there was no witch hunt. Tituba and Osburn were examined again on March 3, and Tituba and Good on March 5. On the seventh the three women were sent to Boston jail. But the only new action taken by the authorities was to appoint Friday, March 11, as a day of prayer and fasting and to call for a consultation of neighboring Essex County ministers.

The fast was held and the ministers consulted. But the important action of that fast day came from the afflicted girls rather than the ministers or magistrates. They had continued to have hallucinations, with someone new appearing in them, and now they "cried out on" her. This time it was not a slave who was accused or a disreputable old woman like Good or Osburn, but Martha Corey, a member in good standing of the church at Salem Village. She had been accused by Ann Putnam, daughter of Sergeant Thomas Putnam, who was parish clerk and whose household was a center for witchcraft accusations from the very beginning. Two of those who heard the accusations were Edward Putnam and Ezekiel Cheever, fellow church members of Martha Corey's, who thought it their "duty to go to her and see what she would say to this complaint, she being in church covenant with us."[11] They agreed, around ten in the morning,

to go about the middle afternoon, and we desired Ann Putnam to take good notice of what clothes Goody Corey [i.e., her apparition] came in, that so we might see whether she was not mistaken in the person. And accordingly we went to the house of Thomas Putnam before we went to Goody Corey to see what Ann could say about her clothes, and she told us that presently after we had told her that we would go and talk with Goody Corey she came and blinded her, but told her that her name was Corey and that she should see her no more before it was night, and then she would come again and pay her off. Then we went both of us away from the home of Thomas Putnam to the house of Giles Corey, where we found . . . the abovesaid Corey all alone in her house. And as soon as we came in, in a smiling manner she saith "I know what you are come for; you are come to talk with me about being a witch, but I am none. I cannot help people's talking of me." Edward Putnam answered her that it was the afflicted person that did complain of her that was the occasion of our coming to her. She presently replied, "But does she tell you what clothes I have on?" We made her no answer to this at her first asking, whereupon she asked again with very great eagerness, "But does she tell you what clothes I have on?" . . . Which questions, with that eagerness of mind with which she did ask, made us to think of what Ann Putnam had told us before we went to her, and we told her no, she did not, for she told us that you came and blinded her and told her that she should see you no more before it was night, that so she might not tell us what clothes you had on. She made but little answer to this but seemed to smile at it, as if she had showed us a pretty trick.

How Martha Corey knew that they would try to identify her by her clothes we do not know for certain, but presumably she had learned it from someone who was present in the Thomas Putnam house that morning. In any case, her "pretty trick" backfired; at her examination, on March 21, Hathorne was more brutal than he had been with the first three.

"You are now in the hands of authority. Tell me now why you hurt these persons."

"I do not."

"Who doth?"

"Pray give me leave to go to prayer."

She asked this several times, and Hathorne told her they had not sent for her to hear her pray.

"But tell me why you hurt these."

"I am an innocent person. I never had to do with witchcraft since I was born. I am a gospel woman."

"Do you not see these complain of you?"

"The Lord open the eyes of the magistrates and ministers; the Lord show his power to discover the guilty."

"Tell us who hurts these children."

"I do not know."

"If you be guilty of this fact, do you think you can hide it?"

"The Lord knows."

"Well, tell us what you know of this matter."

"Why, I am a gospel woman, and do you think I can have to do with witchcraft too?"

"How could you tell, then, that the child was bid to observe what clothes you wore, when some came to speak with you?"

She said she had learned it from Cheever, but he replied that she spoke falsely. Hathorne persisted, and she said her husband had told her.

"Goodman Corey, did you tell her?"

(The old man denied that he told her so.)

"Did you not say your husband told you so?"

(No answer.)

"Who hurts these children? Now look upon them."

"I cannot help it."

"Did you not say you would tell the truth [about] why you asked that question? How came you to the knowledge?"

"I did but ask."

"You dare thus to lie in all this assembly! You are now before authority! I expect the truth. You promised it. Speak now, and tell us who told you [about the] clothes."

"Nobody."

There is much more, but there is no point in going on with it. Hathorne was never more brutal nor more intolerant than in his examination of Martha Corey. Her "pretty trick" was one reason for his brutality; so was her lying, for which it is impossible to assign a certain explanation. Another reason was her skepticism of the examinations, for it was known that Martha Corey had been skeptical. She had even tried to prevent her husband from attending the examinations of Tituba, Good, and Osburn, going so far as to remove the saddle from his horse. And now, during her own examination, she protested "We must not believe all that these distracted children say." Distracted persons, said Hathorne, varied from minute to minute, but these were constant in their accusations. Later he asked her whether she believed "there are witches in the country," to which she answered that she did not know of any.

"Do not you know that Tituba confessed it?"

"I did not hear her speak."

That Martha Corey's skepticism was held against her is clear evidence that by this time the magistrates' attitudes had hardened into those of the witch hunter. Only a witch hunter believes that anyone skeptical of witchcraft must undoubtedly be a witch.

It was at Martha Corey's examination that one typical kind of behavior first appeared. She bit her lip, and several of the afflicted children complained that they were bitten. She was charged with biting her lip, and she quite naturally asked what harm there was in it. The Reverend Mr. Nicholas Noyes of Salem Town explained: "I believe it is apparent she practiseth witchcraft in the congregation; there is no need of images." That is, instead of tormenting images she was using her own body as an image, biting the children by biting her own lips, and later pinching them by clenching her fingers together.

From Martha Corey's examination on, any motion on the part of the accused was apt to produce a corresponding effect in the afflicted children. It must have been a most convincing spectacle, as though black magic were being worked before the very eyes of the beholders. And as the effects produced on the children were obviously painful they were that much more convincing. In some cases there were seen to be marks of bites or pinches on the children's flesh; on other occasions there were pins literally stuck in their flesh.

There are at least three explanations for this behavior. In the first place, hysterics are extremely suggestible, and for hysterics familiar with the idea of image magic it would be easy to assume that an accused person biting her lip was trying to bite them. A similar phenomenon is the "arctic hysteria" of North American Indians, in which the group imitates the motions of the shaman. Secondly, hysterics will often try to injure themselves; they will beat their heads on the floor, or run into fire or water. (But they seldom succeed in injuring themselves seriously because they are most apt to make these attempts when other people are present, and able to stop them.) Surely this is the explanation for the pins in their flesh; the afflicted stuck them there themselves. But this is not to say there was conscious fraud; people in fits are after all not responsible for their actions. Some of the bites and pinches, too, were probably self-inflicted, but it is also probable that some were not. Skin lesions are among the commonest of psychosomatic symptoms, and surely some of these bites and pinches were psychosomatic.

Hathorne and Corwin, of course, thought the cause was witchcraft, and they committed Martha Corey to jail for further examination and eventual trial. And with her commitment to jail, Salem had very nearly committed itself to a witch hunt. Yet there would be moments during the succeeding month when the course of events would seem to hesitate and waver; moments when the slightest change of circumstances might have averted the final catastrophe.

4

❖◦❖◦❖◦❖◦❖

How to Catch a Witch

On Saturday, March 19, two days before the examination of Martha Corey, the Reverend Deodat Lawson arrived in Salem Village. He had been its minister from 1684 to 1688 and had now returned as a visiting preacher and for personal reasons as well; the afflicted girls were saying that his wife and daughter, whom he had buried there, had been killed by witchcraft. He tells us that there were at that time ten afflicted persons —three girls from nine to twelve years old: Elizabeth Parris, Abigail Williams, and Ann Putnam; three adolescent girls: Mary Walcott, Mercy Lewis, and Elizabeth Hubbard; and four married women: Goodwives Putnam, Pope, Bibber, and Goodall. He conducted both the morning and the afternoon services on Sunday, but not without incident. Several of the afflicted persons were present.

They had several sore fits in the time of public worship, which did something interrupt me in my first prayer, being so unusual. After Psalm was sung Abigail Williams said to me, "Now stand up and name your text." And after it was read she said "It is a long text." In the beginning of sermon Mrs. Pope . . . said to me "Now there is enough of that." And in the afternoon Abigail Williams, upon my referring to my doctrine said to me "I know no doctrine you had. If you did name one I have forgot it." In sermon time when Goodwife Corey was present in the meeting-house Abigail Williams called out "Look where Goodwife Corey sits on the beam, suckling her yellow bird between her fingers!" Ann Putnam . . . said there was a yellow bird sat on my hat as it hung on the pin in the pulpit, but those that were by [her] restrained her from speaking aloud about it.[1]

This was not Lawson's first introduction to the behavior of the afflicted. He had lodged the night before at Ingersoll's

Tavern, and there had seen Mary Walcott, who, "as she stood by the door was bitten, so that she cried out of her wrist, and looking on it with a candle we saw apparently the marks of teeth, both upper and lower set, on each side of her wrist." He had also visited the parsonage, where Abigail Williams "had a grievous fit." He would see more on Monday, at Martha Corey's examination, and on Wednesday, when he went to Thomas Putnam's to see his wife, Ann Putnam, Senior.

I found her lying on the bed, having had a sore fit a little before. She spake to me and said she was glad to see me. Her husband and she both desired me to pray with her while she was sensible, which I did, though the apparition said [i.e., to Ann Putnam, Senior] I should not go to prayer. At the first beginning she attended but after a little time was taken with a fit, yet continued silent and seemed to be asleep. When prayer was done, her husband going to her found her in a fit. He took her off the bed to set her on his knees, but at first she was so stiff she could not be bended. But she afterwards set down, but quickly began to strive violently with her arms and legs.

Shortly afterward she began to argue with an apparition, and she thought that telling it a passage from the Bible would make it vanish.

Said she, "I am sure you cannot stand before that text!" Then she was sorely afflicted, her mouth drawn on one side and her body strained for about a minute, and then said "I will tell, I will tell; it is, it is, it is!" three or four times, and then was afflicted to hinder her from telling. At last she broke forth and said "It is the third chapter of the Revelations." I did something scruple the reading it. [Lawson was reluctant because in this case reading the Bible might be construed as using it as a charm.] . . . However, though not versed in these things, I judged I might do it this once for an experiment. I began to read, and before I had read through the first verse she opened her eyes and was well. This fit [had] continued near half an hour. Her husband and the spectators told me she had often been so relieved by reading texts that she named, something pertinent to her case.

The next day was Lecture Day at Salem Village and Lawson preached the sermon, which he published shortly thereafter under the title *Christ's Fidelity the Only Shield Against Satan's Malignity*. Historians have consistently represented it as an attempt to stir up the emotions of the community, but in fact it was nothing of the sort. To be sure, Lawson did reaffirm that the girls' afflictions were the "effects of Diabolical malice and operations, and that it cannot rationally be imagined to proceed from any other cause whatsoever." He did urge the magistrates to care for the afflicted girls and do their utmost to find the cause of their afflictions, and he also urged them to do severe justice: "to approve yourselves a terror of and punishment to evil-doers, and a praise to them that do well." But if this was a severe concept of justice it was also even-handed. Furthermore, Lawson was far from depending on the magistrates to cure the country of its troubles. In fact he warned the community that there was ultimately no legitimate secular defense against witchcraft. There was, for example, no legitimate means of testing to see whether an accused person was a witch: "we find no means instituted of God to make trial of witches." Nor could one rightly defend oneself against witchcraft with white magic, such as boiling one's urine or nailing a horseshoe over the door, because such charms were in themselves "a kind of witchcraft," and might well give a more secure foothold to the Devil.

Careless accusations of suspected persons might also backfire, Lawson warned. "Rash censuring of others, without sufficient grounds, or false accusing any willingly . . . is indeed to be like the Devil, who . . . is a calumniator, or false accuser." Most important, he warned his listeners that the Devil might appear in the shape of an innocent person. Indeed, he suspected this was precisely what had happened when church members saw the apparitions of other church members afflicting them. The Devil had taken "some of the visible subjects of our Lord Jesus and [used] at least their shapes and appearances . . . to afflict and torture other visible subjects of that same Kingdom. Surely his design is that Christ's Kingdom may be divided against itself." Given all these difficulties the only sure protection against witchcraft, the "Only Shield Against Satan's Malignity," was faith in Christ, and the application of that faith in prayer. And such prayer would be answered, particularly if it came from a people bound to the worship of God, like those of New England, by their church covenants: "whensoever God hath declared a person or people to be in covenant with Him, as the objects of His special mercy and favor, he will assuredly and shortly suppress the malice of Satan, however violently engaged against them."

If Lawson, like Cotton Mather with the Goodwin children, thought prayer a more certain cure for witchcraft than anything the magistrates might do, it was partly because it was so difficult to catch a witch. She would not, after all, sign her pact with Satan on Main Street in broad daylight, nor practice her black arts there. Witchcraft was by its nature secret, and hard to be found out. Yet witches had been caught, and many examples were a matter of record, as were many theories on catching them.

There were, to begin with, commonly recognized grounds for investigation. If an apparition was appearing to the citizenry and afflicting them, one would surely want to investigate the person represented in that apparition. One would also look for evidence of malice, since witchcraft was an expression of ultimate malice, the diametrical opposite to Christian charity. And one could hope that an investigation would produce credible confessions. Confessions were often easy to obtain, particularly if one used the technique of "cross and swift questions" recommended by virtually all authorities from *Malleus Maleficarum* to Cotton Mather, but it was not always easy to judge whether they were credible. Satan was the Prince of Lies and witches were his servants; the word of confessed witches was therefore suspect in their accusations both of others and themselves. Furthermore, it was known that desperate persons had sometimes confessed to witchcraft as a bizarre means of committing suicide. And the mentally disturbed had also been known to imagine themselves witches and confess. In spite of all these difficulties, however, confession was often the best evidence one could hope for.

More concrete evidence was occasionally to be had. A diligent search, for example, might turn up some of the tools of the witch's trade: images with fins on them, ointments and potions, books of instruction in the magical arts. And one could search the body of the accused for the so-called Devil's Mark. It was believed that when a pact was made the Devil placed upon the witch's body a piece of flesh from which He, in His own person or that of a familiar, might suck the blood of the witch. (The blood has traditionally been thought to be the carrier of the spirit; in sucking blood the Devil was feeding on the witch's soul.) Since this "witch's tit" was created by the Devil rather than by God it lacked the warmth of normal flesh (hence the still-current expression about being cold as a witch's tit). It also lacked sensation, and one could test for that by running a pin through it to see whether it was a genuinely preternatural excrescence or only a wart or a hemorrhoid.

This "pricking" as a test for witchcraft sometimes had a kind of rough validity, as the psychologist Pierre Janet observed. Witches were often hysterics, like their victims, and one common symptom of hysteria is local anesthesia, particularly if the limits of the anesthetic area make no sense in terms of nerve structure. Thus both Charcot and Janet probed for anesthetic areas in testing for hysteria, and Janet remarked that

in our clinics, we are somewhat like the [medieval] woman who sought for witches. We blindfold the subject, we turn his head away, rub his skin with our nail, prick it suddenly with a hidden pin, watch his answers or starts of pain; the picture has not changed.[2]

Yet pricking for the Devil's Mark was most haphazard and uncertain. It was common for examiners, physicians included, to disagree over whether an excrescence was natural or preternatural. And it was not unheard of for them to find what they thought to be a Devil's Mark on one occasion, only to discover that there was nothing left of it but a piece of dried skin on a second examination.

The common people believed in a number of tests for witches. The best known was the water-ordeal, in which the suspect was bound and "swum": thrown into or dragged by a rope through the nearest body of water. If she floated she was a witch; the water was rejecting her as she had rejected Christian baptism. If she sank, she was innocent; the mob would try to drag her out before she drowned and profess to be sorry if they failed. (It *was* generally mob-action when a witch was swum; the courts seldom countenanced it, even when the accused requested it as a means of proving her innocence.)

Another such test was asking the accused to repeat the Lord's Prayer. It was believed that a witch could not say it correctly, even after prompting, since she regularly said it backwards at her witches' Sabbaths. It was also believed that a witch could not weep. Because she had rejected Christian charity in favor of demonic malice she would remain dry-eyed at the most heart-rending spectacles. Many of the learned, including Increase Mather and Deodat Lawson, rejected such tests outright as superstitions or as white magic or both. Others, like Cotton Mather, were willing to countenance experiments with them but refused to accept them as certain evidence.

There was one test for witchcraft that had a wide following among the learned as well as the common people. This was a kind of laying-on-of-hands in which the suspected person was made to touch an afflicted person in the midst of a fit. If the touch seemed to cure, the theory was that the spell had been taken back into the body of the witch from whom it came. Laying-on-of-hands is, of course, one of the commonest kinds of faith-healing. It was practiced by Christ, and anyone who wishes to can watch it being practiced on television today by an evangelist with the surprising name of Oral Roberts. When the disease is psychosomatic and the sick person believes in the power of the healer there is no question that laying-on-of-hands frequently works. As a test for witchcraft it had been admitted as valid evidence by no less a person than Sir Matthew Hale, Chief Baron of the Exchequer, who presided at the witchcraft trial at Bury St. Edmunds in 1664 (where Sir Thomas Browne provided the expert medical opinion noted in the first chapter). Cotton Mather tells us that the accounts of this trial were "much considered by the judges of New England."[3]

All things considered, however, it was clearly more difficult to prove witchcraft than to prove most other crimes. It is hardly surprising that the Reverend Deodat Lawson thought prayer more efficacious than the law.

When Lawson warned his audience that the Devil could impersonate the innocent, suggested he had done so, and attributed to the Devil the motive of trying to cause division among church members, he may have been thinking of Martha Corey. And he was certainly thinking of another church member, Rebecca Nurse, who was being cried out on by the afflicted on the very day Lawson returned to Salem. One would not expect witches to be church members, since they were supposed to have renounced Christianity in giving their allegiance to the Devil; neither would one expect them to have Rebecca Nurse's reputation for benevolence, since their trade was by its nature an expression of malice. A woman named Sarah Holton did testify that Rebecca Nurse acted maliciously on one occasion, accusing her of "railing and scolding"[4] against her husband. But her more usual demeanor seems to have been the meekness and humility she displayed when she was told she had been accused:

We whose names are underwritten being desired to go to Goodman Nurse his house, to speak with his wife, and to tell her that several of the afflicted persons mentioned her; and accordingly we went, and we found her in a weak and low condition in body as she told us, and had been sick almost a week. And we asked her how it was otherwise with her: and she said she blessed God for it, she had more of his presence in this sickness than sometime she have had, but not so much as she desired; but she would, with the apostle, press forward to the mark; and many other places of Scripture to the like purpose. And then, of her own accord, she began to speak of the affliction that was amongst them, And in particular of Mr. Parris his family, and how she was grieved for them, though she had not been to see them, by reason of fits that she formerly used to have; for people said it was awful to behold: but she pitied them with all her heart, and went to God for them. But she said she heard that there was persons spoke of that were as innocent as she was, she believed; and, after much to this purpose, we told her that she was spoken of also. "Well," she said, "if it be so, the will of the Lord be done." She sat still a while, being as it were amazed; and then she said, "Well, as to this thing I am as innocent as the child unborn; but surely," she said, "what sin hath God found out in me unrepented of, that he should lay such an affliction upon me in my old age?" And, according to our best observation, we could not discern that she knew what we came for before we told her.

Israel Porter
Elizabeth Porter

To the substance of what is above, we, if called thereto, are ready to testify on oath.

Daniel Andrew
Peter Cloyse

Elizabeth Porter was the sister of magistrate John Hathorne, and this says much for the community's uncertainties over the accusation of Rebecca Nurse. Hathorne himself was, for the first time, plainly unsure of himself when he conducted her examination on March 24. When he first asked her what she had to say to the accusations she answered "I can say before my eternal Father I am innocent, and God will clear my innocency." And to this he replied "Here is never a one in the assembly but desires it. But if you be guilty, pray God discover you." He was to repeat this sentiment later in the examination: "I pray God clear you if you be innocent, and if you be guilty discover you."

But how was one to decide whether she was innocent or guilty? Here on the one hand were the afflicted girls, plainly enduring the most frightful tortures and crying out that Rebecca Nurse was the cause of them, echoing in the twistings and turnings of their grotesque postures the most casual movement of Rebecca Nurse's body. There on the other hand was Rebecca Nurse, as unlikely a candidate for witchhood as anyone in Essex County, meekly calling on her God for help in the midst of the demonic uproar. Hathorne plainly did not know what to make of it. Rebecca Nurse's Christian character (and perhaps Lawson's sermon as well) temporarily cast doubt on his previously clear faith in the validity of apparitions as evidence.

"What uncertainty there may be in apparitions I know not, yet this with me strikes hard upon you, that you are at this very present charged with familiar spirits. This is your bodily person they speak to; they say now they see these familiar spirits come to your bodily person. Now what do you say to that?"

That is, the afflicted girls had not only testified that the apparition of Rebecca Nurse was tormenting them; they said they had seen it leave her body and return to it. But she denied it, and it was at this point that Hathorne for the second time prayed that she be cleared if innocent and discovered if guilty.

If he could not doubt that the girls' afflictions were genuine, neither could he doubt that Rebecca Nurse was telling the truth, at least so far as she knew it. Perhaps, he thought, the Devil had made her a witch without her knowledge. Therefore he said to her "Possibly you may apprehend you are no witch, but have you not been led aside by temptations that way?"

"I have not," she answered, and Hathorne could reply only by reflecting on "what a sad thing" it was to see church members accused of such a crime. What, he asked, did she make of the girls' behavior? "They accuse you of hurting them, and if you think it is not unwillingly, but by design, you must look upon them as murderers."

"I cannot tell what to think of it."

Nothing testifies more to the genuineness of the fits than the fact that Rebecca Nurse, like the majority of the accused persons, could not tell what to think of them. Later, when Hathorne asked whether she thought the afflicted persons bewitched, she answered yes, "I do think they are." So he appealed to her again.

"When this witchcraft came upon the stage there was no suspicion of Tituba. . . . She professed much love to that child,

Betty Parris, but it was her apparition that did the mischief. And why should not you also be guilty, for your apparition doth hurt also."

"Would you have me belie myself?" said Rebecca Nurse. To repeated testimony that her apparition was tormenting people she replied "I cannot help it. The Devil may appear in my shape." In the end the magistrates committed her for further examination.

Rebecca Nurse's arrest and examination did more than raise temporary doubts in the mind of John Hathorne; it evoked the first open expression of opposition to the witchcraft proceedings. Mary Warren, one of the afflicted girls, was the servant of a farmer named John Procter. On the morning after Rebecca Nurse's examination he came to Salem Village "to fetch home his jade,"[5] as he put it. He expressed his opinion of the afflicted persons' testimony in no uncertain terms. "If they were let alone," he said, "we should all be devils and witches quickly. They should rather be had to the whipping post. But he would fetch his jade home and thrash the Devil out of her. And more to the like purpose, crying 'Hang them! Hang them!' " He added that when Mary Warren "was first taken with fits he kept her close to the wheel and threatened to thrash her, and then she had no more fits till the next day [when] he was gone forth. And then she must have her fits again, forsooth."

Historians have taken John Procter's statement as evidence that Mary Warren's fits were false, and in this they have been quite wrong. The seventeenth-century community took them as evidence of Procter's malice and brutality, and they were partly right. But only partly. Because however brutal it may be to beat the hysterical out of their fits, the fact remains that such treatment often works. A fit of uncontrolled laughter can often be stopped with a judiciously timed slap in the face. And we should remember that in the eighteenth century one of the commonest treatments for many forms of insanity was beating the patient. Such treatment was probably motivated in part by the "normal" person's exasperation with the insane for so conspicuously losing their rationality. But surely it was also motivated by the fact that it frequently worked. And for that matter, it should be recognized that we are still beating the insane. We no longer administer the blows ourselves; we do it technologically, and with more precision than our ancestors. But this should not disguise the fact that electric shock is just as brutal for the patient as the thrashing John Procter proposed for Mary Warren. Perhaps he did thrash her, and perhaps it did in part work, because as we shall shortly see, Mary Warren was the only person who even temporarily recovered from her affliction.

There are several points at which, had circumstances been slightly different, the course of events at Salem might have changed entirely, and one of these is the examination of Rebecca Nurse. If she had held the stage alone her evident sincerity might have convinced the community that they had been mistaken. But unfortunately someone else was arrested and examined at the same time. This was Dorcas Good, the five-year-old daughter of Sarah Good, and within two days of her arrest she had provided Salem its second confession. Oh yes, she told the examining magistrates, she had a familiar. It was a little snake that used to suck her at the lowest joint of her forefinger. Here, as on a number of other occasions, the examiners were not at first willing to take a confession at face value. Where did the snake suck, they asked; Was it here? "pointing to other places"[6] on the child's body. No, said the child, not there. Here. And she pointed to her forefinger, where the examiners "observed a deep red spot, about the bigness of a flea bite."

Probably it was a flea bite, and the child had only imagined that she had a familiar who sucked her blood there. At this distance in time it is impossible to know for certain what caused that deep red spot. But there is no difficulty in imagining the feelings of the examiners when they saw it. All of them had heard that a demon in the shape of an animal came to the witch and sucked her blood, and here was what seemed to be the physical evidence of just such an "accursed suckage" on the

finger of a five-year-old child, pointed out by the child herself
as corroboration of her confession, corroboration which the
examiners had at first been hesitant to accept. They must have
been thoroughly horrified. If five-year-old children were suckling demons, then the Devil had a far surer foothold in Massachusetts than anyone had imagined, and strenuous investigation would be necessary to discover its extent. Yet their horror
must have been mixed with triumph, for Dorcas Good's confession confirmed the rightness of their procedure in imprisoning her mother, since the child accused her mother as well as
herself and did it without prodding. Who had given her the
little snake, they asked her. Was it the Black Man? Oh no,
Dorcas replied, it wasn't the Black Man; it was her mother,
whom she continued to accuse, testifying at her trial that she
had three familiars, birds, "one black, one yellow and that
these birds hurt the children and afflicted persons."

Dorcas Good's confession, with the accompanying physical
evidence of her Devil's mark, must have quieted the doubts of
the investigation that many had felt at the arrest of Rebecca
Nurse. Because from this time on expressions of sympathy for
Rebecca Nurse were met not with doubt but with suspicion. On
Sunday, April 3, Parris preached on John 6, 70: Have not I
chosen you twelve, and one of you is a Devil. The implication
of the text was clear. The Puritans believed that church members had been chosen—elected—by God. Thus Parris' text
suggested that a church member had betrayed her election just
as Judas had betrayed Christ's choice. In short, it suggested
that Rebecca Nurse was guilty before she had been tried.
As soon as he had spoken, Sarah Cloyse, a sister of Rebecca
Nurse, rose from her seat, left the meetinghouse and slammed
the door behind her "to the amazement of the congregation."[7]
They were amazed, of course, not at her resentment of Parris
but at her public expression of it in the midst of a church
service, a virtually unheard of action in Puritan Massachusetts.

It was quite enough to call Sarah Cloyse to the attention of
the afflicted girls, who shortly began to see her apparition in
their fits, taking the Devil's sacrament of "red bread and

drink." "Oh Goodwife Cloyse," said one, "I did not think to see you here! Is this a time to receive the sacrament? You ran away on the Lord's Day, and scorned to receive it in the meetinghouse, and is this a time to receive it? I wonder at you!" This was the third time in four days that the girls had mentioned a witches' sacrament. The confessions of Tituba and Dorcas Good were beginning to bear fruit; the girls and the community were no longer thinking in terms of individual witches but were beginning to think of an organized society of witches with its own structure and its own sacraments.

In spite of the growing belief that they were facing a diabolical conspiracy the community was still moving relatively slowly. Goodwife Cloyse slammed the door of Salem Village meetinghouse on April 3. The girls must have seen her apparition within twenty-four hours, because it was on April 4 that Jonathan Walcott and Nathaniel Ingersoll entered complaints against her and Elizabeth Procter, the wife of John Procter. Yet warrants were not issued until the eighth, and examinations were not conducted until the eleventh. At least a part of the delay may have been occasioned by the community's decision to take this next examination more seriously than the early ones, perhaps as a result of the belief that they were facing an organized conspiracy. In any case, for this examination Hathorne and Corwin were joined on the bench by four other magistrates, including Samuel Sewall of Boston and Thomas Danforth, the deputy-governor of the colony, who acted as presiding magistrate.

Anyone who has read anything of Sewall's *Diary*—even the brief excerpts that find their way into the typical anthology of American literature—will know that he was a person of considerable shrewdness, kindness, and common sense. But the presence of Sewall and the other three new magistrates made no difference in the procedures of the examination. The transcript does not say who asked the questions, but we may assume from the similarity of this to the earlier transcripts that most of the questions still came from Hathorne. He began by

asking John, Parris' Carib Indian slave, who had hurt him?
Goody Procter, said John, and then Goody Cloyse. What had
they done to him? Choked him, he said, and brought him the
book [the Devil's book] to sign. (This choking is, of course, one
more instance of the *globus hystericus*, the hysterical lump in the
throat, coupled with an hallucination.) Did he know Goody
Cloyse and Goody Procter? (That is, did he know the persons
themselves or had he only seen their apparitions?) Yes, he
answered. "Here is Goody Cloyse."

At this point Goodwife Cloyse could contain herself no
longer, and burst out, "When did I hurt thee?"

"A great many times."

"Oh," said Sarah Cloyse, "you are a grievous liar."[8]

The bench questioned John further, then turned to Mary
Walcott, whose testimony was interrupted by her falling into
fits, and to Abigail Williams. It was these two who testified that
they had seen Sarah Cloyse at a meeting of witches (including
Rebecca Nurse, Martha Corey, and Sarah Good) at Deacon
Ingersoll's, upon which "Sarah Cloyse asked for water, and sat
down as one seized with a dying fainting fit ["dying" here has
the now archaic meaning of losing consciousness; "fainting"
does not mean to lose consciousness but to lose strength]; and
several of the afflicted fell into fits, and some of them cried out,
Oh! her spirit is gone to prison to her sister Nurse."

The bench then turned to the case of Elizabeth Procter.

"Elizabeth Procter, you understand whereof you are charged, viz.
to be guilty of sundry acts of witchcraft; what say you to it? Speak
the truth. And so you that are afflicted, you must speak the truth, as
you will answer it before God another day. Mary Walcott, doth this
woman hurt you?"

"I never saw her so as to be hurt by her."

"Mercy Lewis, does she hurt you?"

Her mouth was stopped.

"Ann Putnam, does she hurt you?"

She could not speak.

"Abigail Williams, does she hurt you?"

Her hand was thrust in her own mouth.

"John (Indian), does this woman hurt you?"

"This is the woman that came in her shift and choked me."

"Did she ever bring the book?"

"Yes sir."

"What to do?"

"To write."

"What, this woman?"

"Yes, sir."

"Are you sure of it?"

"Yes sir."

Again Abigail Williams and Ann Putnam were spoke to by the court, but neither of them could make any answer, by reason of dumbness or other fits.

"What do you say, Goody Procter, to these things?"

"I take God in heaven to be my witness that I know nothing of it, no more than the child unborn."

The bench returned to questioning the girls, and this time they were able to answer. Yes, Goody Procter had afflicted them, and many times. Upon this she looked at them, and they fell into fits. When they recovered they were asked, had she brought the book to them to sign? Yes, and boasted that her maid, Mary Warren, had signed it. When Abigail Williams asked her to her face whether she had not told her that Mary Warren had signed the book, Elizabeth Procter answered, "Dear child, it is not so. There is another judgment, dear child." Abigail's reply was to fall again into fits, in which Ann Putnam joined her, and soon both were crying out that they saw Goodwife Procter's apparition perched above the spectators on a beam. Soon they were crying out of John Procter as well, saying he was a wizard, and at this "many, if not all of the bewitched had grievous fits." Then they saw Procter's apparition. Abigail Williams called out, "There is Goodman Procter going to Mrs. Pope," and immediately Goodwife Pope fell into a fit. "There is Goodman Procter going to hurt Goody Bibber," and immediately Goodwife Bibber fell into a fit.

Elizabeth Procter's demeanor had been as meek and as Christian as that of Rebecca Nurse, but how many would remember it after such a horrendous display of fits and such graphic hallucinations? Certainly Samuel Sewall did not. His brief diary entry for April 11 reads:

Went to Salem, where, in the Meeting-house, the persons accused of witchcraft were examined; was a very great assembly; 'twas awful to see how the afflicted persons were agitated. Mr. Noyes prayed at the beginning, and Mr. Higginson concluded.[9]

Indeed, the outcry against John Procter was so terrible that he was committed with his wife, and the following day the Procters, with Sarah Cloyse, Rebecca Nurse, Martha Corey, and Sarah Good were sent to Boston jail.

The accusation that Mary Warren, the Procters' maidservant, had signed the Devil's book had a special significance, because she had previously been one of the afflicted girls. But lately she had taken to denying both her own testimony and that of others. The girls' evidence was false, she said; they "did but dissemble."[10] By this she did not mean that they were simply lying. She meant that they were living in two different worlds of experience—that of their fits, and that of normal perception —and the world of their fits was false. She told several people that

"the magistrates might as well examine Keysar's daughter that had been distracted many years and take notice of what she said as well as any of the afflicted persons. For," said Mary Warren, "when I was afflicted I thought I saw the apparitions of a hundred persons" (for she said her head was distempered [so] that she could not tell what she said). And . . . when she was well again she could not say that she saw any of the apparitions aforesaid.

One of the other girls, Mercy Lewis, was also capable at this time of distinguishing between the hallucinations of her fits and the world of ordinary perception. A young man named Ephraim Sheldon testified that

I, this deponent, being at the house of Lieutenant Ingersoll when Mercy Lewis was in one of her fits, I heard her cry out of Goodwife Cloyse. And when she came to herself she was asked who she saw. She answered, she saw nobody. They demanded of her whether or no she did not see Goodwife Nurse, or Goodwife Cloyse, or Goodwife Corey. She answered, she saw nobody.[11]

But Mercy Lewis was seldom asked to choose between her hallucinations and her ordinary perceptions. She was a maid in the household of Thomas Putnam, whose daughter, Ann Putnam, Jr., was one of the most violently afflicted girls and one of the most ready in making accusations, and whose wife, Ann Putnam, Sr., was not far behind. The Putnam household was in fact as much a center for hysterical fits and accusations as the Parris household, and given such a home environment it is scarcely surprising that Mercy Lewis never reached the point that Mary Warren achieved, of denying the general validity of her hallucinations.

But the Procter household was a very different matter. John Procter may, as has been suggested, have beaten Mary Warren out of some of her fits. Certainly he often threatened her with beating, and with worse; on one occasion he threatened to burn her out of her fit with a pair of hot tongs. Another time he threatened to drown her. In her fits she had tried to run into the fire and into water, and he had prevented her, but he told her once that if it happened again he would let her destroy herself. Once he was in the room while she was in a fit and said to her, "If you are afflicted, I wish you were more afflicted." Indeed, he added, he wished all the afflicted persons were worse afflicted.

"Master," she asked, "what makes you say so?"

"Because," said John Procter, "you go to bring out innocent persons."

Mary Warren answered that "that could not be."

But her hysteria was vulnerable to his persistent skepticism, or to his threats, or to his violence, or to a combination of the three. She did return to sanity, and she did deny the validity of her hallucinations. This is another of those points at which the course of Salem witchcraft might have changed. If Cotton Mather, who had shown himself in Boston more interested in curing the Goodwin children than in catching witches, had been present then Mary Warren would probably have retained her sanity. If Samuel Willard had been present, who at Groton had seized on and explored every contradiction in the testimony of Elizabeth Knapp, she might also have remained sane. But Mather and Willard were not present, and the magistrates and ministers of Salem and of Salem Village were not interested in the fact that Mary Warren had recovered from her fits and was, correctly, calling them insanity. They were interested in the fact that Mary Warren's specter was now engaged in tormenting the other afflicted persons.

They were not instantly sure of themselves; Mary Warren was accused of signing the Devil's book on April 11, and she was not examined until the nineteenth. But by that date the magistrates had plainly made up their minds.

"You were a little while ago an afflicted person," said Hathorne. "Now you are an afflicter. How comes this to pass?"

"I look up to God," said Mary Warren, "and take it to be a great mercy of God."

"What!" said Hathorne, "Do you take it to be a great mercy to afflict others?"

The afflicted persons had begun having fits as soon as Mary Warren approached the bar; shortly they were all in fits. Hysteria is communicable, and Mary Warren had previously been subject to it.

Shortly Mary Warren fell into a fit, and some of the afflicted cried out that she was going to confess, but Goody Corey and Procter and his wife came in, in their apparition, and struck her down and said she should tell nothing.

Mary Warren continued a good space in a fit [so] that she did neither see, nor hear, nor speak. Afterwards she started up and said, "I will speak," and cried out "Oh! I am sorry for it, I am sorry for it," and wringed her hands, and fell a little while into a fit again, and then came to speak, but immediately her teeth were set. And then she fell into a violent fit and cried out, "Oh Lord help me! Oh good Lord save me!" And then afterwards cried again, "I will tell, I will tell," and then fell into a dead fit again. And afterwards cried, "I will tell! They did! They did! They did!" and then fell into a violent fit again. After a little recovery she cried, "I will tell! They brought me to it!" and then fell into a fit again, which fits continuing she was ordered to be had out. . . .

When Mary Warren had been returned to prison she again recovered her sanity and again denied the validity of what she saw and said in her fits. The magistrates continued to examine her—sometimes in prison and sometimes in public—for the next three weeks, continually refusing to accept her denials and continually demanding that she confess. By the end of the process she had incriminated herself, her mistress, and finally her master. Once, she said, she had caught at an apparition that looked like Goody Corey, but pulling it down into her lap had found it to be John Procter. By the time she gave up her denials she was having fits so violent that her legs could not be uncrossed without breaking them.

5

❖❖❖❖❖❖

Witchcraft at Salem

It is plain that Mary Warren was literally driven insane by the refusal of the magistrates, the ministers, and the afflicted girls to accept her sanity. If her case had been an isolated one the community's treatment of her would be very nearly incredible. But just as the community's attitudes toward Rebecca Nurse had probably been influenced by her being examined on the same day as the second confessor, Dorcas Good, their attitudes toward Mary Warren were probably influenced by the fact that three other persons were examined on April 19: Giles Corey, Abigail Hobbes, and Bridget Bishop. Giles Corey had been very ready to testify against his wife, Martha, and to speak against her out of court as well as in: he had told several people that he knew things that would "do his wife's business."[1] Now he was admirably, if belatedly, protesting her innocence as well as his own. But he did it stupidly; he denied having said things which witnesses had heard him say, and thus was several times caught lying. Since lying was a serious matter in Puritan Massachusetts and perjury is a serious matter in any age, Giles Corey must have made a very bad impression.

Abigail Hobbes was a wild and irreverent young girl who on one occasion had parodied the sacrament of baptism by sprinkling water on her mother and pronouncing the words of baptism over her.[2] And she had cultivated the reputation of a witch. When Lydia Nichols had asked her "how she durst lie out of nights in the woods alone," she replied that "she was not afraid of anything, for . . . she had sold herself body and soul to the Old Boy." On another occasion she had told Lydia to hold her tongue or she would "raise all the folks thereabouts" [i.e., summon all the spirits thereabouts], and told her to look

—"there was old Nick[3] . . . over the bedstead." Her mother was present and said to Abigail that "she little thought to have been mother to such a daughter." On another occasion a woman named Priscilla Chubb was scolding her "about her wicked carriage and disobedience to her father and mother," and Abigail replied that "she did not care what anybody said to her, for she had seen the Devil and had made a covenant or bargain with him." She confessed immediately, at her first examination, but it is most unlikely that she was actually a witch. Far too often she did not know what to answer to her examiners' questions, and they had to supply her the details of her supposed craft with their leading questions.

But there was more than Giles Corey's dogged lying and Abigail Hobbes' willingness to acquire a wicked reputation on display in Salem Village on April 19. There was Bridget Bishop. And Bridget Bishop was in all probability a practicing witch. She had a long-standing reputation for witchcraft; it was rumored that she had bewitched her first husband (a Goodman Wasslebee) to death.[4] In 1679/80, during her second marriage (to Thomas Oliver), she had been brought before the Court of Assistants for witchcraft. The records of that trial do not survive, but it is probable that a major factor in her release at the time was the good opinion of her clergyman, John Hale of Beverly, who was then "hoping better of Goody Bishop" than others in the community. But Hale had changed his mind by 1692. Her present husband, Edward Bishop, had accused her of witchcraft; two women testified that he had said "the Devil did come bodily unto her, and that she was familiar with the Devil, and that she sat up all the night long with the Devil." She was well aware of her reputation. Once she had asked William Stacey "whether his father would grind her grist. He put it to her why she asked. She answered, because folks counted her a witch." She also had the malice requisite to the craft. During her examination, when Hathorne used the bullying techniques he had used on others, she startled him with an open threat. "If I were any such person [a witch]," she told him, "you should know it." [I.e., she would *make* him know it.]

But there was much more against Bridget Bishop than her reputation and her malice. Two men testified that

> being employed by Bridget Bishop, alias Oliver, of Salem to help take down the cellar wall of the old house she formerly lived in, we the said deponents, in holes in the old wall belonging to the said cellar, found several puppets made up of rags and hogs' bristles with headless pins in them with the points outward. . . .

The doll with pins in it is the classic charm of black magic, and burying it in a wall is still a technique of witches; such charms have been found in the walls of rural English cottages in the twentieth century. To be sure, the evidence was circumstantial—nobody had seen Bridget Bishop stick the pins in the dolls or bury them in the walls. But she could, according to Cotton Mather, give no account of them to the court "that was reasonable or tolerable."[5] Coupled with the other testimony against her, that concerning the dolls was extremely incriminating. It would have been quite enough to get her hanged in seventeenth-century England or burned in Scotland or on the Continent. It is probable that Bridget Bishop was indeed a practicing witch.

There is one more piece of evidence which probably applies to her use of image magic. Samuel Shattuck, a Quaker who was the local dyer, testified that she had brought him for dyeing "sundry pieces of lace, some of which were so short that I could not judge them fit for any use." Upham, in the nineteenth century, interpreted this to mean that Bridget Bishop was wearing clothing of a style incomprehensible to a simple Quaker[6] and later writers have followed him in this interpretation, coupling with it the fact that Bridget Bishop often wore a "red paragon bodice" and leaving the impression that she dressed in a higher or more flashy fashion than the community thought proper. But red was not an unusual color for clothing in seventeenth-century New England, and Shattuck said nothing about the cut of the laces she brought him for dyeing. He said the pieces were *too small* to be of any use. If Bridget Bishop had been dressing extravagantly wouldn't her laces have been *larger* than usual? It would seem that what Shattuck meant was that the pieces of lace were too small to be worn by a human being. But they would not have been too small for dressing a witch's doll, which is often clothed in the same materials and colors as the clothing worn by the victim.

Shattuck, like other seventeenth-century common folk, had quite a smattering of occult information, which he was not above putting to use. One of his children had, years ago, been unaccountably ill of fits; "his mouth and eyes drawn aside . . . in such a manner as if he was upon the point of death." A passing stranger suggested the child was bewitched and offered to take the boy to Goodwife Bishop's and scratch her face (drawing blood from a witch's face was a common means of breaking her spells). Shattuck agreed, and added some white magic of his own: "I gave him money and bid him ask her for a pot of cider." (Obtaining property and subjecting it to occult abuse was a common technique of both white and black magic.) But Goodwife Bishop was not to be taken in. She refused to sell the cider and chased the stranger off with a spade. Not only did she avoid having her face scratched; she scratched the face of Shattuck's son. "And ever since," said Shattuck,

this child hath been followed with grievous fits as if he would never recover more, his head and eyes drawn aside so as if they would never come to rights more; lying as if he were in a manner dead; falling anywhere, either into fire or water if he be not constantly looked to; and generally in such an uneasy and restless frame, almost always running to and fro, acting so strange that I cannot judge otherwise but that he is bewitched, and by these circumstances do believe that the aforesaid Bridget Oliver, now called Bishop, is the cause of it. And it has been the judgment of doctors . . . that he is under an evil hand of witchcraft.

Notice again how willing the medical profession was to diagnose witchcraft. In fact, the seventeenth-century physician was apt to attribute everything he could not explain organically to witchcraft, just as the twentieth-century physician is apt to call whatever he cannot understand psychosomatic. But notice also that the child's symptoms are identifiably hysterical, and therefore may well have been due to his frightening experience with Bridget Bishop.

Certainly other persons were terrified of her and had hysterical hallucinations as a result of their terror. Richard Coman testified that about eight years before he had been in bed with his wife, with a light burning in the room.

I being awake did then see Bridget Bishop of Salem, alias Oliver, come into the room we lay in and two women more with her, which two women were strangers to me. I knew them not, but said Bishop came in her red paragon bodice and the rest of her clothing which she then usually did wear. . . . And quickly after they appeared the light was out, and the curtains at the foot of the bed opened, where I did see her. And presently [she] came and lay upon my breast or body and so oppressed me that I could not speak nor stir, no not so much as to awake my wife, although I endeavored much so to do it. The next night they all appeared again in like manner and the said Bishop, alias Oliver, took hold of me by the throat and almost hauled me out of the bed. The Saturday night following, I having been that day telling of what I had seen and how I suffered the two nights before, my kinsman William Coman told me he would stay with me and lodge with me and see if they would come again, and advised me to lay my sword athwart my body. [The hilt of a sword, being shaped like a cross, was thought to be a protection against witches and evil spirits.] Quickly after we went to bed that said night, and both well awake and discoursing together, in came all the three women again, and said Bishop was the first as she had been the other two nights. So I told him, "William, here they be all come again." And he was immediately struck speechless and could not move hand or foot. And immediately they got hold of my sword and strived to take it from me, but I held so fast as they did not get it away. And I then had liberty of speech [having been able to hold on to the sign of the cross; notice again how magic works in a society which believes in it] and called William, also my wife, and Sarah Phillips that lay with my wife, who all told me afterwards they heard me but had not power to speak or stir. . . . And the first that spake was Sarah Phillips, and said, "In the name of God, Goodman Coman, what is the matter with you?" So they all vanished away.[7]

Presumably the hallucination ended because the name of God had been invoked, just as Coman had regained his speech by holding to the symbol of the cross.

Samuel Gray had a similar experience fourteen years before, when he woke to

see a woman standing between the cradle in the room and the bedside and [she] seemed to look upon him. So he did rise up in his bed and it vanished. . . . Then he went to the door and found it locked. And unlocking and opening the door he went to the entry door and looked out, and then again did see the same woman he had a little before seen in the room, and in the same garb she was in before. Then he said to her, "In the name of God, what do you come for?" Then she vanished away. So he locked the door again and went to bed. And between sleeping and waking he felt something come to his mouth or lips, cold, and thereupon started and looked up, and again did see the same woman with something between both her hands, holding [it] before his mouth. Upon which she moved, and the child in the cradle gave a great screech out, as if it was greatly hurt, and she disappeared. And taking the child up [he] could not quiet it in some hours. From which time the child, that before was a very likely thriving child, did pine away and was never well (although it lived some months after, yet in a sad condition) and so died. Some time after, within a week or less, he did see the same woman in the same garb or clothes that appeared to him as aforesaid, . . . although he knew not her nor her name before. Yet both by her garb and countenance doth testify that it was the same woman that they now call Bridget Bishop, alias Oliver, of Salem.

The death of the child cannot be explained on natural grounds except by suggesting that there was something wrong with it quite unrelated to its father's experience. Nor can one account for Gray's having hallucinations of Bridget Bishop before he knew her or knew her name except by suggesting that he was mistaken. But the next experiences—those of John Louder—need no explanation. They fit the pattern of hysterical hallucinations we have seen before.

About seven or eight years since, I then living with Mr. John Gedney in Salem . . . had some controversy with Bridget Bishop, the wife of Edward Bishop of Salem, sawyer, about her fowls that used to come into our orchard or garden. Some little time after which, I going well to bed, about the dead of the night felt a great weight upon my breast, and awakening looked and, it being bright moonlight, did clearly see said Bridget Bishop or her likeness sitting upon my stomach. And putting my arms off of the bed to free myself from that great oppression, she presently laid hold of my throat and almost choked me, and I had no strength or power in my hands to resist or help myself. And in this condition she held me to almost day. Some time after this my mistress, Susannah Gedney, was in our orchard and I was then with her, and said Bridget Bishop being then in her orchard which was next adjoining to ours, my mistress told said Bridget that I said or affirmed that she came one night and sat upon my breast as aforesaid, which she denied and I affirmed to her face to be true, and that I did plainly see her, upon which discourse with her she threatened me. And some time after that I, not being very well, stayed at home on a Lord's Day. And on the afternoon of said day, the doors being shut, I did see a black pig in the room coming towards me. So I went towards it to kick it and it vanished away. [Notice again that hallucinations vanish if the subject is able to speak or move.] Immediately after I sat down . . . and did see a black thing jump into the window. And [it] came and stood just before my face. . . . The body of it looked like a monkey, only the feet were like a cock's feet with claws, and the face somewhat more like a man's than a monkey's. And I being greatly affrighted, not being able to speak or help myself by reason of fear, I suppose, so the thing spoke to me and said, "I am a messenger sent to you. For I understand you are troubled in mind, and if you will be ruled by me you shall want for nothing in this world." Upon which I endeavored to clap my hands upon it, and said, "You Devil, I will kill you," but could feel no substance. And it jumped out of the window again and immediately came in by the porch, although the doors were shut, and said, "You had better take my counsel." Whereupon I struck at it with a stick but struck the groundsill and broke the stick, but felt no substance, and that arm with which I struck was presently disenabled. Then it vanished away and I opened the back door and went out, and going towards the house-end I espied said Bridget Bishop in her orchard going towards her house, and seeing her had no power to set one foot forward but returned in again. And going to shut the door I again did see that or the like creature that I before did see within doors, in such a posture as it seemed to be going to fly at me. Upon which I cried out, "The whole armor of God . . . be between me and you!" So it sprang back and flew over the appletree, flinging the dust with its feet against my stomach, upon which I was struck dumb and so continued for about three days time. And also [it] shook many of the apples off from the tree which it flew over.

At her trial Bridget Bishop denied knowing John Louder, although it was common knowledge that they had been next-door neighbors and had frequently quarreled. The gratuitous lie must have hurt her, but not nearly so much as the other evidence against her.

There is, unfortunately, no way of knowing whether Bridget Bishop was actually using charms or spells against Richard Coman, or Samuel Gray, or John Louder. But their testimony is eloquent evidence of the power which accompanied a reputation for witchcraft. And the dolls, the pieces of lace too short for use, and the scratching of the Shattuck child's face all suggest that Bridget Bishop had consciously sought such power, that she was in fact a witch, as the community believed her to be.

Bridget Bishop was not the only witch in Essex County; before they were through the magistrates had found others who were guilty of practicing black magic. One of them was Candy, a Negro slave from Barbados, who was examined on the fourth of July. Yes, she said, she was a witch. But she had not been a witch in Barbados, nor had her mother been a witch. Her mistress, Mrs. Hawkes, had made her a witch in this country, by bringing her a book in which she made her mark. "How did you afflict or hurt these folks?" Hathorne asked her. "Where are the puppets you did it with?"[8] She asked permission to leave the room, and get them. The magistrates sent someone with her and she returned shortly carrying "a handkerchief wherein several knots were tied, rags of cloth, a piece of cheese and a piece of grass." At the sight of these

Mary Warren, Deliverance Hobbes, and Abigail Hobbes . . . were greatly affrighted and fell into violent fits. And all of them said that [the specters of] the Black Man and Mrs. Hawkes and the Negro stood by the puppets or rags and pinched them, and then they were afflicted. And when the knots were untied yet they continued as aforesaid.

The accounts do not tell us what the cheese was used for. But Candy was forced to swallow the grass "and that night she was burned in her flesh." The magistrates had, apparently, decided to experiment rather thoroughly with these charms. A piece of one of the rags was burned "and one of the afflicted . . . was presently burned on the hand." Another piece was put under water and two of the afflicted "were choked, and strived for breath as if under water." Another ran down to the river "as if she would drown herself," but they stopped her. It does not seem to have occurred to anyone at the time that in experimenting with these charms the magistrates were themselves practicing witchcraft, and with dramatic and conspicuous success. Nor did it occur to anyone to notice that the experiments suggested that the malignant power must reside not in the witch but in the charms themselves or in the Devil's power that lay behind them, since they worked equally well whether they were manipulated by a confessed witch or by a godly magistrate. John Hale was to reflect on these experiments months later and reach a startling and original conclusion.

Another person who had clearly practiced witchcraft was Wilmot "Mammy" Redd, who had for many years been the town witch of Marblehead. The most interesting and most damning evidence against her concerned a quarrel she had with a Mrs. Simms of Salem Town, who suspected Mammy Redd's maid of stealing her linen. The quarrel grew so hot that Mrs. Simms threatened to swear out a warrant against the maid, upon which Mammy Redd pronounced a curse. Two witnesses swore to the substance of the curse, which was that Mrs. Simms "might never *mingere* [urinate] nor *cacare* [defecate]"[9] until she let her alone. And sure enough, Mrs. Simms was shortly "taken with the distemper of the dry belly-ache, and so continued many months" until she left the area. At her preliminary examination, on May 31, Mammy Redd was reserved if not downright evasive. Hathorne may well have been interested in her professional opinion on the condition of the afflicted persons. In any case, he asked her repeatedly what she thought ailed them. But she would only answer, "I cannot tell." Finally he asked her directly whether she did not think it was witchcraft, but again she replied, "I cannot tell." "And being [again] urged for her opinion in the case, all she would say was, 'My opinion is they are in a sad condition.' "

Bridget Bishop, Candy, and Wilmot Redd had practiced malefic witchcraft. There were others who may or may not have practiced it—the evidence is insufficient—but who had clearly used their reputation for occult power to gain illegitimate personal ends. One of these was Dorcas Hoar of Beverly, a parishioner of the Reverend John Hale. She had been dabbling in the occult for years; Hale testified that "about twenty-two years ago"[10] she told him she had borrowed a book on palmistry, containing rules on how to know the future. "But I telling her it was an evil book and evil art, she seemed to me to renounce or reject all such practices, whereupon I had great charity for her several years." Hale's charity was wasted, however, since Dorcas Hoar continued telling people's futures, sometimes through reading their faces as well as through reading their palms. Fortunetelling is often only white magic. But it easily becomes black magic when it concerns itself with the time or manner of the subject's death. In such cases the fortuneteller is often suspected, and not without reason, of assisting fortune. Precisely this had happened with Dorcas Hoar, who had told it about "that she should live poorly so long as her husband William Hoar did live, but the said Will should die before her and after that she should live better." He did die before her (not the only instance in which she had correctly foretold the order of death), and the community was so suspicious that an autopsy was held. She was enraged at that, but nothing had ever come of it.

Eight years after Hale first remonstrated with Dorcas Hoar he discovered

an evil practise [which] had been between a servant of mine and some of said Hoar's children in conveying goods out of my house to the said Hoars. And I had a daughter Rebecca, then between eleven and twelve years old, whom I asked if she knew of the Hoars' stealing. She told me yea, but [she] durst not reveal it to me. And one reason was [that] she was threatened that Goody Hoar was a witch, and had a book by which she could tell what said Rebecca did tell me in my house. And if the said Rebecca told me of the stealing, the said Hoar would raise the Devil to kill her or bewitch her or words to that effect. But whether the said Dorcas herself or her children told Rebecca these words I remember not. I asked Rebecca if she saw the book. She said yes, she was showed that book, and there were many streaks and pictures in it by which (as she was told) the said Hoar could reveal and work witchcrafts. . . . [Both fortune-telling manuals and grimoires are, of course, full of diagrams.] "And," said she, "now I have told you of the stealing Goody Hoar will bewitch me." I [tried to persuade] my daughter not to think so hardly of Goody Hoar. But she replied, "I know Goody Hoar is a witch" (or to that effect), and then told stories of strange things that had been acted in or about my house when I and my wife were abroad to fright[en] said Rebecca into silence about the theft, which said Rebecca judged to be acts of witchcraft. The particulars I have now forgotten. . . . And after my daughter's death a friend told me that my daughter said to her [that] she went in fear of her life by the Hoars till quieted by the scripture, "Fear not them which can kill the body. . . ."

Theft was not a capital crime in seventeenth-century New England (although it was in seventeenth-century England, and remained so into the nineteenth century). But theft under these particularly repulsive circumstances would have been enough to get Goodwife Hoar executed in any part of seventeenth-century Western civilization. Indeed, the wonder is that Hale had not prosecuted her at the time. The most likely explanation of his failure to do so is his frequently demonstrated benevolence. He was always "hoping better" of people—even of such reprobates as Bridget Bishop and the Hoars.

The other person who used a reputation for occult power for illegitimate ends was the Reverend George Burroughs, who had been minister of Salem Village from 1680 to 1682 and was now serving a parish in Maine. On April 20 the apparition of a minister appeared to Ann Putnam, Jr. (who had been only two years old when Burroughs left Salem Village), at which "she was grievously affrighted and cried out, 'Oh dreadful, dreadful! Here is a minister come. What, are ministers witches too?' "[11] Like other witch apparitions he tortured her, and the torture included choking, as in so many other cases. He also tempted her "to write in his book," but she refused, scolding him "that he which was a minister, that should teach children to fear God, should come to persuade poor creatures to give their souls to the Devil." She asked him to tell her who he was so that she might complain of him to the authorities. Rather inconsistently, he told her, and went on to volunteer the information that he had bewitched many people to death, including his first two wives. (This was only one of several occasions when specters incriminated the persons they represented.)

Two weeks later the apparition was back, telling Ann that the specters of his first two wives would shortly appear to her but that they would tell a great many lies, to which she must not listen.

Then immediately appeared to me the form of two women in winding-sheets, and napkins about their heads, at which I was greatly affrighted. And they turned their faces towards Mr. Burroughs and looked very red and angry and told him that he had been a cruel man to them, and that their blood did cry for vengeance against him, and also told him that they should be clothed with white robes in Heaven when he should be cast into Hell. And immediately he vanished away. And as soon as he was gone the two women turned their faces towards me and looked as pale as a white wall, and told me that they were Mr. Burroughs' two first wives and that he had murdered them. And one told me that she was his first wife, and he stabbed her under the left arm and put a piece of sealing-wax on the wound. And she pulled aside the winding-sheet and showed me the place, and also told me that she was in the house [where] Mr. Parris now lived where it was done. And the other told me that Mr. Burroughs and that wife which he hath now killed her in the vessel as she was coming to see her friends, because they would have one another.

Burroughs' specter appeared in the hallucinations of a number of other people, including Susannah Sheldon, who reported that his specter told her he "had killed two of his wives—the first he smothered and the second he choked." Nobody seems to have noticed that the specters differed about the means by which the supposed murders were done. Or perhaps the discrepancy was attributed to the fact that it was Burroughs' specter speaking on one occasion and those of his wives on the other. In any case, it is easy to discover the source for these particular hallucinations, since Burroughs had indeed been a cruel man to his wives. Among other things, he was constantly suspicious of them and of others. He tried to force them to "write, sign, seal, and swear a covenant never to reveal any of his secrets." And whenever he was absent from them he would, on his return, proceed to tell them what they had been saying about him.

The testimony of his brother-in-law, Goodman Ruck, is particularly enlightening here. Ruck and his sister and Burroughs had gone out to gather strawberries, and Burroughs

stepped aside a little into the bushes, whereupon they halted and hallooed for him. He not answering, they went away homewards with a quickened pace without any expectation of seeing him in a considerable while. And yet when they were got near home, to their astonishment they found him on foot with them, having a basket of strawberries. [Burroughs] immediately then fell to chiding his wife on the account of what she had been speaking to her brother of him on the road, which, when they wondered at [it], he said he knew their thoughts. Ruck, being startled at that, made some reply intimating that the Devil himself did not know so far. But [Burroughs] answered, "My God makes known your thoughts unto me."

What had happened, apparently, was that Burroughs had simply stepped out of sight in the bushes and then followed his wife and his brother-in-law home, keeping within hearing but out of sight. Then he had repeated their conversation to them and made them believe that he knew it not from eavesdropping but from occult powers. When Burroughs said "My God makes known your thoughts unto me," both he and his hearers understood his god to be the Devil; the Christian God does not deal in the occult, particularly at the level of family gossip, but the Devil does. Now he was about to pay for the illegitimate power he had sought, but he tried to evade the payment with a clumsy lie. He had not been left alone, he said. His wife and brother-in-law had left a man with him. Ruck denied it, and when the magistrates asked Burroughs what this man's name was, "his countenance was much altered, nor could he say who 'twas."

Burroughs seems, in fact, to have been an habitual liar. At his trial, as part of his defense, he read a paper arguing that witches cannot send a Devil to torment people by making a covenant with the Devil. The court immediately recognized this paper as copied out of Thomas Ady's *A Candle in the Dark.* Burroughs "said he had taken none of it out of any book." When he was flatly charged with plagiarism he barely wriggled out of the contradiction he had created by saying that "a gentleman gave him the discourse in a manuscript, from whence he transcribed it." This devious half-lie, coupled with his other lies, told very heavily against him—a clergyman especially was supposed to be a man of good faith; it was the Devil who was the Prince of Lies. It is quite possible that George Burroughs was a worshipper of that prince. Certainly he was no orthodox Puritan. He had conspicuously avoided taking communion —he said it was so long since he had taken it that he could not tell how long—and he had baptized only the eldest of his children. But one cannot be certain. Perhaps he was only a liar who liked to boast of occult powers.

Certainly he boasted of his physical powers. He was, apparently, a very strong man, although slightly built. Some of the stories told of him are incredible: that he held up a seven-foot fowling piece by inserting his forefinger in the muzzle, or that he lifted a barrel of molasses by inserting two fingers in the bung. Burroughs had told some of these stories of himself; now they were coming back to haunt him, since they seemed to the community evidence of a strength that was clearly preternatural.

While the accusation of a minister was shocking, it was by no means unusual. Renegade members of the clergy have played a large part in the history of witchcraft both in fact and in fiction. It should be remembered that Morgan le Fay, King Arthur's sister, was supposed to have learned her evil craft in the nunnery where she was educated, that Benvenuto Cellini's sorcerer-friend was a priest, and that a renegade priest is supposed to be necessary to the performance of a Black Mass. So Massachusetts found no difficulty in reconciling George Burroughs' occupation with his reputation as a wizard. On the contrary, they felt when they arrested him that they had laid hands on the leader of the demonic conspiracy.

Beside the black magic of Bridget Bishop, Candy, and Wilmot Redd and the illegitimate use of a reputation for occult power by the Hoar family and by George Burroughs, the examining magistrates turned up evidence of much trafficking in the occult that is best classified as white witchcraft. We have seen that the events at Salem began with experiments made by Elizabeth Parris and Abigail Williams with the egg and glass, and that a witch cake was used to find out the names of the first witches. Similar methods of obtaining knowledge were commonly used, especially the sieve and shears, a method of divining not unlike the contemporary ouija board. Two persons are required. Each holds one handle of a pair of shears, and a sieve is held suspended between the points of the shears. Then questions are asked, and the answer depends on the movements of the sieve. Another common method of divining was the key and Bible, in which a key is inserted between the leaves of a Bible and the answer to the question is found in the words to which the key points.

Beside divining, there was much white magic involved in the medical practice of the time, which liberally employed both spells and charms. The most entertaining example of the latter to be found in the Salem documents has to do with what Robert Calef called "the burning [of] the mare's fart." Isaac Cummings, Sr., had a mare which fell suddenly sick—so suddenly that he thought she must have been ridden all night by witches. He sent for Thomas Andrews of Boxford to help cure the animal, and Andrews tried a number of remedies without success.

"But," said he, "I cannot tell but she may have the belly-ache. And," said he, "I will try one thing more." My brother Andrews said he would take a pipe of tobacco and light it and butt it into the fundament of the mare. I told him that I thought it was not lawful. [The idea that this remedy was unlawful is probably a result of the use of tobacco in it. Tobacco was an "Indian weed" and used in Indian ceremony and medicine. The Puritans, like other seventeenth-century Christians, thought the Indians to be Devil worshippers and thought of their medicine men as magicians.] He said it was lawful for man or beast. Then I took a clean pipe and filled it with tobacco and did light it, and went with the pipe lit to the barn. Then the said Andrews did use the pipe as he said before he would, and the pipe of tobacco did blaze and burn blue. [Gaseous nitrogenous waste does burn with a blue color.] Then I said to my brother Andrews, "You shall try no more; it is not lawful." He said, "I will try again once more," which he did. And then there arose a blaze from the pipe of tobacco which seemed to me to cover the buttocks of the said mare. The blaze went upward towards the roof of the barn and in the roof of the barn there was a great crackling, as if the barn would have fallen or been burnt. . . .[12]

At this point, according to Cummings' son, the father declared that "he had rather lose his mare than his barn,"[13] and the experiments ended for that day. But Cummings conquered his misgivings rapidly. "The next day, being Lord's day, I spoke to my brother Andrews at noon to come to see the said mare, and said Andrews came. And what he did I say not."

One of the commonest countercharms for a bewitched animal was to cut a piece off of it—frequently an ear—and burn it or boil it. A neighbor of Cummings', John Hunkins, suggested this countercharm to him in the evening of that same Sunday. But Cummings would have no part in working further magic on the Sabbath. "I said no, not today. But if she lived till tomorrow morning he might cut off a piece of her and burn [it] if he would." No sooner had he said this than the mare fell dead.

This kind of countercharm verged on black magic because it was supposed not only to break the witch's spell but to injure the witch or compel her presence. It could be used with people as well as with animals, although you did not, of course, cut off the person's ear. You cut some of their hair or took some of their urine, and boiled it. The Quaker Samuel Shattuck, whom we have seen before engaged in an occult contest with Bridget Bishop, once tried this countercharm when he thought his child bewitched by one Mary Parker. Directly after Goodwife Parker had visited the Shattuck house the child

was taken in a strange and unusual manner as if his vitals would have broke out his breast-bone, drawn up together to the upper part of his breast, his neck and eyes drawn so much aside as if they would never come to right again. He lay in so strange a manner that the doctor and others did believe he was bewitched. Some days after, some of the visitors cut some of his hair off to boil [in Shattuck's testimony it is always anonymous visitors who work the charms], which they said although they did [it] with great tenderness the child would shriek out as if he had been tormented. They put his hair in a skillet over a fire which stood plain on the hearth. And as soon as they were gone out of the room it was thrown down, and I came immediately into the room and could see no creature in the room.[14]

They put the skillet back on the fire, and after the child's hair had boiled awhile Goodwife Parker came to the house on the pretense of selling chickens, although Shattuck found on later investigation that she had no chickens to sell. So the experiment was considered a success, on the grounds that it had compelled the presence of the witch. Unfortunately it did not help the child, who "continued in a very sad condition followed with very solemn fits, which hath taken away his understanding."

Boiling urine was a far more common countercharm than boiling hair, although it was, in colonial history, often attended with difficulties. In 1682, for example, a meeting of prominent Quakers in New Hampshire, including Samuel Jennings, governor of West Jersey, Walter Clark, deputy governor of Rhode Island, and Thomas Maule of Salem, was troubled by persistent poltergeist activity, especially stone-throwing. The family at whose house they met tried a number of ways to rid themselves of these "lapidary salutations," including the following experiment:

They did set on the fire a pot with urine and crooked pins in it, with [the] design to have it boil, and by that means to give punishment to the witch or wizard (that might be the wicked procurer or contriver of this stone affliction) and take off their own, as they had been advised. This was the effect of it: as the liquor began to grow hot a stone came and broke the top or mouth of it, and threw it down and spilt what was in it; which being made good again, another stone, as the pot grew hot again, broke the handle off; and being recruited and filled the third time was then with a third stone quite broke to pieces and split; and so the operation became frustrate and fruitless.[15]

Another failure was recorded by Cotton Mather in his *Memorable Providences*.[16] A man having fallen ill, and witchcraft being suspected, his friends "went to the traditional experiment of bottling urine; but they could get no urine from him, a strange hole through the urinary passage shedding the water before they could receive it into the vessel." The man died shortly afterward and the body was examined by a jury. "An hole was found quite through his yard, which hindered their saving of any urine and gave a terrible torture to him." Everyone concluded that he had been bewitched, but in the absence of evidence sufficient to convict a witch the case went no further.

Mather did not approve of what he called "the urinary experiment," on the grounds that it was using "a charm against a charm, or . . . a Devil's shield against a Devil's sword." Nevertheless, careful scholar that he was, he recorded the opinion that it was not sufficient to boil steel filings with the urine. "I suppose the urine must be bottled with nails and pins, and such instruments in it as carry a show of torture with them, if it [is to] attain its end."

But the instance of urine-boiling which came before the Salem magistrates was not a failure, but a success. A doctor by the comically appropriate name of Roger Toothaker had boasted to one Thomas Gage

that his daughter had killed a witch. And I asked him how she did it. And said Toothaker answered readily that his daughter had learned something from him. I asked by what means she did it. And he said that there was a certain person bewitched, and said person complained of being afflicted by another person. . . . And further, said Toothaker said that his said daughter got some of the afflicted person's urine and put it into an earthen pot, and stopped said pot very close and put said pot into a hot oven, and stopped up said oven.[17]

The next morning the witch was dead; apparently she was bewitched to death.

Most of the physical effects of witchcraft are attributable to hysteria, but not death. People do not die of hysteria. But death, like the hysterical symptoms of bewitchment, begins with the victim's fear of the witch's power.

Witchcraft deaths have been reported for a very long time, yet it is only recently that they have received serious medical attention. In 1942 Dr. Walter B. Cannon of Harvard Medical School published an article entitled " 'Voodoo' Death,"[18] in which he began by acknowledging that "the phenomenon is so extraordinary and so foreign to the experience of civilized people that it seems incredible." And yet, he thought, it had been so widely reported, for so long, and by such dependable observers that it clearly deserved careful investigation. Cannon was unaware that death is frequently reported in the literature of European and American witchcraft, but he did know that it had been reported from primitive cultures in South America, Africa, Australia, New Zealand, the Pacific islands, and Haiti, over a period of time from 1587 to the present. He quotes several such reports, two of which are well worth repeating here. The first is from Africa:

I have seen more than one hardened old Hausa soldier dying steadily and by inches because he believed himself to be bewitched; no nourishment or medicines that were given to him had the slightest effect either to check the mischief or to improve his condition in any way, and nothing was able to divert him from a fate which he considered inevitable. In the same way, and under very similar conditions, I have seen Kru-men and others die in spite of every effort that was made to save them, simply because they had made up their minds, not (as we thought at the time) to die, but that being in the clutch of malignant demons they were bound to die.[19]

The second describes the effect of magic bone-pointing among Australian aborigines:

The man who discovers that he is being boned by an enemy is, indeed, a pitiable sight. He stands aghast, with his eyes staring at the treacherous pointer, and with his hands lifted as though to ward off the lethal medium, which he imagines is pouring into his body. His cheeks blanch and his eyes become glassy and the expression of his face becomes horribly distorted. . . . He attempts to shriek but usually the sound chokes in his throat, and all that one might see is froth at his mouth. His body begins to tremble and the muscles twist involuntarily. He sways backwards and falls to the ground, and after a short time appears to be in a swoon; but soon after he writhes as if in mortal agony, and, covering his face with his hands, begins to moan. After a while he becomes very composed and crawls to his wurley. From this time onwards he sickens and frets, refusing to eat and keeping aloof from the daily affairs of the tribe. Unless help is forthcoming in the shape of a counter-charm administered by the hands of the Nangarri, or medicine man, his death is only a matter of a comparatively short time. If the coming of the medicine man is opportune he might be saved.[20]

In all cases death comes inexorably and in a relatively short time. As one observer put it, "the victims die . . . as though their strength ran out as water." The only known cure was a countercharm, and when this was successfully employed recovery was so rapid and complete that Western observers found it remarkable. (Since Cannon's article was published, two doctors have reported their experiences in curing bewitched patients. Dr. John E. Snell of Tufts University has successfully used hypnosis to cure both southern whites and Negroes who believed themselves bewitched.[21] A Hawaiian physician, Dr. Harold M. Johnson, has reported both severe skin lesions and death among the victims of Kahuna sorcerers. He has succeeded in curing bewitched patients by giving them methylene blue tablets, which turns their urine blue and persuades them that a powerful countercharm has been worked on their behalf.)[22]

Cannon suggested that witchcraft death might well be a genuine phenomenon, and also put forward a hypothetical explanation. "It may be explained," he thought, "as due to shocking emotional stress—to obvious or repressed terror." It would occur, he felt, chiefly in primitive cultures,

among human beings so primitive, so superstitious, so ignorant that they are bewildered strangers in a hostile world. Instead of knowledge they have a fertile and unrestricted imagination which fills their environment with all manner of evil spirits capable of affecting their lives disastrously.

Therefore he published his article in *American Anthropologist* rather than in one of the medical journals, presumably feeling that an anthropological audience would have better opportunities for testing his hypothesis than a medical one. Yet he did note that there were two "civilized" environments that might produce such deaths. Battlefield deaths had been reported in which the wounds were superficial and a postmortem revealed no serious injury. And apparently some patients found a hospital as terrifying an environment as a battlefield, and at least one doctor was very much aware of this:

That the attitude of the patient is of significant importance for a favorable outcome of an operation is firmly believed by the well-known American surgeon, Dr. J. M. T. Finney, for many years Professor of Surgery at the Johns Hopkins Medical School. He has publicly testified [1934], on the basis of serious experiences, that if any person came to him for a major operation, and expressed fear of the result, he invariably refused to operate.

Cannon's hypothesis was tested in the Psychobiological Laboratory at Johns Hopkins Medical School by Curt P. Richter, who published his findings in 1957 in an article entitled "On the Phenomenon of Sudden Death in Animals and Man."[23] Richter encountered the phenomenon while testing the survival times of wild versus domesticated rats, which he placed in water-filled beakers to swim until they drowned. The statistics he was obtaining were most irregular because some of the rats, especially the wild rats, died much more rapidly than others, and for no assignable reason. It occurred to Richter that these rats might be dying the same psychogenic death as human victims of witchcraft, and he therefore set out to test the cause of death. Cannon had suggested that fear might be the emotional cause, with consequent overstimulation of the sympathicoadrenal system, acceleration of the heart beat, and death with the heart contracted in systole. But Richter found that while acceleration of the heart beat was the initial reaction, it was shortly followed by a steady, gradual decrease in rate, with the heart eventually stopping in diastole, like a run-down clock. This meant that the emotional cause of death was not fear but hopelessness, produced by the rat's conviction that there was no possible means of escape, with consequent overstimulation of the parasympathetic rather than the sympathicoadrenal system.

Richter tested his findings by pretreatment with atropine and with colinergic drugs, and also by adrenalectomy and thyroidectomy. He also tried training the rats. By immersing them briefly and then removing them from water he taught them that their situation was not hopeless. Rats so trained did not die psychogenic deaths but produced constant swimming endurance records. Finally, he discovered that if rats about to die a psychogenic death were removed from the beaker they recovered rapidly, precisely like the human witchcraft victim who has been reprieved by a countercharm.

In short, Richter found that the first response in such cases was fear but that the emotional cause of death was the hopelessness that succeeded fear, and that death could be prevented either by restoring hope or by training the subject to be hopeful in a particular situation. He agreed with Cannon that the incidence of this kind of death would probably vary

inversely as the degree of civilization, or domestication, of the individual, since it occurs more frequently in wild than in domesticated rats and so far has been described chiefly in primitive man, that is to say, in creatures living in precarious situations.

But he noted that there did seem to be instances of the phenomenon in so-called "civilized" contexts, and not only in the hospital or on the battlefield. "Many instances are at hand," he said, "of sudden death from fright, sight of blood, hypodermic injections, or from sudden immersion in water." He concluded by reporting the experience of Dr. R. S. Fisher, coroner of the City of Baltimore, who had found that "a number of individuals die each year after taking small, definitely sublethal doses of poison, or after inflicting small, nonlethal wounds on themselves; apparently they die as a result of the belief in their doom."

Richter's findings throw much new light on the history of Massachusetts witchcraft. They should enable us at long last to take as seriously as it deserves Cotton Mather's detailed account of his treatment of the Goodwin girl. When he gave her religious sustenance by spelling the crucial words she was unable to hear spoken (a technique he would use again, as we shall see, in 1693), he may have been saving his patient from much more than convulsive fits. By giving her continued hope he may literally have been keeping her alive.

Richter's findings also explain the frequent reports of death in both European and American witchcraft cases. There are about a dozen such reports in the documents of Salem witchcraft, but in most instances one cannot be at all certain of the actual cause of death. Even when death does appear to be psychogenic it is usually impossible to say whether the victim's hopelessness was simply a result of private fears or whether those fears had their origin in a specific magical act. But with Roger Toothaker and his daughter there is enough to reconstruct the probable course of events with some degree of accuracy. We have seen, in the deadly earnest contests of charm and countercharm between Samuel Shattuck and Bridget Bishop and between Shattuck and Mary Parker, the seriousness with which seventeenth-century people took occult combat.

Toothaker accepted such a combat on behalf of a person he believed bewitched. He taught his daughter the classic countercharm of boiling the victim's urine in a pot. Probably he threatened the witch with this countercharm, or boasted of it to the neighbors, because the next morning the witch was dead. It is the right period of time for a witchcraft death, and therefore it is quite likely that this woman died of knowing that her victim's urine was being boiled in a pot.

It should be clear by now that our historians have erred in their assumption that there was no witchcraft practiced at Salem, or that if there was it was of little consequence. The documents, rightly read, present us a far different picture. In Bridget Bishop, Candy, and Mammy Redd we have three people who practiced black magic, and with demonstrable success. In the Hoar family and George Burroughs we have people who established a reputation for black magic and then traded on it, although whether they were actually witches remains uncertain. There are other cases, like those of Sarah Good and Samuel Wardwell, which I have not treated in detail because the evidence is suspicious but not conclusive, and one can only guess that some of them were probably practicing witchcraft. Finally, we have a variety and abundance of white magic, some of which merges with the black because it was intended to harm the witch. And if the testimony concerning Roger Toothaker and his daughter may be taken at face value—and there is reason to believe it may—we have one case of murder by witchcraft—one case in which occult means were used to take a human life away.

6

A Country Full of Lies

Our seventeenth-century ancestors differed from us in most ways, but in nothing did they differ more than in their attitude toward the truth. In this they were closer to the Middle Ages than to us. For them a lie—a breaking of one's faith— was the worst of sins. Today we do not regard lying as a serious moral wrong. If the word "morality" is mentioned we think immediately of our bodily appetites, especially of sex, and drugs, and alcohol. We take our appetites very seriously—perhaps too seriously—but we do not regard lying as a mortal sin. We are one of the few civilizations in which entire professions (advertising, for example, and public relations) are seriously devoted to bending the truth.

Dante, in his *Divine Comedy,* divided sins into three kinds: those of lust, those of violence, and those of fraud. The sins of lust—those we tend to take most seriously—were those that Dante thought most trivial; the sins of fraud—which we take lightly—were for Dante the worst of all. To create a "credibility gap" as our revealing phrase has it (as though the only relevant issue is whether a statement will compel belief), to lie, was for the medieval man to break one's faith, and it was faith which constituted the bonds between man and his fellowman, between man and the state, between man and God. To lie was to reduce all the most valuable relationships of life to chaos. And the seventeenth-century Puritan, like Dante, was still living by his faith.

Just how important the truth was to the seventeenth-century Puritan may be gathered from the fact that all of the innocent persons who were executed—and the majority of those executed were innocent—could have saved themselves by lying. After the first execution—that of Bridget Bishop—took place in June it became obvious to everyone that persons who confessed, like Tituba and Dorcas Good, were not being brought to trial. Thus any suspected person might have his life by confessing. Twenty people died, nineteen of them hanged and one pressed for refusing to plead. Bridget Bishop, Mammy Redd, and George Burroughs were three of these. One cannot be at all certain of the guilt or innocence of several more. But at least a dozen now seem to be clearly innocent. Twelve people, and probably more, chose to die rather than belie themselves. It is impressive evidence of the Puritan's attachment to the truth.

Yet it was not really so simple as that, because the truth was not easy to find in Salem in 1692. The greatest difficulty was created by the genuineness of the afflicted persons' fits. Their sufferings were so convincing that they often shook the confidence of the accused. One example is William Hobbes, who began by stoutly denying that he had anything to do with the afflicted girls' convulsions. When he looked at them they fell down in fits, and Hathorne accused him of overlooking them (i.e., of the evil eye), yet still he denied it. Abigail Williams cried out that she saw his specter going to hurt Mercy Lewis "and immediately said Mercy fell into a fit and diverse others."[1]

"Can you now deny it?" said Hathorne.

"I can deny it to my dying day," said William Hobbes.

But he did not. Here, after all, were people in hideous convulsions, and saying that his specter was the cause. How could this be? Hathorne suggested that the Devil might be able to use Hobbes' specter because of Hobbes' sins; he had not observed either public or private worship. Might not the Devil have taken advantage of that? Hobbes "was silent a considerable space—then said yes." The girls' fits shook not only Hobbes' confidence in himself, but also his confidence in his daughter Abigail, the wild young girl who had boasted that she had sold herself "body and soul to the Old Boy." Hathorne wanted to know whether Hobbes had not known for a long time that his daughter was a witch.

"No, sir," was the reply.

"Do you think she is a witch now?" asked Hathorne.

And all that Hobbes could say was, "I do not know."

Abigail Faulkner's experience was similar. At her first examination, on August 11, she firmly denied that she had anything to do with the girls' afflictions. When she looked at them they fell down in fits, and Hathorne asked her, "Do you not see?"[2]

Yes, she saw. But she had nothing to do with it. Yet she could not doubt that the girls were suffering, and saw no reason to doubt their word that it was her specter afflicting them. Therefore the Devil must be appearing in her form: "It is the Devil does it in my shape."

But by August 30 she was no longer so sure of her innocence. It was true, she said, that she had been angry at what people said when her cousin, Elizabeth Johnson, had been arrested. She had felt malice toward the afflicted persons then because they were the cause of her cousin's arrest. She had wished them ill, and "her spirit being raised she did pinch her hands together." Perhaps the Devil had taken advantage of that to pinch the girls, thus exploiting her malice.

Even those whose confidence was not shaken bore testimony to the impressiveness of the fits. Mary Easty knew that she had not bewitched the girls, and she was confident as well of the innocence of her sisters, Rebecca Nurse and Sarah Cloyse. Yet she had to grant that there was something preternatural in the girls' behavior. "It is an evil spirit," she said, "but whether it be witchcraft I do not know."[3] Even George Burroughs, who had been audacious enough to boast of occult powers, found himself stunned by the girls' behavior. "Being asked what he thought of these things he answered it was an amazing and humbling Providence, but he understood nothing of it."[4]

Indeed, these courtroom fits were so convincing that most of the indictments were for witchcraft committed during the preliminary examination rather than for the offenses named in the original complaint. The typical order of events in the Salem witchcraft cases was: (1) the swearing out of a complaint for acts of witchcraft; (2) a preliminary examination during which the afflicted persons had convulsive fits; (3) an indictment for acts of witchcraft performed during the preliminary examination; and (4) the trial.

The direct cause of these fits, in the courtroom or out of it, was, of course, not witchcraft itself, but the afflicted person's fear of witchcraft. If fits were occasioned by fear of someone like Bridget Bishop, who was actually practicing witchcraft, they might also be occasioned by fear of someone who was only suspected of practicing it. For example, we have every reason to believe that John Procter and his wife Elizabeth were innocent of witchcraft. But in the month after they had been accused and imprisoned, one Joseph Bailey, with his wife, was on his way to Boston.

When I came in sight of the house where John Procter did live there was a very hard blow struck on my breast which caused great pain in my stomach and amazement in my head. But [I] did see no person near me, only my wife behind me on the same horse. And when I came against said Procter's house, according to my understanding I did see John Procter and his wife at said house. [They were, remember, in prison at this time.] Procter himself looked out of the window and his wife did stand just without the door. I told my wife of it, and she did look that way and could see nothing but a little maid at the door. I saw no maid there, but Procter's wife according to my understanding did stand at the door. Afterwards, about half a mile from the aforesaid house, I was taken speechless for some short time. My wife did ask me several questions and desired me that if I could not speak I should hold up my hand, which I did. And immediately I could speak as well as ever. [Notice again that the fit is broken when the subject is able to move or speak.] And when we came to the way where Salem Road cometh into Ipswich Road, there I received another blow on my breast which caused much pain, [so] that I could not sit on my horse. And when I did alight off my horse, to my understanding I saw a woman coming towards us about sixteen or twenty pole from us, but did not know who it was. My wife could not see her. When I did get up on my horse again, to my understanding there stood a cow where I saw the woman. [Witches were thought capable of transforming their shapes.] After that we went to Boston without any further molestation, but after I came home again to Newbury I was pinched and nipped by something invisible for some time. But now through God's goodness to me I am well again.[5]

Testimony like this is careful and honest, and historians have been wrong in refusing to take it seriously. Bailey was quite aware that he had been ill, and that the illness had created a difference between his perceptions and those of his wife. But the fatal distinction between his understanding of the event and ours is that his culture led him to attribute his illness to witchcraft whereas ours permits us to attribute it to his fear of witchcraft.

There are many similar instances of the specters of innocent people appearing to afflict the citizenry once they were suspected of witchcraft. One of the more interesting involves John Willard, who had at first been a deputy-constable employed in arresting persons who had been complained of. According to Calef he became dissatisfied after being sent to arrest persons he believed innocent, and resigned his position.[6] This immediately brought him under suspicion, and soon the afflicted girls were crying out against him. Shortly thereafter his grandfather, Bray Wilkins, was ready for dinner, when

John Willard came into the house with my son Henry Wilkins, before I sat down, and said Willard to my apprehension looked after such a sort upon me as I never before discerned in any. [That is, Wilkins thought Willard had "overlooked" him—given him the evil eye.] I did but step into the next room and I was presently taken so that I could not dine nor eat anything. I cannot express the misery I was in, for my water was suddenly stopped and I had no benefit of nature, but was like a man in a rock. And I told my wife immediately that I was afraid that Willard had done me wrong. My pain continuing and finding no relief my jealousy [i.e., suspicion] continued. Mr. Lawson and others there were all amazed and knew not what to do for me. There was a woman accounted skilful [who] came hoping to help me, and after she had used means she asked me whether none of those evil persons had done me damage. I said I could not say they had but I was sore afraid they had. She answered, she did fear so too. As near as I remember I lay in this case three or four days at Boston, and afterwards, with the jeopardy of my life (as I thought), I came home. And then some of my friends coming to see me (and at this time John Willard was run away) one of the afflicted persons, Mercy Lewis, came in with them, and they asked whether she saw anything. She said, "Yes, they are looking for John Willard but there he is on his grandfather's belly." (And at that time I was in grievous pain in the small of my belly.) I continued so in grievous pain and my water much stopped till said Willard was in chains. And then as near as I can guess I had considerable ease. But on the other hand, in the room of a stoppage I was vexed with a flowing of water so that it was hard to keep myself dry. On the fifth [of] July last, talking with some friends about John Willard, some pleading his innocency and myself and some others arguing the contrary, within about one-quarter of an hour after that . . . I was taken in the sorest distress and misery, my water being turned into real blood, or of a bloody color, and the old pain returned excessively as before, which continued for about twenty-four hours together.[7]

The hysterical loss of appetite which was Wilkins' first symptom we have seen before and shall see again. The inability to urinate we have seen in Mrs. Simms as a result of Mammy Redd's curse. But there was clearly something organic as well as psychosomatic wrong with Bray Wilkins. The blood in the urine coupled with the extreme pain of relatively short duration suggests that it may have been a kidney stone. But whatever it was, both Wilkins and the community at large were by this time ready to attribute it to witchcraft.

John Hale, whose *Modest Enquiry Into the Nature of Witchcraft* is the most balanced contemporary account of the Salem trials, says that the "matter was carried on . . . chiefly by the complaints and accusations of the afflicted . . . and . . . by the confessions of the accused, condemning themselves and others."[8] Nothing is at first sight more surprising than the number of the confessors and the character of their confessions. There were about fifty of them, and the statements which they made far exceeded in color and detail the simple statements of personal guilt that were necessary to save their lives. William

Barker's confessions provide an excellent example. At his preliminary examination he testified that

he has been in the snare of the Devil three years; that the Devil first appeared to him like a black man, and [he] perceived he had a cloven foot; that the Devil demanded of him to give up himself soul and body unto him, which he promised to do. [The Devil promised in return to pay Barker's debts and see that he lived comfortably. Barker signed the contract in blood.] Satan's design was to set up his own worship, abolish all the churches in the land, to fall next [i.e., first] upon Salem and so go through the country. He saith the Devil promised that all his people should be equal, that there should be no day of resurrection or of judgment, and neither punishment nor shame for sin.[9]

Barker said that the demonic "Grandees" had told him there were "about 307 witches in the country" and he volunteered his opinion that all the persons arrested and imprisoned to date (August 29) were guilty. But an oral confession was not enough for him. Hale prints another "which he wrote himself in prison, and sent to the magistrates to confirm his former confession."

God having called me to confess my sin and apostasy in that fall in giving the Devil advantage over me, appearing to me like a Black, in the evening, to set my hand to his book, as I have owned to my shame. He told me that I should not want [in] so doing. At Salem Village, there being a little off the Meeting-House about an hundred five blades [i.e., young bucks], some with rapiers by their sides, which was called (and might be more for ought I know) by B[ishop] and Bu[rroughs]. And the trumpet sounded, and [there was] bread and wine which they called the Sacrament, but I had none, being carried over all on a stick, never being at any other meeting. I being at cart[ing] a Saturday last, all the day, of hay and English corn, the Devil brought my shape to Salem and did afflict M[artha] S[prague] and R[ose] F[oster] by clitching my hand. And a Sabbath day my shape afflicted A[bigail] M[artin], and at night afflicted M[artha] S[prague] and A[bigail] M[artin]. E[lizabeth] J[ohnson] and A[bigail] F[aulkner] have been my enticers to this great abomination, as one have owned and charged her to her sister with the same. And the design was to destroy Salem

Village, and to begin at the minister's house, and to destroy the Church of God, and to set up Satan's kingdom, and then all will be well. And now I hope God in some measure has made me something sensible of my sin and apostasy, begging pardon of God, and of the Honorable Magistrates and all God's People, hoping and promising by the help of God to set to my heart and hand to do what in me lieth to destroy such wicked worship, humbly begging the prayers of all God's People for me [that] I may walk humbly under this great affliction and that I may procure to myself the sure mercies of David and the blessing of Abraham.[10]

There are other confessions which support Barker's, both in general and in detail. And there is not a word of truth in any of them. While there were many individual acts of witchcraft in seventeenth-century Massachusetts there was never an attempt or a plot to make witchcraft a formal religion which would supplant Christianity. Yet we need not conclude that Barker and his fellow-confessors were lying. It is probable that they, like the afflicted girls, were hysterics subject to hallucinations. Certainly that is the conclusion to be drawn from Thomas Brattle's opinion of them in his "Letter": "my faith is strong concerning them that they are deluded, imposed upon, and under the influence of some evil spirit, and therefore unfit to be evidences either against themselves or anyone else."[11]

Brattle wrote this in October, when Massachusetts was returning to stability. But at the height of the excitement confessions like Barker's seemed convincing enough. For one thing, they had a curious precision: he did not say there were about three hundred witches in the country but "about three hundred and seven"; he did not say there were about a hundred young wizards at the mustering of the Satanic militia but "about an hundred five." But what made these confessions most believable was that they offered a simple and comprehensive explanation for all the frightening events at Salem, at a time when explanations were not easy to discover.

Barker's confessions are now readily identifiable as false, if only for their extravagance, but there is some testimony which remains ambiguous even today. Samuel Wardwell, for example, at his preliminary examination confessed himself a wizard. He had begun, he said, with white magic, "with telling of fortunes which sometimes came to pass."[12] And, he said, "he used also when any creature came into his field to bid the Devil take it, and it may be the Devil took advantage of him by that." Eventually he had signed a pact: "he convenanted with the Devil until he should arrive to the age of sixty years." He renounced this confession at his trial, saying that he had made it, but that he had belied himself. He added that it was all one: "he knew he should die for it whether he owned it or no."

Ordinarily one would simply accept his renunciation. But there are several puzzling circumstances here. For one thing, it was not all one whether he maintained or renounced his confession. People who maintained their confessions were not being brought to trial, much less executed. For another, at least a part of his confession was true; he had dabbled in the occult for some time, telling a great many fortunes, and boasting that he could make animals come to him when he wished. Finally, Wardwell was executed. But in 1693, when the panic had subsided and the climate of opinion totally changed, there were three people who held to their confessions. Two of them were women long thought to be "senseless and ignorant creatures." The third was Wardwell's wife. All of these circumstances are puzzling and some of them are suspicious. But on the other hand there is no evidence to support his confession of having made a pact. The only possible conclusion, it would seem, is that in this case the truth is not obtainable.

In a situation where the truth was so difficult to find the people of Massachusetts did what anybody else would do— they sought expert advice. In matters of witchcraft the experts were the clergy, and ultimately the advice was sought of the most distinguished clergymen in the colony. Indeed, at least one member of the trial court, Judge John Richards, asked the Reverend Cotton Mather to be present at the first trial. Mather was too ill to attend, but he did everything he could under the circumstances. He had suggested earlier (the exact date is not known) that the afflicted persons should be separated and an attempt made to cure them with prayer and fasting.[13] He volunteered to take in as many as six of them himself. He had cured the Goodwin children, and he might well have cured the Salem girls as well; certainly separation and private care would have been better treatment for hysterical fits than the excitements of a public courtroom. But unfortunately Mather's offer had not been accepted. Now, although he could not attend the first sitting of the court he wrote Richards a letter offering him his opinions.[14]

In the first place, he expected that God would smile upon the labors of the court: "His people have been fasting and praying before Him for your direction, and yourselves are persons whose exemplary devotion disposeth you to such a dependence on the Wonderful Counselor, for his counsel in an affair thus full of wonder, as He doth usually answer with the most favorable assistances." Yet he wanted to warn Richards, and the warning, which is his second point, is so important that it needs reprinting in full:

And yet I must most humbly beg you that in the management of the affair in your most worthy hands, you do not lay more stress upon pure specter testimony than it will bear. When you are satisfied or have good plain legal evidence that the Demons which molest our poor neighbors do indeed represent such and such people to the sufferers, though this be a presumption, yet I suppose you will not reckon it a conviction that the people so represented are witches to be immediately exterminated. It is very certain that the Devils have sometimes represented the shapes of persons not only innocent but very virtuous, though I believe that the just God then ordinarily provides a way for the speedy vindication of the persons thus abused. Moreover, I do suspect that persons who have too much indulged themselves in malignant, envious, malicious ebullitions of their souls may unhappily expose themselves to the Judgment of being represented by Devils, of whom they never had any vision and with whom they have much less written any covenant. I would say this: if upon the bare supposal of a poor creature's being represented by a specter too great a progress be made by the Authority in ruining a poor neighbor so represented, it may be that a door may be thereby opened for the Devils to obtain from the Courts in the Invisible World a license to proceed unto most hideous desolations upon the repute and repose of such as have yet been kept from the great transgression. If mankind have thus far once consented unto the credit of Diabolical representations, the Door is opened! Perhaps there are wise and good men that may be ready to style him that shall advance this caution a witch advocate, but in the winding up this caution will certainly be wished for.

Mather's third point is that although he believes that Devils have sometimes afflicted men on their own initiative, without being called up by witches, in this case he thinks that witches are involved: "there is cause enough to think that it is a horrible witchcraft which hath given rise to the troubles wherewith Salem Village is at this day harrassed, and the indefatigable pains that are used for the tracing this witchcraft are to be thankfully accepted and applauded among all this people of God." Fourth, he points out that although witchcraft is a spiritual matter and therefore "very much transacted upon the stage of imagination," its effects are "dreadfully real" and therefore criminally punishable. "Our dear neighbors are most really tormented, really murdered, and really acquainted with hidden things which are afterwards proved plainly to have been realities."

In his fifth and sixth sections he suggests what evidence may be used for convictions. The best evidence, he says, is "a credible confession. . . . And I say a credible confession because even confession itself is sometimes not credible." He was confident of Richards' ability to judge such matters: "a person of a sagacity many times thirty furlongs less than yours will easily perceive what confession may be credible and what may be the result of only a delirious brain or a discontented heart." In obtaining confessions he was "far from urging the un-English method of torture," but he thought that "cross and swift questions" might be used, along with anything else that "hath a tendency to put the witches into confusion" and thus might bring them to confession. If the suspect had made threats or boasts which seemed to require occult power and which came true, this was valid evidence. So were such concrete matters as "puppets" (for image magic) and witch marks on the body. Mather had never seen such a mark, but he thought a surgeon ought to be able to tell if a bodily excrescence were magical. Finally, he was willing to countenance as experiments (but not as full evidence) some witch-finding techniques which themselves partook of the occult: setting a suspect to repeating the Lord's Prayer; trying to wound a witch through striking her specter; putting the suspect to the water ordeal.

Seventh, and finally, he recommended clemency for "some of the lesser criminals." If such persons were not executed but "only scourged with lesser punishments, and also put upon some solemn, open, public, and explicit renunciation of the Devil" he thought it might discourage the Devils from afflicting those neighborhoods in which they had been publicly renounced.

Mather's letter was written within the context of a Puritan method for arriving at the truth, and it can be fully understood only within that context. In dealing with the American Puritans we must remember always that they had rejected the formidable hierarchies of the Medieval and Renaissance church and state, with all their authority of tradition and inherited position. They had replaced these hierarchies with bodies of ministers and magistrates which, if they were not fully democratic in the twentieth-century sense of the word, were nevertheless elected. The clergyman was called to his position by the members of the church; the magistrate was elected by his constituency. Furthermore, the church had no central administration; every congregation was a law unto itself. The state did have a central administration—a governor and lieutenant-governor and their council—but this administration had nothing even faintly resembling the authority of a royal government.

If serious differences of opinion arose over any public matter, whether religious or secular or both, it could not be settled as in authoritarian Europe by Papal Bull or royal decree.

Differences could be settled only by arriving at consensus through discussion. If the matter were purely religious and disagreement was fundamental, then a synod might be called—an informal council of all ministers—and the matter would be thrashed out until consensus was arrived at. What was expected was absolute consensus—discussion would proceed until opinion was unanimous, and the final product was therefore seen as a truth as absolute for the Puritan as any Papal Bull for the Catholic. If the matter were secular, or like the present one, a matter for secular decision with strong religious issues at stake, then business would proceed through normal governmental channels, with the clergy being called on for advice. Again, it was expected that final opinions and decisions would be absolute and unanimous. For the Puritans were not prepared to admit that their church and state proceeded by a light less certain than that of a European hierarchy. They were prepared to argue (and vehemently did) that the true method of arriving at absolute opinions was their method of consensus through discussion.

Reinforcing their belief in the possibility of achieving such absolute consensus was their conviction that they were God's Chosen People, directly comparable to the Old Testament Jews. Thus the ministers and magistrates had their authority not simply from the people but from God's People, and had thus been called to their offices by God. "It is yourselves who have called us to this office," said John Winthrop to the people's representatives, "and being called by you, we have our authority from God."[15] Surely God would give the ministers and magistrates of His own people enough light so that they could govern themselves with certainty.

This complex of beliefs put a tremendous obligation on the Puritans to achieve consensus, and explains why they so frequently did. It also explains some aspects of their history difficult for the twentieth-century mind to understand: why, for example, they chose to exile such dissidents as Roger Williams and Anne Hutchinson rather than accept their refusal to agree with the majority opinion. There were, of course, occasions when we find the Puritans pretending that consensus had been achieved although in fact no such thing had happened, when otherwise honest men lied to themselves in order to protect the sanctity of their most basic decision-making process. We shall presently see both Cotton Mather and his father involved in precisely such a predicament. At the moment, however, let us return to what this process of consensus tells us both about Cotton Mather's letter and about the state of opinion in Massachusetts at the end of May, 1692.

Mather was fully aware that his advice was being sought, as the most brilliant young member of the Massachusetts clergy, in precisely such a decision-making process. Yet as became a younger man he was careful in framing his advice to take account of ideas different from his own. Thus we can see reflected in his letter a wide spectrum of opinions, some of which would otherwise have been lost to us. We can see, for example, that there were some persons opposed to prosecuting in any witchcraft case, on the grounds that witchcraft was a spiritual matter, a sin rather than a crime, and thus outside the domain of criminal law. Mather made short shrift of this argument: to be sure, he wrote, witchcraft was spiritual, but the effects of it were dreadfully physical, and thus punishable at law. One has to admit that, given the facts of witchcraft, his logic was superior here. And he might easily have summoned authority to his side as well as logic. The laws of every civilized nation provided the death penalty for witchcraft, and so did the Bible (Exodus xxii, 18: "Thou shalt not suffer a witch to live").

Another opinion Mather deals with is that the troubles at Salem were caused by Devils, but not by witches. That is, the idea had already been advanced that the afflicted girls were possessed—infested by Demons—but not bewitched; that the Devils had acted on their own initiative rather than that of witches. This is the idea that was eventually adopted by virtually all of Massachusetts to explain the events at Salem, once it was recognized that most of those executed had been innocent. It was the explanation advanced by Thomas Brattle, the most serious critic of the Massachusetts establishment at the conclusion of the trials, and was later adopted not only by Brattle's disciple, Robert Calef, but also by Cotton Mather himself. In May of 1692, however, it was distinctly a minority opinion, and Mather dismissed it simply by saying there was "cause enough" to think the troubles at Salem Village had been caused by witchcraft. Again, given the times and the circumstances, one has to admit that Mather's opinion seems the right one. After all, he was writing to a court that was preparing to try Bridget Bishop, and as we have seen, she probably was a witch.

Neither of these opinions—that witchcraft was a sin rather than a crime, and that the afflicted persons were possessed rather than bewitched—seem to Mather worthy of much refutation. But there is an opinion he takes elaborate pains to refute, so elaborate that the matter requires more space than any other topic in his letter. This is the idea that specter evidence (the appearance of the specter of a suspected person in the hallucinations of the afflicted) is sufficient proof of guilt. The basic question, as the seventeenth century understood it, was whether God would permit the Devil to assume the shape of an innocent person. Most authorities, and especially most Protestant authorities, believed that He would, and thus held, like Hamlet, that "the Devil hath power/ to assume a pleasing shape."

Mather agreed with the majority, although he added that "I believe the just God then ordinarily provides a way for the speedy vindication of the persons thus abused." He was probably thinking here of the case at Groton, where innocent persons' specters had appeared in the hallucinations of Elizabeth Knapp, but through Samuel Willard's sane handling of the case the suspects had been quickly cleared. Indeed, Mather probably expected John Richards and his fellow-judges to be the means for clearing the innocent; he was plainly confident that Richards' sagacity would be more than equal to judging whether or not confessions were credible, and thus it should also be equal to judging the credibility of apparitions.

But Richards would not be capable of clearing anybody if he was going to accept the appearance of a person's specter as conclusive proof of guilt. If such infernal testimony were accepted, nobody could be safe from accusation. Mather put it forcefully enough. "If mankind have thus far once consented unto the credit of Diabolical representations, the Door is opened!" But Mather knew there were people at Salem so committed to the validity of spectral evidence that they were willing to call anyone who challenged it, including himself, a "witch advocate." All he could do was warn such people that when matters were finished "this caution will certainly be wished for." And in this he could not possibly have been more right.

7

⟐⟐⟐⟐⟐

The Door Is Opened

Mather's warning came far too late to change the course of events. There had been a time when Justice Hathorne admitted some doubt of the validity of spectral evidence; on March 24 he had said to Rebecca Nurse, "What uncertainty there may be in apparitions I know not."[1] But he had gone on to say why he found spectral evidence so persuasive:

this with me strikes hard upon you, that you are at this very present charged with familiar spirits. This is your bodily person they speak to. They say now they see these familiar spirits come to your bodily person. Now what do you say to that?

Hathorne was paying tribute to the dramatic effectiveness of the girls' hallucinations. One of them would cry out that she saw the specter of the accused woman leaving her body and going to afflict another, and immediately the girl named would go into hideous convulsions. Neither Hathorne nor any of the other spectators could believe that the girls were acting. The fits were far too violent for that. Nor could they see any other cause for the fits except the one they had been offered. This was spectral evidence, to be sure, but it was terribly "real" and convincing. Especially since the fits could invariably be cured by bringing the suspect to touch the afflicted girl, at which, it was believed, the tormenting specter was taken back into the body of the witch.

The suspect could only protest that in spite of appearances she was innocent—she had done nothing. Frequently suspects did appeal to the doctrine that the Devil could appear in any shape, and insisted He was appearing in theirs. Hathorne listened to the evidence throughout March and April, and always he and his colleague, Corwin, decided there was reason enough to commit the accused person to prison, either for further investigation or for trial. Nor was the pattern broken when other magistrates sat with Hathorne and Corwin on the Salem bench, even though these visitors included persons of much distinction and much common sense, like Judge Samuel Sewall of Boston and Deputy-Governor Thomas Danforth, who presided over the examinations of Sarah Cloyse and the Procters on April 11. By the end of April warrants were no longer being issued singly, but in groups of half a dozen or more, so sharply had the tempo of the accusations increased. And by early May Hathorne (like most of the other eyewitnesses to the events at Salem) had made up his mind about spectral evidence. On May 10 he was examining George Jacobs, Sr., pressing hard the accusations against him.

"You tax me for a wizard," said Jacobs. "You may as well tax me for a buzzard. I have done no harm."

"Is it no harm to afflict these?"

"I never did it."

"But how comes it to be in your appearance?"

"The Devil can take any [person's] likeness."

"Not," said Hathorne, "without their consent."[2]

There it was, flatly stated. Spectral evidence was now for Hathorne conclusive proof that the person represented had been trafficking with the Devil. It was not, as Mather was to recommend, merely a reason for further investigation, but evidence of guilt. From this time onward Hathorne would show no uncertainties. Once he had obtained the spectral evidence his sole concern would be to obtain whatever confirmation of it he could, resolutely ignoring all evidence that cast doubt upon it. In this he was joined by his silent partner, Corwin, and eventually by all the judges of the witchcraft court except, perhaps, for one. The magistrates' view was supported by the local ministers: John Hale of Beverly, Samuel Parris of Salem Village, and Nicholas Noyes of Salem (the other minister of Salem, John Higginson, took little part in the witchcraft proceedings because, as he himself tells us, of "the infirmities of a decrepit old age"[8]). It was also supported by the people at large, at least through the executions of August 19.

If spectral evidence was convincing to the magistrates, the ministers, and the people at large, it was a nightmare to the suspects. That it sometimes shook their own confidence in themselves we have already seen, but the full horror of it can be conceived only through an account like that of Captain Nathaniel Cary of Charlestown, whose wife was examined at the end of May.

I having heard some days that my wife was accused of witchcraft, being much disturbed at it, by advice we went to Salem Village, to see if the afflicted did know her. We arrived there 24 May; it happened to be a day appointed for examination. Accordingly, soon after our arrival Mr. Hathorne and Mr. Corwin, etc., went to the Meeting-House, which was the place appointed for that work. The minister began with prayer. And having taken care to get a convenient place, I observed that the afflicted were two girls of about ten years old, and about two or three other of about eighteen. One of the girls talked most, and could discern more than the rest. The prisoners were called in one by one and as they came in were cried out of, etc. The prisoner was placed about seven or eight foot from the justices and the accusers between the justices and them. The prisoner was ordered to stand right before the justices, with an officer appointed to hold each hand lest they should there with afflict them [c.g., by clenching their hands, thus pinching the afflicted]. And the prisoner's eyes must be constantly on the justices, for if they looked on the afflicted they would either fall into their fits or cry out of being hurt by them. After examination of the prisoners [as to] who it was afflicted these girls, etc., they were put upon saying the Lord's Prayer as a trial of their guilt. After the afflicted seemed to be out of their fits they would look steadfastly on some one person, and frequently not speak (and then the justices said they were struck dumb), and after a little time would speak again. Then the justices said to the accusers, "Which of you will go and touch the prisoner at the bar?" Then the most courageous would adventure, but before they had made three steps would ordinarily fall down, as in a fit. The justices ordered that they should be taken up and carried to the prisoner, that she might touch them. And as soon as they were touched by the accused the justices would say, "They are well," before I could discern any alteration, by which I observed that the justices understood the manner of it. Thus far I was only as a spectator. My wife also was there part of the time, but no notice taken of her by the afflicted except once or twice they came to her and asked her name.

But I having an opportunity to discourse [with] Mr. Hale (with whom I had formerly acquaintance), I took his advice what I had best to do, and desired of him that I might have an opportunity to speak with her that accused my wife, which he promised should be, I acquainting him that I reposed my trust in him.

Accordingly he came to me after the examination was over and told me I had now an opportunity to speak with the said accuser, viz. Abigail Williams, a girl of eleven or twelve years old, but that we could not be in private at Mr. Parris' house as he had promised me. We went therefore into the alehouse, where an Indian man attended us who it seems was one of the afflicted. To him we gave some cider. He showed several scars that seemed as if they had been long there, and showed them as done by witchcraft, and acquainted us that his wife, who also was a slave, was imprisoned for witchcraft. And now instead of one accuser they all came in, who began to tumble down like swine, and then three women were called in to attend them. We in the room were all at a stand to see who they would cry out of, but in a short time they cried out, "Cary." And immediately after a warrant was sent from the justices to bring my wife before them, who were sitting in a chamber nearby waiting for this.

Being brought before the justices, her chief accusers were two girls. My wife declared to the justices that she never had any knowledge of them before that day. She was forced to stand with her arms stretched out. I did request that I might hold one of her hands, but it was denied me; then she desired me to wipe the tears from her eyes and the sweat from her face, which I did; then she desired she should lean herself on me, saying she should faint.

Justice Hathorne replied, she had strength enough to torment those persons and she should have strength enough to stand. I speaking something against their cruel proceedings, they commanded me to be silent or else I should be turned out of the room. The Indian before mentioned was also brought in to be one of her accusers. Being come in, he now (when before the justices) fell down and tumbled about like a hog, but said nothing. The justices asked the girls who afflicted the Indian. They answered, "She" (meaning my wife), and [she] now lay upon him. The justices ordered her to touch him, in order to his cure, but her head must be turned another way lest instead of curing she should make him worse by her looking on him, her hand being guided to take hold of his. But the Indian took hold on her hand and pulled her down on the floor in a barbarous manner. Then his hand was taken off and her hand put on his and the cure was quickly wrought. I being extremely troubled at their inhumane dealings uttered a hasty speech (that God would take vengeance on them, and desired that God would deliver us out of the hands of unmerciful men). Then her *Mittimus* was writ. I did with difficulty and charge obtain the liberty of a room, but no beds in it. If there had, could have taken but little rest that night. She was committed to Boston Prison, but I obtained a *Habeas Corpus* to remove her to Cambridge Prison, which is in our County of Middlesex. Having been there one night, next morning the jailer put irons on her legs (having received such a command). [It was the curious theory that chaining the prisoner would prevent her specter from afflicting anyone.] The weight of them was about eight pounds. These irons and her other afflictions soon brought her into convulsion fits, so that I thought she would have died that night. I sent to entreat that the irons might be taken off, but all entreaties were in vain, [even] if it would have saved her life, so that in this condition she must continue. . . .[4]

Captain Cary was the only contemporary ever to accuse everyone concerned—the afflicted persons, the magistrates, and the ministers—of bad faith. Clearly he thought the whole business was nothing but connivance. There is, of course, nothing surprising in his reacting that way; a little paranoia is more than understandable under the appalling circumstances. Similar charges of bad faith and connivance were made by Captain John Alden[5] (who was examined seven days after Mrs. Cary), in an account curiously written in the third person. His charges were not so comprehensive as Cary's, and they were weakened by his offering alternate explanations (besides fraud) for the behavior of the afflicted persons. They were "distracted," he suggested, or possessed. Or perhaps they were themselves witches.

John Alden, Senior, of Boston, in the County of Suffolk, Mariner, on the 28th day of May, 1692, was sent for by the Magistrates of Salem, in the County of Essex, upon the accusation of a company of poor distracted or possessed creatures, or witches, and being sent by Mr. Stoughton [the deputy-governor] arrived there the 31st of May and appeared at Salem Village before Mr. Gedney, Mr. Hathorne, and Mr. Corwin. [Bartholomew Gedney, a Salem magistrate, frequently joined Hathorne and Corwin as an examiner.]

Those wenches being present, who played their juggling tricks, falling down, crying out, and staring in people's faces, the magistrates demanded of them several times who it was of all the people in the room that hurt them. One of these accusers pointed several times at one Captain Hill, there present, but spake nothing. The same accuser had a man standing at her back to hold her up; he stooped down to her ear; then she cried out, Alden, Alden afflicted her. One of the magistrates asked her if she had ever seen Alden. She answered, no. He asked her how she knew it was Alden. She said, the man told her so.

Then all were ordered to go down into the street, where a ring was made and the same accuser cried out, "There stands Alden, a bold fellow with his hat on before the judges. He sells powder and shot to the Indians and French, and lies with the Indian squaws and has Indian papooses." Then was Alden committed to the marshall's custody and his sword taken from him, for they said he afflicted them with his sword. After some hours Alden was sent for to the Meeting-House in the Village before the Magistrates, who required Alden to stand upon a chair, to the open view of all the people.

The accusers cried out that Alden did pinch them then, when he stood upon a chair in the sight of all the people, a good way distant from them. One of the magistrates bid the marshall to hold open Alden's hands, that he might not pinch those creatures. Alden asked them why they should think that he should come to that village to afflict those persons that he never knew or saw before. Mr. Gedney bid Alden confess and give glory to God. Alden said he hoped he should give glory to God and hoped he should never

1. Witches receiving images from a Devil, for use in their charms. From John Ashton, *Chap-Books of the Eighteenth Century* (London, 1882). *Pennsylvania State University Still Photography Studios.*

2. A witch accepts a familiar from the Black Man. From Ashton. *Pennsylvania State University Still Photography Studios.*

3. An hysterical fit, from J.-M. Charcot, *Lectures on the Diseases of the Nervous System* (London, 1877). Notice the extruded tongue, reported during the seventeenth century in witchcraft cases at Groton, Boston, Salem, and elsewhere. Notice also the legs crossed in spasm; at one time Mary Warren's legs could not be uncrossed without breaking them. *Pennsylvania State University Still Photography Studios.*

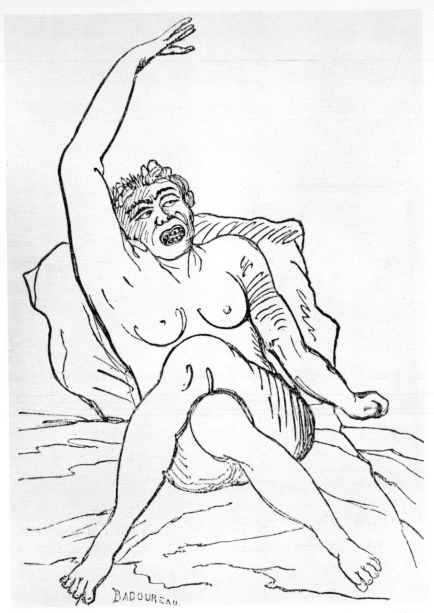

4. Charcot's patient Ler— during an hysterical attack. Her postures reminded him "of the attitudes which history assigns to the demoniacs" (*Lectures on the Diseases of the Nervous System*, v. 1, p. 280). *Pennsylvania State University Still Photography Studios.*

Witches Apprehended, Examined and Executed, for notable villanies by them committed both by Land and Water.

With a strange and most true triall how to know whether a woman be a Witch or not.

Printed at London for *Edward Marchant*, and are to be sold at his shop ouer against the Crosse in Pauls Church-yard. 1 6 1 3.

5. Swimming a witch in seventeenth-century England. Swimming was not employed at Salem, although it was in Connecticut and Virginia. Mobs swam suspected witches as late as the nineteenth century in both England and America. *Reproduced by permission of The Huntington Library, San Marino, California.*

ROBIN
Good-Fellovv,

His Mad Prankes, and merry Iests,

Full of honest Mirth, and is a fit Medicine for Melancholy.

LONDON,
Printed for *F. Groue* dwelling on Snow-hill
ouer against the Sarasens head. 1628.

6. A seventeenth-century English version of the deified herd animal (see pp. 3–5). His attributes make it plain that he is a fertility god. Like his relative the Devil, he is a trickster. He must be called Goodfellow to propitiate him. *Reproduced by permission of The Huntington Library, San Marino, California.*

7. Krampus, an Austrian version of the deified herd animal who has survived into the twentieth century. The twigs are explained on pp. 3–4. The object in his left hand may be related to the Devil's pitchfork, or to the horned moon, or to the diphallus of Dionysus. It and his horns are gilded, like the horns and hooves of the Irish Puck-goat. *John P. Mertz, Pennsylvania State University Still Photography Studios.*

THE
DISPLAYING,
OF SUPPOSED
WITCHCRAFT.

Wherein is affirmed that there are many sorts of

Deceivers and Impostors,

AND

Divers persons under a passive *Delusion* of

MELANCHOLY and *FANCY.*

But that there is a *Corporeal League* made betwixt the
DEVIL and the WITCH,

Or that he sucks on the *Witches Body*, has *Carnal Copulation*, or
that *Witches* are turned into *Cats, Dogs,* raise Tempests, or
the like, is utterly denied and disproved.

Wherein also is handled,

The Existence of Angels and Spirits, the truth of Apparitions, the Nature of
Astral and Sydereal Spirits, the force of Charms, and Philters;
with other abstruse matters.

By *John Webster*, Practitioner in Physick.

---

*Falsæ etenim opiniones Hominum præoccupantes, non solùm surdos, sed & cæcos faciunt, ità ut
videre nequeant, quæ aliis perspicua apparent.* Galen. lib. 8. de Comp. Med.

LONDON,

Printed by *J. M.* and are to be sold by the Booksellers in *London.* 1677.

---

8. The title page of the most important attack on witchcraft beliefs to
be published in late seventeenth-century England. It suggests the
severe limits of skepticism at that time. *Pennsylvania State University
Still Photography Studios. From the Rare Books Room of the Pennsylvania State University Libraries.*

9. Increase Mather. *American Antiquarian Society*.

10. Cotton Mather. *American Antiquarian Society*.

11. Samuel Sewall. *American Antiquarian Society*.

12. William Stoughton. *American Antiquarian Society*.

gratify the Devil, but appealed to all that ever knew him if they ever suspected him to be such a person, and challenged anyone that could bring in anything upon their own knowledge that might give suspicion of his being such an one. Mr. Gedney said he had known Alden many years, and had been at sea with him, and always looked upon him to be an honest man, but now he did see cause to alter his judgment. Alden answered, he was sorry for that, but he hoped God would clear up his innocency [so] that he would recall that judgment again, and added that he hoped that he should with Job maintain his integrity till he died. They bid Alden look upon the accusers, which he did, and then they fell down. Alden asked Mr. Gedney what reason there could be given why Alden's looking upon *him* did not strike *him* down as well, but no reason was given that I heard. But the accusers were brought to Alden to touch them, and this touch they said made them well. Alden began to speak of the Providence of God in suffering these creatures to accuse innocent persons. Mr. Noyes asked Alden why he would offer to speak of the Providence of God. "God by his Providence," said Mr. Noyes, "governs the world and keeps it in peace," and so went on with discourse and stopped Alden's mouth as to that. Alden told Mr. Gedney that he could assure him that there was a lying Spirit in them, "for I can assure you that there is not a word of truth in all these say of me." But Alden was again committed to the marshall, and his *Mittimus* written. . . .[6]

Rationalist historians have taken Cary's and Alden's accusations of bad faith at face value, but there is little reason to do so. Not only does Alden offer conflicting explanations (e.g., that the girls are possessed, with "a lying Spirit in them"), but were his charges consistent they would still be part of a very small minority opinion, even among those accused of witchcraft. And surely their sense of outraged helplessness is explanation enough for the charges they made. That sense is the chief burden of both accounts, and both men eventually acted upon it. Nathaniel Cary waited until the trials had begun. When he saw that the trial procedures were essentially similar to those of the preliminary examinations, and failed in his attempts to have Mrs. Cary tried in Middlesex County rather than Essex, he contrived her escape from prison on July 30 and fled with her to New York. Alden followed his example in September, as had a number of others before him.

We have seen more than enough to demonstrate that the acceptance of specter evidence led to continual bullying of the accused during the preliminary examinations. And we must remember that these examinations were not confined to the courtroom. Typically, if an accused person refused to confess in the formal hearing before the magistrates she could expect many hours of further examinations in prison, some of them formal and some of them informal. In the latter both the jailers and the ministers took their turns at threatening and grilling the suspects, as the following undated testimony shows:

The deposition of Sarah Ingersoll, aged about thirty years, saith that seeing Sarah Churchill after her examination, she came to me crying and wringing her hands, seeming to be much troubled in spirit. I asked her what she ailed. She answered, she had undone herself. I asked her in what? She said in belying herself and others, in saying she had set her hand to the Devil's book, whereas she said she never did. I told her I believed she had set her hand to the book. She answered crying, and said, "No, no, no! I never, I never did!" I asked, then what made her say she did? She answered, because they threatened her and told her they would put her into the dungeon, and put her along with Mr. Burroughs. And thus several times she followed me up and down, telling me that she had undone herself in belying herself and others. I asked her why she did write it [i.e., her confession]? She told me, because she had stood out so long in it that now she durst not. She said also that if she told Mr. Noyes but once she had set her hand to the book, he would believe her, but if she told the truth and said she had not set her hand to the book a hundred times he would not believe her.[7]

Furthermore, the bullying of the accused was not confined to magistrates, ministers, and jailers. The population in general accepted the validity of specter evidence, and as a result the relatives of the accused frequently joined in pressing them relentlessly to confess. Captain Cary's sturdy defense of his wife's innocence was unusual; much more common was the experience of an Andover woman:

Goodwife Tyler did say that when she was first apprehended she had no fears upon her and did think that nothing could have made her confess against herself, but since, she had found to her great grief that she had wronged the truth and falsely accused herself. She said that when she was brought to Salem her brother Bridges rode with her and that all along the way from Andover to Salem her brother kept telling her that she must needs be a witch, since the afflicted accused her and at her touch were raised out of their fits, and urging her to confess herself a witch. She as constantly told him that she was no witch, that she knew nothing of witchcraft, and begged of him not to urge her to confess. However, when she came to Salem she was carried to a room where her brother on one side and Mr. John Emerson on the other side did tell her that she was certainly a witch, and that she saw the Devil before her eyes at that time (and accordingly the said Emerson would attempt with his hand to beat him away from her eyes), and they so urged her to confess that she wished herself in any dungeon rather than be so treated. Mr. Emerson told her once and again, "Well! I see you will not confess! Well! I will now leave you, and then you are undone, body and soul, forever!" Her brother urged her to confess and told her that in so doing she could not lie, to which she answered, "Good brother, do not say so. For I shall lie if I confess, and then who shall answer unto God for my lie?" He still asserted it, and said that God would not suffer so many good men to be in such an error about it, and that she would be hanged if she would not confess, and continued so long and so violently to urge and press her to confess that she thought verily her life would have gone from her, and became so terrified in her mind that she owned at length almost anything that they propounded to her. But she had wronged her conscience in so doing; she was guilty of a great sin in belying of herself, and desired to mourn for it as long as she lived. This she said and a great deal more of the like nature, and all of it with such affection, sorrow, relenting, grief, and mourning, as that it exceeds any pen for to describe and express the same.[8]

Nor was Goodwife Tyler the only Andover woman so abused by her relatives. According to Thomas Brattle

Deacon Fry's wife, Captain Osgood's wife, and some others, remarkably pious and good people in repute . . . [were] first brought [to confession] by the urgings and arguings of their good husbands, who, having taken up that corrupt and highly pernicious opinion that whoever were accused by the afflicted were guilty, did break charity with their dear wives upon their being accused and urge them to confess their guilt, which so far prevailed with them as to make them say they were afraid of their being in the snare of the Devil, and which, through the rude and barbarous methods that were afterwards used at Salem, issued in somewhat plainer degrees of confession and was attended with imprisonment.[9]

Every confession reinforced the conviction of the magistrates, the ministers, and the community that they were on the right track. It is by no means impossible to understand their conviction. They were uncovering indisputable evidence of witchcraft. Also, it was true that arresting and confining a suspect always relieved the afflicted persons of their fits. (The relief was unfortunately temporary, because no sooner had one suspect been confined than the specter of a new one would appear, although surely there must have been a limit to the supply of witches in Massachusetts?) Moreover, the confessions themselves seemed most convincing. To be sure, some of them, like those we have just been considering, had been produced under duress. But the majority were made quite freely, without any compulsion at all. It is Brattle, a sharp critic of the witchcraft proceedings, who tells us that a majority of the confessors were, like the afflicted girls, "possessed." That is, they were hysterics, and their confessions were the product of their hysteria rather than of duress.

Some concrete evidence of genuine witchcraft; many confessions, the majority of them freely given; the therapeutic success of imprisoning those whose specters appeared to the afflicted—such are the basic elements in the community's conviction that its behavior was right. This conviction was so firmly seated that all through the summer of 1692 the community resisted any evidence which suggested it might be mistaken.

We have seen how strongly this conviction operated when Mary Warren had doubts of the validity of her hallucinations; she was forced back into those hallucinations, out of touch with the reality which had led her to question them. It is scarcely

surprising that nobody pursued Sarah Ingersoll's testimony that
Sarah Churchill had recanted her confession, or weighed the
other evidence that the testimony of the afflicted persons was
not, after all, very reliable.

There was, however, clear evidence of contradictions in
this testimony. Robert Moulton, Sr., testified that

watching with Susanna Sheldon since she was afflicted, I heard her
say that the witches hauled her upon her belly through the yard like
a snake and hauled her over the stone wall, and presently I heard
her contradict her former discourse and said that she came over the
stone wall herself.[10]

There was also evidence that at least some of the accusations
were the result of malicious suggestions.

The testimony of Samuel Phillips, aged about 67, minister of the
Word of God in Rowley, who saith that Mr. Payson (minister of
God's Word also in Rowley) and myself went, being desired, to
Samuel Perley of Ipswich to see their young daughter, who was
visited with strange fits, and in her fits (as her father and mother
affirmed) did mention Goodwife Howe, the wife of James Howe,
Jr., of Ipswich, as if she was in the house and did afflict her. When
we were in the house the child had one of her fits but made no
mention of Goodwife Howe, and when the fit was over, and she
came to herself, Goodwife Howe went to the child and took her by
the hand and asked her whether she had ever done her any hurt.
And she answered, "No, never. And if I did complain of you in my
fits I knew not that I did so." I further can affirm upon oath that
young Samuel Perley, brother to the afflicted girl, looking out of a
chamber window (I and the afflicted child being without doors
together) . . . said to his sister, "Say Goodwife Howe is a witch. Say
she is a witch." And the child spake not a word that way, but I
looked up to the window where the youth stood and rebuked him
for his boldness to stir up his sister to accuse the said Goodwife
Howe, whence she had cleared her from doing any hurt to his sister
in both our hearing. And, I added, no wonder that the child in her
fits did mention Goodwife Howe, when her nearest relations were
so frequent in expressing their suspicions in the child's hearing
when she was out of her fits. . . .[11]

The Reverend Mr. Phillips' testimony is practicably telling for the twentieth-century reader because we know that hysterics are notoriously suggestible. Unfortunately it was weakened for the seventeenth century by the fact that Phillips' colleague, Edward Payson, could corroborate most of the central events within doors but could not recall the Perley boy's malicious suggestions. Yet such suggestions (most of them, of course, less directly and less blatantly put) probably played a large part in the process of accusation. Certainly this seems to have been the case in the household of Thomas Putnam, which was the greatest single source for accusations.

John Tarbell being at the house of Thomas Putnam upon the 28th day of this instant March, being the year 1692, upon discourse of many things, I asked them some questions. And among others I asked this question: whether the girl that was afflicted [Ann Putnam, Jr.] did first speak of Goody Nurse before others mentioned her to her. They said she told them she saw the apparition of a pale-faced woman that sat in her grandmother's seat, but did not know her name. I replied and said, "But who was it that told her that it was Goody Nurse?" Mercy Lewis said it was Goody Putnam that said it was Goody Nurse. Goody Putnam said it was Mercy Lewis that told her. Thus they turned it upon one another, saying "It was you," and "It was you that told her." This was before any was afflicted at Thomas Putnam's beside his daughter. . . .[12]

Then, too, there was evidence that some of the afflicted persons (though not, so far as we know, any of the most important ones) were thoroughly undependable. Six people, for example, testified that Goodwife Sarah Bibber was a person of turbulent and malicious character, and that she had been subject to strange fits long before the witchcraft investigation. Thomas and Mary Jacobs, in whose house she had lived, reported that she "would be very often speaking against one and another, very obscenely, and those things that were very false, and wishing very bad wishes."[13] Ann Pudeator protested, in a petition to the judges, that John Best, who had given evidence against her, had formerly been convicted and whipped as a liar.[14]

Robert Calef, in his *More Wonders of the Invisible World,*

maintains that the court once glossed over a blatant falsehood.

At the trial of Sarah Good one of the afflicted fell in a fit, and after coming out of it she cried out of the prisoner for stabbing her in the breast with a knife, and that she had broken the knife in stabbing of her. Accordingly a piece of the blade of a knife was found about her. Immediately, information being given to the court, a young man was called who produced a haft and part of the blade, which the court having viewed and compared found to be the same. And upon inquiry the young man affirmed that yesterday he happened to break that knife, and that he cast away the upper part, this afflicted person then being present. The young man was dismissed, and she was bidden by the court not to tell lies, and was improved (after, as she had been before) to give evidence against the prisoners.[15]

One other incident recorded in the documents suggests that at least a few of the accusations were the result of outright lying rather than of hysteria.

The testimony of Daniel Eliot, aged twenty-seven years or thereabouts, who testifieth and saith, that I being at the house of Lieutenant Ingersoll on the 28th of March in the year 1692, there being present one of the afflicted persons, which cried out and said, "There's Goody Procter." William Raymond being there present told the girl he believed she lied, for he saw nothing. Goody Ingersoll told the girl she told a lie. Then the girl said that she did it for sport—they must have some sport.[16]

A second version of this incident varies in several details.

The testimony of William Raymond, aged twenty-six years or thereabout, testifieth and saith that I being at the house of Lieutenant Ingersoll some time in the latter end of March, there discoursing concerning the examining of several persons suspected for witches, I was saying that I heard that Goody Procter was to be examined tomorrow, to which Goody Ingersoll replied she did not believe it, for she heard nothing of it. Some of the afflicted persons being present, one of them or more cried out, "There, Goody Procter, there, Goody Procter," and "Old witch, I'll have her hang." Goody Ingersoll sharply reproved them. Then they seemed to make a joke of it.[17]

If all that happened was that the girls "seemed to make a joke of it" then we may be dealing simply with hysterical laughter. But if one of them actually said "she did it for sport" then it is clearly fraud, and it would be helpful to know which one it was. It is unlikely that it was any of the main accusers—Abigail Williams, or Ann Putnam, Jr., or Mercy Lewis—because this testimony was offered in defense of Elizabeth Procter, and if one of the main accusers had been involved her name would surely have been mentioned. Whoever it was, the magistrates do not seem to have pursued the matter further.

But then, why would they? They had not pursued Mary Warren's doubts of the validity of her hallucinations, and since Mary had been persuaded to abandon those doubts she had become a constant proof of the genuineness of the girls' behavior. Her own seizures had increased in violence; we have seen that on one occasion her legs were crossed with such force that they could not be uncrossed without breaking them. The violence continued throughout the summer, until on September 2 she was reported as having "a pin run through her hand and blood running out of her mouth."[18] *A pin run through her hand and blood running out of her mouth.* No impartial observer of Mary Warren could entertain, even for one moment, the idea that the afflicted girls' behavior was fraudulent.

8

❦❦❦❦❦

Witch Hunt

When a community looks only for evidence of guilt and ignores or suppresses all contradictory evidence, the result is a witch hunt. And a witch hunt was developing in Salem as the community felt itself so beset by evil that it was no longer capable of perceiving the good.

The primary causes should now be clear. There was an outbreak of epidemic hysteria in Salem Village which originated in experiments with the occult. And the hysterical hallucinations of the afflicted persons were confirmed by some concrete evidence of actual witchcraft and by many confessions, the majority of them also hysterical. A number of other explanations have been offered, but most of them are more or less unconvincing. It has been argued, for example, that the outbreak was the result of the malice accumulated during a long series of village quarrels, and it is true that there had been no scarcity of petty quarreling in Salem Village. But many small towns have such a history, and few of them have witch hunts. It has also been argued that the outbreak was due to Puritanism. Puritans, we have all been taught, were repressive; thus the Salem witchcraft was a kind of insanity resulting from Puritanical sexual repression.

Several major objections can be raised to this explanation beside the obvious one that it is grossly simplistic. In the first place, the degree of repressiveness in Puritan society is a matter of debate. Then, too, the demonstrably hysterical behavior at Salem was the result of fear rather than of sexual repression. Finally, and most damagingly, proponents of the Puritan theory seem to be ignorant of the fact that outbreaks of witchcraft occurred throughout Western civilization during the seventeenth century, and in every kind of religious community, Lutheran, Anglican, and Catholic as well as Puritan. If Puritanism was responsible for the hanging of nineteen people in Salem, what was responsible for the burning of nine hundred people in Bamberg?[1]

It has also been argued that the outbreak owed much to the fact that Massachusetts at this time felt itself gravely threatened. There is much to be said for this argument. What more likely time would Massachusetts' arch-enemy, the Devil, choose for his attack than precisely that time when she was beset by all her other enemies? The Salem witchcraft occurred at a time when the very existence of the colony had been threatened for more than a generation.

Massachusetts had begun her existence in 1630 when a group of English Puritans, thinking it impossible to live any longer in the England of Charles I, had obtained a royal charter for trading and planting in New England and had then emigrated to Massachusetts, taking their charter with them. As long as they could retain the charter which was the legal basis of their existence, they could exist as an English colony independent of any English authority. They had managed to maintain this position throughout the troubled reign of Charles I; that monarch was too occupied with problems at home to bother with exerting his authority over a small group of religious dissenters across so wild and vast an ocean. They had held it also through the years of revolution and during the existence of Cromwell's Puritan Commonwealth.

But with the restoration of the monarchy in 1660 and the accession of Charles II a new act of religious uniformity was passed, and both English and New English Puritans felt themselves in danger. Fortunately for Massachusetts, Charles II spent most of his reign consolidating his power at home. It was not until 1684 that he felt secure enough to exert his authority over the Massachusetts Bay Company; in that year he recalled the charter.

The accession of James II the following year presented a far greater danger than had Charles II. James was an avowed Catholic and an exponent of Divine Right. On his accession rebellions broke out in England, led by Monmouth and by Argyll; James put them bloodily down. And in 1686 he put down Massachusetts; he appointed a royal governor, Sir Edmund Andros, who was during his short rule the most hated man in all the English colonies. But James's attempt at absolute monarchy was a failure. By 1688 it became apparent that he could no longer govern and he fled the country in the bloodless "Glorious Revolution." In 1689, before the news of that event had reached New England, Massachusetts had its own revolution; the royal government was overthrown and Governor Andros imprisoned.

With the accession of William and Mary in 1689, at the invitation of parliament, the threat of religious suppression passed. The Act of Toleration specifically excluded Catholics, Unitarians, and Jews, but it guaranteed freedom of worship to all Protestants except Unitarians. However, the Test Act of 1673, requiring Anglican communion for civil or military office, remained in force. This left Massachusetts in an extremely ticklish situation. Not only was she without her charter, but she was—as she had been doing since 1631—excluding everyone but Puritans both from civil office and from the franchise. This was entirely unacceptable to the English government.

Massachusetts sent a commission to negotiate a new charter, with the Reverend Increase Mather in charge. It was the first time a clergyman had performed so important a civil function, and Mather performed it well. He did not achieve what Massachusetts had wanted—the restoration of the old charter—but no man could have achieved that; the Throne was not prepared to charter any more independent commonwealths. But they were prepared to negotiate a compromise. The Throne would no longer tolerate a situation in which members of the Church of England were excluded from the franchise, so Massachusetts had to accept a property qualification for the vote rather than the religious one it desired. In return, the Throne was willing to give tacit acknowledgment to the fact that the Test Act was unenforceable in Massachusetts. Thus, although Puritans could not hold office in England, the charter permitted them to continue holding office in Massachusetts. Since they constituted an overwhelming majority there, they could reasonably expect to continue electing Puritan representatives and magistrates. The Throne was unwilling to be excluded from the government, however, and therefore insisted on the power of appointing the governor. In return for this basic concession the governor was to exercise far less power than Andros had, and Massachusetts was consulted in making the appointment. In fact, it was Increase Mather who nominated the first governor under the new charter: Sir William Phips, who was New England born, an ardent Puritan, and a protégé of the Mathers.

It was a major diplomatic triumph. Indeed, it is unlikely that anyone could have obtained more liberal terms for Massachusetts than had Increase Mather. But no diplomatic triumph could obscure the fact that in obtaining the new charter he had been forced to acknowledge the end of Massachusetts' former independence. There could be little joy in Zion when it became apparent that the price of her continued existence had been a yielding to and toleration of her ancient enemies.

And then there were troubles with the French and Indians on the frontier. No wonder the Powers of the Air chose such a time to descend on Massachusetts, and particularly on Salem, which had been colonized in 1628 as a kind of pilot settlement for Boston. "An army of Devils," wrote Cotton Mather, "is horribly broke in upon that place which is the center, and after a sort, the first-born of our English settlements."[2]

Phips and Increase Mather arrived in Boston with the new charter on May 14, 1692. Massachusetts had been without a charter for the past eight years, but she proceeded to work out an orderly plan for transition to the new one. All of the old charter laws not repugnant to the laws of England were to continue in force—the General Court passed a resolution to that effect on June 8—while new laws were written during the summer and fall. No major legal business had been expected until January, when the Superior Court of Judicature was scheduled to meet, and by that time the new laws would be in force.

But the witchcraft situation complicated matters. The jails were filling up with suspects; according to Calef there were about a hundred of them by the end of May. Being incarcerated in a seventeenth-century jail was a genuine hardship. Not only was it apt to be more unpleasant than a twentieth-century jail in all the more obvious ways, but seventeenth-century prisoners were required to pay for their lodging, so that lengthy imprisonment could bring terrible economic hardships. If all these people were held in prison until January some of the more infirm among them would surely die—Sarah Osburn had already died, on the tenth of May—and many more would be impoverished. It had been the policy of both England and New England to mitigate such hardships by trying indicted prisoners as soon as practicable. And in this case there seemed to be perfectly sound legal grounds for trials, since both the old charter law and English law provided death for malefic witchcraft. If anything, the English law was the more comprehensive. The first section read:

One that shall use, practise, or exercise any invocation or conjuration of any evil or wicked spirit, or consult, covenant with, entertain or employ, feed or reward any evil or wicked spirit, to or for any intent or purpose; or take up any dead man, woman, or child, out of his, her, or their grave, or any other place, where the dead body resteth; or the skin, bone, or other part of any dead person, to be employed or used in any manner of witchcraft, sorcery, charm or enchantment; or shall use, practise, or exercise any witchcraft, enchantment, charm, or sorcery, whereby any person shall be killed, destroyed, wasted, consumed, pined, or lamed in his or her body, or any part thereof: such offenders duly and lawfully convicted and attainted, shall suffer death.[3]

Therefore Phips acted. On May 27 the Governor's Council established a Special Court of Oyer and Terminer with the following order:

Upon consideration that there are many criminal offenders now in custody, some whereof have lain long, and many inconveniences attending the thronging of the jails at this hot season of the year, there being no judicatories or courts of justice yet established: Ordered, that a Special Commission of Oyer and Terminer be made out to William Stoughton, John Richards, Nathaniel Saltonstall, Wait Winthrop, Bartholomew Gedney, Samuel Sewall, John Hathorne, Jonathan Corwin and Peter Sergeant, Esquires, assigning them to be justices, or any five of them (whereof William Stoughton, John Richards and Bartholomew Gedney Esq's to be one), to inquire of, hear and determine for this time, according to the law and custom of England and of this their Majesties' Province, all manner of crimes and offenses had, made, done or perpetrated within the counties of Suffolk, Essex, Middlesex, and each of them.[4]

Stoughton was Phips' lieutenant-governor, and acted as chief-justice. He was from Dorchester. Richards, Winthrop, Sergeant, and Sewall were from Boston. Saltonstall was from Haverhill, and Hathorne, Corwin, and Gedney from Salem. All were experienced magistrates. Thomas Newton was appointed King's Attorney; he was a leading member of the Boston bar and had served as King's Attorney in New York in 1691. He served until July 27, when he was replaced by Anthony Checkley, the newly recommissioned Attorney-General of Massachusetts. Samuel Sewall's brother, Captain Stephen Sewall, was appointed clerk of the court. No more experienced or distinguished a court could have been assembled anywhere in English America, and Phips had every right to expect that they would deal adequately with the problem of witchcraft. He was himself leaving for the frontier to deal with the French and the Indians.

The court sat on June 2, tried one person—Bridget Bishop —and sentenced her to death. She was hanged on June 10. That only one person was tried at the first session, and that it should be Bridget Bishop, are both significant facts. They suggest that at first the court took Cotton Mather's letter to Judge Richards extremely seriously. They had, for example, decided to follow his advice that lesser criminals should not be put to death. Most seventeenth-century witchcraft courts executed everyone who confessed themselves a witch. But this court, good Puritans that they were, had apparently decided that confession was evidence of possible regeneration. Therefore confessors like Tituba and Dorcas Good—both of whom would have been burned by a European court—were not brought to trial. The court was also following Mather's advice that specter evidence was not sufficient for conviction. Bridget Bishop was far from the first person to be examined; she had been arrested more than six weeks after Sarah Good, who was still in prison and would not hang until July 19. But against Bridget Bishop there was the damning evidence of the dolls with pins in them and her scratching of the Shattuck child's face in what was clearly a contest of occult power. Against Sarah Good there was nothing so concrete.

The trouble was, however, that of all the hundred or so then in prison there was this kind of concrete evidence *only* against Bridget Bishop. When the court adjourned, it was not at all sure what to do next. Therefore the government did what Massachusetts governments had always done in times of uncertainty; it asked the advice of the Boston clergy. In a document drawn up by Cotton Mather and dated Boston, June 15, 1692, the clergy gave its reply:

The Return of Several
Ministers Consulted
by his Excellency, and the Honorable Council,
upon the present Witchcrafts in Salem Village

I. The afflicted state of our poor neighbors that are now suffering by molestations from the invisible world, we apprehend so deplorable that we think their condition calls for the utmost help of all persons in their several capacities.

II. We cannot but with all thankfulness acknowledge the success which the merciful God has given unto the sedulous and assiduous endeavours of our honorable rulers to detect the abominable witchcrafts which have been committed in the country, humbly praying that the discovery of these mysterious and mischievous wickednesses may be perfected.

III. We judge that in the prosecution of these, and all such witchcrafts, there is need of a very critical and exquisite caution, lest by too much credulity for things received only upon the Devil's authority there be a door opened for a long train of miserable consequences, and Satan get an advantage over us, for we should not be ignorant of his devices.

IV. As in complaints upon witchcrafts there may be Matters of Inquiry which do not amount unto Matters of Presumption, and there may be Matters of Presumption which yet may not be reckoned Matters of Conviction, so 'tis necessary that all proceedings thereabout be managed with an exceeding tenderness towards those that may be complained of, especially if they have been persons formerly of an unblemished reputation.

V. When the first inquiry is made into the circumstances of such as may lie under any just suspicion of witchcrafts, we could wish that there may be admitted as little as is possible of such noise, company, and openness as may too hastily expose them that are examined, and that there may be nothing used as a test for the trial of the suspected the lawfulness whereof may be doubted among the People of God, but that the directions given by such judicious writers as Perkins and Bernard be consulted in such a case.

VI. Presumptions whereupon persons may be committed, and, much more, convictions whereupon persons may be condemned as guilty of witchcrafts, ought certainly to be more considerable than barely the accused person being represented by a specter unto the afflicted, inasmuch as 'tis an undoubted and a notorious thing that a Demon may, by God's permission, appear even to ill purposes in the shape of an innocent, yea, and a virtuous man. Nor can we esteem alterations made in the sufferers by a look or touch of the accused to be an infallible evidence of guilt, but frequently liable to be abused by the Devil's legerdemains.

VII. We know not whether some remarkable affronts given to the Devils by our disbelieving those testimonies whose whole force and strength is from them alone may not put a period unto the progress of the dreadful calamity begun upon us in the accusation of so many persons, whereof we hope some are yet clear from the great transgression laid unto their charge.

VIII. Nevertheless, we cannot but humbly recommend unto the

government the speedy and vigorous prosecution of such as have rendered themselves obnoxious, according to the direction given in the Laws of God and the wholesome statutes of the English nation for the detection of witchcraft.[5]

It is a polite and tactful document. It begins by sympathizing with the afflicted persons and commending the magistrates for their efforts to date, and ends by urging the prosecution "of such as have rendered themselves obnoxious." The ministers had to be polite and tactful. Because in the heart of this document, in sections III through VII, they rejected virtually all of the techniques the magistrates had been using in the preliminary examinations. They firmly rejected not only specter evidence but also all other "things received only upon the Devil's authority," which would include the testimony of confessed witches. They warned against precisely the kind of noisy and disorderly hearings Nathaniel Cary had found so offensive, and against all tests for witchcraft that might be suspect (i.e., that might themselves be a kind of charm). This latter warning, which is so obviously at variance with the advice given by Cotton Mather in his letter to John Richards, reflects the presence of Increase Mather, who, in contrast to his son, was vehemently opposed to such tests as saying the Lord's Prayer or the water ordeal. And finally, in section VII, they suggested that refusing to believe specter evidence and the testimony of confessed witches might "put a period" to the affair, including the accusations. In referring the judges to William Perkins' *Discourse of the Damned Art of Witchcraft* (London, 1608) and Richard Bernard's *Guide to Jury-Men . . . in Cases of Witchcraft* (1627) they were underlining their own reservations, since these writers, as Calef puts it, "made it their business and main work herein to oppose such [ways of trying witches] as they found to be pernicious."[6]

There is no account of the judges' deliberations, either in court or out of it, and it is unlikely that such a transcript was ever made. Many documents do survive from the trials, but aside from indictments and other court orders they consist entirely of evidence presented for and against the accused. But

"The Return of Several Ministers Consulted" can be used, like Cotton Mather's letter to John Richards, to reconstruct the course of the debate over how to conduct the witchcraft trials. It is obvious that, although the magistrates had observed Cotton Mather's warnings against depending on specter evidence when they chose to try Bridget Bishop first, they were anxious to make more use of it in future trials. And it is also obvious that a major difference of opinion was developing between the ministers and the magistrates, with the ministers flatly recommending that the magistrates try disbelieving all "things received only upon the Devil's authority."

It seems probable that at first the debate existed among the judges as well as between the judges and the Boston clergy. We know that Judge Nathaniel Saltonstall resigned from the court and that he was "very much dissatisfied with the proceedings of it."[7] We do not have the date of his resignation, but tradition says it was early, and the most likely time was during the last two weeks in June, between "The Return of Several Ministers Consulted" and the second sitting of the court, on the thirtieth of June. The court that met on that date appears to have made up its mind. It held three sessions—beginning on June 30, August 5, and September 9—and at none of these sessions was there the slightest evidence of judicial dissent. To a man the judges had committed themselves to the validity of specter evidence.

At the sessions of June 30 five people were tried: Sarah Good, Rebecca Nurse, Susannah Martin, Elizabeth Howe, and Sarah Wildes. All of them were condemned. And on July 19 all of them were executed. At the gallows the Reverend Nicholas Noyes called on Sarah Good to confess, telling her she was a witch and she knew she was a witch. Her reply is justly famous. "You are a liar," she told him. "I am no more a witch than you are a wizard, and if you take away my life God will give you blood to drink."[8] It must have sent a chill through the crowd assembled on Gallows Hill, because it was not the sort of thing a dying Christian would say. Seventeenth-century Christians at their death would try to forgive even their bitterest enemies; only a witch would die with a curse upon her lips—a witch, or a malevolent old woman.

There is not evidence enough to say for certain that Sarah Good was one or the other. But tradition has it that twenty-five years later, when Nicholas Noyes lay dying, he choked upon the blood that poured copiously from his mouth. And when that happened Salem remembered Sarah Good's words with feelings that were more than a little ambiguous. Hutchinson, who reported the tradition in his *History* of 1750, says that the people of Salem in his day still considered Sarah Good "if not a witch, a Pythonissa" [someone possessed by a spirit and prophesying by its aid.]⁹ This is, of course, the incident Hawthorne adapted for *The House of the Seven Gables.*

The most important of the trials at this session was not Sarah Good's, but that of Rebecca Nurse. We have seen that John Hathorne's sister and brother-in-law testified for her at her preliminary examination, and that Hathorne was not at all sure of himself while examining her. In the meantime thirty-nine of her neighbors had signed a petition stating that according to their observation "her life and conversation were according to her profession [as a Christian], and we never had any cause or grounds to suspect her of any such thing as she is now accused of."¹⁰ One of the signers was Jonathan Putnam, who had with Edward Putnam sworn out the original complaint against her but had since, apparently, changed his mind. The jury too found it hard to believe Rebecca Nurse a witch, and they brought her in not guilty. When their verdict was announced

immediately all the accusers in the court, and suddenly after all the afflicted out of court, made an hideous outcry, to the amazement not only of the spectators but the court also. . . .¹¹

Nobody could have expected the afflicted persons to be happy with a verdict that would release Rebecca Nurse. On June 1, when she had been taken out of prison only long enough to be brought before a grand jury and indicted, Ann Putnam, Sr., testified that the apparition of Rebecca Nurse did again fall upon me and almost choke me. And she told me that now she was come out of prison she had power to afflict me, and that now she would afflict me all this day long, and would kill me if she could.[12]

So the "amazement" of the spectators and the court must have been due to the volume and hideousness of the outcry rather than to the fact that an outcry was made. In any case, the judges were almost as unhappy with the verdict as the afflicted persons. "One of the judges expressed himself not satisfied. Another of them, as he was going off the bench, said they would have her indicted anew." (This would have been relatively easy to do. Since the specters of the accused persons appeared frequently to many of the afflicted, it would only have been necessary to base the new indictment on new appearances.) Chief-Justice Stoughton "said he would not impose upon the jury," but asked whether they had considered the implications of something Rebecca Nurse had said.

When one Hobbes, who had confessed herself a witch, was brought into the court to witness against her, the prisoner turning her head to her said, "What, do you bring her? She is one of us," or [words] to that effect.

The implication, Stoughton thought, was that Rebecca Nurse was acknowledging her membership in a coven of witches. Actually, all she had meant was that Hobbes was a fellow-prisoner, and she did not think a fellow-prisoner could be a legal witness against her. But the phrase sounded suspicious enough to the jury, coupled with the outcry of the afflicted, so that they asked leave to reconsider. On reconsideration they found they could not agree, and they returned to court to request that Rebecca Nurse be asked to explain her words. The question was put to her. But she was old, and partially deaf, and wrung with the day's experiences. She did not hear the question. The jury took her silence for evidence of guilt, and changed their verdict to guilty.

It has been suggested that Stoughton's procedure in this case was illegal, but this is not so. It was not at all unusual for a judge to ask a jury to reconsider. They might, of course, have refused the request, or they might have reconsidered and returned the same verdict. Had they done that, Stoughton would have had one more recourse. He could have refused the verdict, thus throwing the case into the General Court (as had happened in 1655, when the judges had refused to accept a verdict of guilty in the Hibbins case).

Now that a verdict of guilty was in, however, Rebecca Nurse's relatives immediately did what they could to rectify what must have seemed to them a simple but frightful mistake. They obtained the following statement from the foreman of the jury:

July 4, 1692. I, Thomas Fisk, the subscriber hereof, being one of them that were of the jury the last week at Salem court upon the trial of Rebecca Nurse, etc., being desired by some of the relations to give a reason why the jury brought her in guilty after her verdict [of] not guilty, I do hereby give my reasons to be as follows, *viz.*

When the verdict not guilty was [brought in] the honored Court was pleased to object against it, saying to them that they think they let slip the words which the prisoner at the bar spake against herself, which were spoken in reply to Goodwife Hobbes and her daughter, who had been faulty in setting their hands to the Devil's Book as they have confessed formerly. The words were, "What, do these persons give in evidence against me now? They used to come among us." After the honored Court had manifested their dissatisfaction of the verdict several of the jury declared themselves desirous to go out again, and thereupon the honored Court gave leave. But when we came to consider of the case I could not tell how to take her words as an evidence against her till she had a further opportunity to put her sense upon them, if she would take it. And then, going into court, I mentioned the words aforesaid, which by one of the Court were affirmed to have been spoken by her, she being then at the bar, but made no reply nor interpretation of them, whereupon these words were to me a principal evidence against her.

Thomas Fisk

From Goodwife Nurse herself they obtained this statement:

These presents do humbly show to the honored court and jury that, I being informed that the jury brought me in guilty upon my saying that Goodwife Hobbes and her daughter were of our company, but I intended no otherways than as they were prisoners with us, therefore did then, and yet do, judge them not legal evidence against their fellow-prisoners. And I being something hard of hearing, and full of grief, none informing me how the court took up my words, and therefore had not opportunity to declare what I intended when I said they were of our company.

Whether or not they took these documents to Chief-Justice Stoughton is not known. But they probably took them to Governor Phips, because Phips granted Rebecca Nurse a reprieve. No sooner had he done so than—before the official news had reached Salem—the afflicted complained of being freshly tormented. This was not the first time they had performed such a feat. Often they had complained that someone in prison was tormenting them, and then had been released from their torments at precisely the hour when that person was put in irons. Nor is there any difficulty in seeing how this could happen. They would have known when the order to chain a prisoner went out, and would have been able to estimate about how long it would take to carry it out. Expecting relief when the order was carried out, they would get it. One must never forget the hysteric's susceptibility to suggestion. And the same explanation probably accounts for this incident. The girls must have known that Rebecca Nurse's kinsmen were on their way to obtain a reprieve from the governor, and must have been able to estimate about how long it would take. Expecting to be tormented at the time the reprieve would be granted, they were tormented.

But this very plausible twentieth-century explanation of the girls' renewed torments was not, of course, available in the seventeenth century. The renewal of the torments as soon as the reprieve was granted seemed to most people a conclusive demonstration of Rebecca Nurse's guilt. A "Salem gentleman" —his name is unknown—remonstrated with the governor and persuaded him to recall his reprieve. Furthermore the church in Salem Town, of which Rebecca Nurse was a member, voted to excommunicate her, and did so without a single dissenting vote. The church record reads:

1692, July 3. After sacrament the elders [Higginson and Noyes] propounded to the church—and it was by an unanimous vote consented to—that our sister Nurse, being a convicted witch by the court and condemned to die, should be excommunicated, which was accordingly done in the afternoon, she being present.[18]

On July 19 she was put to death with the others, the most conspicuously innocent person of all those who died at Salem. On the gallows she was, in contrast to Sarah Good, a model of Christian behavior.

9

⟡⟡⟡⟡⟡

The Witch Hunt Debated

The execution of Rebecca Nurse must have been shocking news to everyone in prison on suspicion of witchcraft. She had enjoyed the greatest reputation for benevolence and piety of all those accused. If the court could hang her and if the church could excommunicate her what hope was there for anybody else? The question answered itself. There was one group in Massachusetts known to have serious reservations about the conduct of the witchcraft examinations and trials, and that was the Boston clergy. Four days after the execution of Rebecca Nurse, John Procter, who was to be tried at the next session of the court, addressed a letter on behalf of himself and his fellow-prisoners to five members of the Boston clergy.

Salem Prison, July 23, 1692

Mr. [probably Increase] Mather, Mr. Allen,
Mr. Moody, Mr. Willard, and
Mr. Bailey.
Reverend Gentlemen.

The innocency of our case, with the enmity of our accusers and our judges and jury, whom nothing but our innocent blood will serve their turn, having condemned us already before our trials, being so much incensed and enraged against us by the Devil, makes us bold to beg and implore your favorable assistance of this our humble petition to his Excellency [Governor Phips], that if it be possible our innocent blood may be spared, which undoubtedly otherwise will be shed if the Lord doth not mercifully step in, the magistrates, ministers, juries, and all the people in general being so much enraged and incensed against us by the delusion of the Devil, which we can term no other, by reason we know in our own consciences we are all innocent persons. Here are five persons who have lately confessed themselves to be witches and do accuse some of us of being along with them at a Sacrament [i.e., a witches' Sabbath] since we were committed into close prison, which we know to be lies. Two of the five are (Carrier's sons) young men who would not confess anything till they tied them neck and heels till the blood was ready to come out of their noses. And 'tis credibly believed and reported this was the occasion of making them confess that [which] they never did, by reason they said one had been a witch a month and another five weeks, and that their mother had made them so, who has been confined here nine weeks. My son, William Procter, when he was examined, because he would not confess that he was guilty when he was innocent, they tied him neck and heels till the blood gushed out at his nose, and would have kept him so twenty-four hours if one more merciful than the rest had not taken pity on him and caused him to be unbound. These actions are very like the Popish cruelties. They have already undone us in our estates, and that will not serve their turn without our innocent blood. If it cannot be granted that we can have our trials at Boston, we humbly beg that you would endeavor to have these magistrates changed and others in their rooms, begging also and beseeching you would be pleased to be here, if not all, some of you at our trials, hoping thereby you may be the means of saving the shedding of our innocent blood, desiring your prayers to the Lord in our behalf, we rest your poor afflicted servants,

John Procter, etc.[1]

The issue of torture, which Procter raises, is one that needs to be considered here. Cotton Mather had declared against it in his letter to Richards, calling it "un-English," and it is true that neither English nor New English law sanctioned it. The latter expressly forbade it, except for extorting the names of accomplices from convicted criminals, and even in that case it forbade "such tortures as be barbarous and inhumane."[2] What men of this age meant by "barbarous and inhumane" tortures may be realized by citing one example of the tortures used in Scotland and on the Continent. To make the comparison as just as possible, let us choose a witchcraft case, a Scottish one in which King James the Sixth (later James the First of England) took a personal interest. In 1591 a Doctor Fian had, under torture, confessed himself a witch. He had subsequently escaped. On his recapture he repudiated his confession,

whereupon the King's Majesty perceiving his stubborn wilfulness, conceived and imagined that in the time of his absence he had entered into a new conference and league with the Devil his master, and that he had been again newly marked, for the which he was narrowly searched, but it could not in any wise be found. Yet for more trial of him to make him confess he was commanded to have a most strange torment [strange to the anonymous writer, who was English], which was done in this manner following.

His nails upon all his fingers were riven and pulled off with an instrument called in Scottish a *Turkas*, which in England we call a pair of pincers, and under every nail there was thrust in two needles ... even up to the heads. At all which torments notwithstanding the doctor never shrunk any whit. Neither would he then confess it the sooner, for all the tortures inflicted upon him.

Then was he with all convenient speed, by commandment, conveyed again to the torment of the boots, wherein he continued a long time, and did abide so many blows in them that his legs were crushed and beaten together as small as might be, and the bones and flesh so bruised that the blood and marrow spouted forth in great abundance, whereby they were made unserviceable forever. And notwithstanding all these grievous pains and cruel torments he would not confess anything, so deeply had the Devil entered into his heart. ...[3]

Nothing of that sort ever occurred in New England, although it was routine practice on the Continent and in Scotland throughout the sixteenth and seventeenth centuries; similar tortures, for example, were liberally employed during the witchcraft scandal that shook the court of Louis XIV in 1679 to 1682. But it was a brutal age, and practices we consider barbarous and inhumane were still freely employed in both England and New England, not only during interrogation but also as punishments administered by the courts—branding, for example, or the pillory, in which the torture was left to the spontaneous imagination of passersby. Tying neck and heels (which means exactly what it says; the neck and the heels were tied together) was a legal punishment in Virginia, and thus it is not entirely surprising to find it being used by overenthusiastic jailers in Salem.

Another kind of duress that seems to have been freely employed at Salem was prolonged and aggressive interrogation. Sometimes this was combined with "watching," in which the suspect was observed throughout the night to see whether a familiar appeared to her. Watching could be simply converted into a kind of third degree by keeping the suspect as well as the watcher awake, poking and prodding her whenever she dozed. And Brattle says that a "blade was employed"[4] in forcing confessions from several Andover women, although precisely what he means by this is not known.

Nevertheless, torture was not really a central issue at Salem. It should be remembered that the majority of the confessions were free and unforced. And since Procter could have been condemned by such confessions as well as by those extorted under duress, the chief significance of the use of torture at Salem is that it gives us one more indication of the state of mind prevailing there during the month of July—a state of mind in which "the magistrates, ministers, juries, and all the people in general" were "so much enraged and incensed" against Procter and his fellow-prisoners that they could not believe them anything but guilty, and were willing to employ torture to extort what they believed to be the truth.

It is this prejudgment which is the central issue. The community had "condemned us," as Procter rightly said, "before our trials." In such circumstances the best hope for a fair trial lay in a change of venue from Salem to Boston, or, failing that, in a change of judges, bringing in men not conditioned by the hysterical fits of the afflicted. The only person who could command either of these changes was Governor Phips, and therefore Procter addressed his petition to Phips. But he was not going to make the mistake of Rebecca Nurse's family, and therefore he sent his petition through people who would have more influence upon the governor than any "Salem gentleman" —the ministers of Boston.

It was probably in response to Procter's petition that eight ministers, including Increase Mather, met at Cambridge on August 1. Unfortunately there is little known about their deliberations; the only account of the meeting is a brief paragraph in Increase Mather's *Cases of Conscience,* which does not even give us the names of the other seven ministers. Apparently, however, they took up the central issue in Procter's letter, the issue of prejudgment, and that issue led them directly to the means of prejudgment—the old question of spectral evidence. Mather tells us that

the question then discoursed on was whether the Devil may not sometimes have a permission to represent an innocent person as tormenting such as are under diabolical molestations.

and he adds that

the answer which they all concurred in was in these words, *viz.* "That the Devil may sometimes have a permission to represent an innocent person as tormenting such as are under diabolical molestations, but that such things are rare and extraordinary, especially when such matters come before civil judicatures."[5]

That last clause, of course, represented a major change in position for the clergy. They were backing down. To understand this we must recognize the difference between their previous situation and the one in which Procter had put them. Before this time their opinion had been solicited by the judges themselves, or by the governor's council acting for the judges, and they had been free to offer what was nothing more than expert advice. Procter was not asking for advice. He was asking the clergy to recognize that their advice had not been taken and that a serious division of opinion between the Boston ministers and the magistrates had split the leadership of Massachusetts. Furthermore, he was asking them to act on that recognition and advise the governor to take the remaining witchcraft cases out of the hands of the erring magistrates.

This the clergy was not willing to do. Few establishments are, of course, willing to admit that they are fundamentally divided. This was particularly true for Massachusetts, where, as we have seen, all the hierarchical authority of the past had been rejected in favor of the view that Massachusetts' literate and intelligent leadership would be able to reach an absolute consensus on every important issue. Now Procter was asking for the admission that no such consensus existed, or in other words that the Massachusetts way of life was, in this case, a failure. It is hardly surprising that the clergy tried to squirm their way out of the position in which he had put them. But there is no question that they squirmed. Why of course, they were in effect saying, the Devil can impersonate the innocent, just as we've said all along. But surely he wouldn't do such a horrid thing before Massachusetts magistrates? God might permit Satan to impersonate the virtuous. But surely he would not permit discord in Zion?

The ministers probably sent their newly equivocal judgment to Governor Phips along with Procter's petition. Four days later, on August 5, the Special Court of Oyer and Terminer sat for the third time at Salem. They tried six persons: John and Elizabeth Procter, George Burroughs, John Willard, George Jacobs, Sr., and Martha Carrier. All were found guilty, and all were condemned to death. Elizabeth Procter "pleaded her belly." In both England and New England a pregnant woman would not be executed, on the ground that the child she was carrying was an innocent person; the mother would be executed shortly after the child was born. Elizabeth Procter escaped that fate; her child was not born until January of 1693, and by that time the witch hunt was over. But her husband had long been dead. He and the others were hanged on August 19.

The Boston ministers had not simply abandoned Procter and the others to their fate when they delivered their equivocal judgment of August 1. Increase Mather did heed Procter's plea that "you would be pleased to be here, if not all, some of you at our trials, hoping thereby you may be the means of saving the shedding of our innocent blood." But apparently he hadn't time to attend all of them, and unfortunately the one he chose to attend was not that of John Procter, whom we now have every reason to think innocent, but that of George Burroughs, who may very well have been guilty.

As we have seen, Burroughs made a very poor performance at his trial, where his malice and his habitual lying were clearly demonstrated. He had helped to create his reputation for preternatural powers and then traded on it; now that reputation had returned to condemn him, not only in the judges' eyes but also in those of Increase Mather. "Had I been one of his judges," Mather wrote, "I could not have acquitted him, for several persons did upon oath testify that they saw him do such things as no man that has not a Devil to be his familiar could perform."[6] Apparently Mather also asked the judges to what extent they had depended upon specter evidence, because he added that "the judges affirm that they have not convicted anyone merely on the account of what specters have said, or of what has been represented to the eyes or imaginations of the sick bewitched persons." It was literally true, but it was no better than a half-truth, because in many cases the judges had nothing but confessions to back the testimony of the afflicted girls, and what appeared to the imaginations of the confessors was little better than a kind of specter evidence. But Mather was not aware of that. He had seen one man tried who appeared to be guilty, and he had received the reassurances of his friends among the judges. His investigation was hasty and superficial, but everything he did see and hear must have confirmed him, for the time being, in the opinion that the Boston ministers had been right in backing down on the question of specter evidence.

Yet if the Boston clergy were temporarily satisfied with the procedures of the court, there were others who were becoming increasingly dissatisfied. One of these was Robert Pike, a magistrate of Salisbury who had, in his official capacity, taken and attested evidence both for and against some of the people of his district. On August 9 he wrote a long letter to Judge Corwin, respectfully but firmly taking issue with the methods of the court. The crux of Pike's position was his view that the afflicted persons were subject to diabolical torments; that making evidence of such torments was accepting the word of the Devil; worse, that accepting such evidence was holding commerce with the Devil, and therefore in itself a kind of witchcraft. Pike had no personal experience of what had been happening at Salem. But, he wrote,

that which I have heard here is this: first, that they [the afflicted persons] do tell who are witches, of which, some they know and some they do not. Secondly, they tell who did torment such and such a person, though they know not the person. Thirdly, they are tormented themselves by the looks of persons that are present, and recovered again by the touching of them. Fourthly, that if they [the accused] look to[ward] them, they fall down tormented. But if the persons accused look [away] from them, they recover, or do not fall into that torment. Fifthly, they can tell when a person is coming before they see them, and what clothes they have [on], and some, what they have done for several years past, which nobody else ever accused them with nor do not yet think them guilty of. Sixthly, that the dead out of their graves do appear unto them and tell them that they have been murdered, and require them to see them to be revenged on the murderers, which they name to them, some of which persons are well known to [have] die[d] their natural deaths, and [been] publicly buried in the sight of all men. Now if these things be so, I thus affirm:

First, that whatsoever is done by them that is supernatural is either divine or diabolical.

Secondly, that nothing is or can be divine but what ha[s] God's stamp upon it, to which he refers for trial (Isaiah viii. 19,20): If they speak not according to these, there is no light in them.

Thirdly, and by that rule none of these actions of theirs have any warrant in God's Word, but [are] condemned wholly.

First, it is utterly unlawful to inquire of the dead or to be informed by them (Isaiah viii. 19). It was an act of the Witch of Endor to raise the dead, and of a reprobate Saul to inquire of him (1 Samuel xxviii.8, 11–14; Deuteronomy viii.11).

Secondly, it is a like evil to seek to them that have familiar spirits (Leviticus xix.31). It was the sin of Saul in the forementioned place (1 Samuel xxviii.8) and of wicked Manasses (2 Kings xxi.6).

Thirdly, no more is it likely that their racking and tormenting should be done by God or good angels, but by the Devil, whose manner ha[s] ever been to be so employed. Witness his dealing with the poor child (Mark v.2–5) besides what he did to Job (Job ii.7) and all the lies that he told against him to the very face of God.

Fourthly, the same may be rationally said of all the rest. Who should tell them things that they do not see but the Devil, especially when some things that they tell are false and mistaken?

His opinion of the confessors' testimony was just as low:

May we believe the [confessed] witches that do accuse anyone . . . ? Can the fruit be better than the tree? If the root of all their knowledge be the Devil, what must their testimony be? . . . Their testimony may be legal against themselves, because they know what themselves do. . . .

But their word should not, he thought, be taken against those who denied the charges and whose previous behavior had been blameless.

Pike had a new interpretation of the fits to which the afflicted and some of the confessors were subject; they were, he thought, the Devil's way of forcing them to accuse the innocent. "We see by woeful and undeniable experience, both in the afflicted persons and the confessors, some of them, that he torments them at his pleasure to force them to accuse others." The accusation of the apparently innocent was beginning to make some people think that both the afflicted and the confessors were liars. Pike disagreed; he thought their sufferings were pitiable and genuine. But he thought the Devil was lying through them. And no matter who was lying, the effect of the lie was still the same:

For if they counterfeit, the wickedness is the greater in them and the less in the Devil; but if they be compelled to it by the Devil against their wills, then the sin is the Devil's and the suffering theirs. But if their testimonies be allowed of, to make persons guilty by, the lives of innocent persons are alike in danger by them, which is the solemn consideration that do[th] disquiet the country.

Finally, Pike found it impossible to believe that any person pleading innocent would at the same time perform acts of witchcraft in the courtroom, as all of them had been accused of doing.

It is directly contrary to the use of reason, the law of nature, and principles of humanity, to deny it and plead innocent when accused of witchcraft, and yet at the same time to be acting witchcraft in the sight of all men, when they know their lives lie at stake by doing it. Self-interest teaches everyone better.[7]

John Foster, a member of the governor's council, was also disturbed over the possibility that Massachusetts might be shedding innocent blood, disturbed enough so that he asked the opinion of Cotton Mather. Mather replied in a letter dated August 17, two days before the execution of Procter, Burroughs, Willard, Jacobs, and Carrier.

Sir:

You would know whether I still retain my opinion about the horrible witchcrafts among us, and I acknowledge that I do.

I do still think that when there is no further evidence against a person but only this, that a specter in their shape does afflict a neighbor, that evidence is not enough to convict the [person] of witchcraft.

That the Devils have a natural power which makes them capable of exhibiting what shape they please I suppose nobody doubts, and I have no absolute promise of God that they shall not exhibit *mine*.

It is the opinion generally of all Protestant writers that the Devil may thus abuse the innocent; yea, 'tis the confession of some Popish ones. And our honorable judges are so eminent for their justice, wisdom, and goodness, that whatever their own particular sense [i.e., belief] may be, yet they will not proceed capitally against any upon a principle contested with great odds on the other side in the learned and Godly world.

Nevertheless, a very great use is to be made of the spectral impressions upon the sufferers. They justly introduce and determine an inquiry into the circumstances of the person accused, and they strengthen other presumptions.

When so much use is made of those things, I believe the use for which the great God intends them is made. And accordingly you see that the excellent judges have had such an encouraging presence of God with them as that scarce any, if at all any, have been tried before them against whom God has not strangely sent in other, and more human, and most convincing testimonies.

If any persons have been condemned about whom any of the judges are not easy in their minds that the evidence against them has been satisfactory, it would certainly be for the glory of the whole transaction to give that person a reprieve.

It would make all matters easier if at least bail were taken for people accused only by the invisible tormentors of the poor sufferers, and not blemished by any further grounds of suspicion against them.

The odd effects produced upon the sufferers by the look or touch of the accused are things wherein the Devils may as much impose upon some harmless people as by the representation of their shapes.

My notion of these matters is this. A suspected and unlawful communion with a familiar spirit is the thing inquired after. The communion on the Devil's part may be proved while, for aught I can say, the man may be innocent. The Devil may impudently impose his communion upon some that care not for his company. But if the communion on the man's part be proved, then the business is done.

I am suspicious lest the Devil may at some time or other serve us a trick by his constancy for a long while in one way of dealing. We may find the Devil using one constant course in nineteen several [i.e., separate] actions, and yet he be too hard for us at last, if we thence make a rule to form an infallible judgment of a twentieth. It is our singular happiness that we are blessed with judges who are aware of this danger.

For my own part, if the Holy God should permit such a terrible calamity to befall myself as that a specter in my shape should so molest my neighborhood as that they can have no quiet, although there should be no other evidence against me, I should very patiently submit unto a judgment of transportation [i.e., exile], and all reasonable men would count our judges to act as they are, like the fathers of the public, in such a judgment. What if such a thing should be ordered for those whose guilt is more dubious and uncertain, whose presence yet perpetuates the miseries of our sufferers? They would cleanse the land of witchcrafts and yet also prevent the shedding of innocent blood, whereof some are so apprehensive of hazard. If our judges want any good bottom to act thus upon, you know that besides the usual power of governors to relax many judgments of death our General Court can soon provide a law.

Sir,

You see the incoherency of my thoughts, but I hope you will also find some reasonableness in those thoughts.

In the year 1645 a vast number of persons in the county of Suffolk [England, not New England] were apprehended as guilty of witchcraft, whereof some confessed. The Parliament granted a Special Commission of Oyer and Terminer for the trial of those witches, in which commission there were a famous divine or two, Mr. Fairclough particularly, inserted. That excellent man did preach two sermons to the court before his first sitting on the bench, wherein having first proved the existence of witches he afterwards showed the evil of endeavoring the conviction of any upon defective evidence. The sermon had the effect that none were condemned who could be saved without an express breach of the law. And then, though 'twas possible some guilty did escape, yet the troubles of those places were, I think, extinguished.

Our case is extraordinary. And so you and others will pardon the extraordinary liberty I take to address you on this occasion. But after all, I entreat you that whatever you do, you strengthen the hands of our honorable judges in the great work before them. They are persons for whom no man living has a greater veneration than

Sir,
Your servant
C. Mather[8]

It is a remarkable letter, and it is full of good advice. Specter evidence may be grounds for investigation, and may strengthen other presumptions, but it is not evidence on which to convict. (Mather's example that the Devil might, for all he knew, impersonate Mather himself was to come true within a year, although his specter did not go so far as to disrupt an entire neighborhood—it appeared only in the hallucinations of one afflicted girl. If it had only appeared earlier it might have saved some lives, by changing the judges' minds about the validity of specter evidence.) Experiments on the afflicted with the look and touch of the accused were quite as unreliable as specter evidence. Given the unreliability of such evidence wasn't caution and leniency advisable? Shouldn't bail be taken for those against whom there was only specter evidence? And if their specters continued to afflict the girls, wouldn't exile be a better way of dealing with that problem than execution? Exile had always been New England's favorite solution for its most inconvenient problems. It had disposed of Ann Hutchinson, and Roger Williams, and a number of Quaker missionaries. Some of the latter, to be sure, had been hanged, but not until they had persisted in returning while they were under sentence of exile. Mather may have been thinking not only of such precedents but also of the example of Nathaniel Cary and his wife, who had by this time fled to New York, whereupon Mrs. Cary's shape had ceased from troubling citizens of Massachusetts. Finally, he suggests that with those who have already been sentenced, it would be wise to reprieve anyone of whose guilt there is doubt.

But the most remarkable advice of all is the hint contained in his remarks about the English witchcraft case of 1645, in which Parliament had placed "a famous divine or two" upon the bench, one of whom explicitly advised the court on the dangers of defective evidence, with the net result that although some guilty persons may have gone unpunished the disturbances of witchcraft were quieted. Mather was, of course, suggesting that Massachusetts follow England's example, and in making such a suggestion to a member of the governor's council he was indeed taking an "extraordinary liberty." Although the civil influence of the clergy had always been considerable, no minister had ever held an important domestic civil office in Massachusetts. The appointment of Increase Mather to an important foreign post—head of the commission to obtain a new charter—had come only because the elder Mather was so obviously the most distinguished and talented person available and because the task itself was so extraordinary. Now his son was suggesting that Massachusetts' case was once more extraordinary. Unfortunately the council did not accept that suggestion. If they had done so, and taken the unprecedented (in New England) course of appointing one or both of the Mathers to the bench, there is no question that lives would have been saved.

Perhaps one reason the council did not act is that Mather's position, however extraordinary, was still equivocal. Although he could make it plain that he and the judges were in fundamental disagreement on the validity of specter evidence, and could even hint broadly that appointing "a famous divine or two" to the Special Court of Oyer and Terminer would remove the danger of shedding innocent blood, he could not bring himself to flatly condemn the judges. One reason for this we have seen before; he had been raised in a culture which expected its leaders to reach a consensus, and expected that consensus to be right. Another, and perhaps even more powerful reason, was that many of the judges were his personal friends. Furthermore, he thought all of them, as he put it, to be men of such "justice, wisdom, and goodness" that he could not believe they would "proceed capitally against any" merely upon a principle so contested as that of specter evidence. In short, at the very time that he is recommending reprieves in doubtful cases he is also specifying that the doubt must exist in the minds of the judges.

But apparently there were no doubts in the minds of the judges. Because there were no reprieves.

10

❖❖❖❖❖❖

Cases of Conscience

While the debate continued, opinion was beginning to change, and the change was sharply accelerated by what happened at the third hanging. We have no account of the first Salem hanging. Bridget Bishop's passing from this world seems to have made little impression on her contemporaries.

At the second hanging, on July 19, the central event was Sarah Good's cursing of the Reverend Nicholas Noyes, and her curse—that God would give him blood to drink—was far more dramatic than the quietly Christian behavior of Rebecca Nurse. But all of those who died on August 19—Procter, Burroughs, John Willard, George Jacobs, Sr., and Martha Carrier—seem to have died well. Judge Samuel Sewall tells us that "all of them said they were innocent, Carrier and all."[1] (Sewall was particularly surprised at Martha Carrier's protestations of innocence because she had enjoyed so long and so thorough a reputation for witchcraft.)[2]

Procter, Willard, and Burroughs made particularly strong impressions. According to Thomas Brattle,

in the opinion of many unprejudiced, considerate, and considerable spectators, some of the condemned went out of the world not only with as great protestations but also with as good shows of innocency as men could do.

They protested their innocency as in the presence of the great God whom forthwith they were to appear before. They wished, and declared their wish, that their blood might be the last innocent blood shed upon that account. With great affection [i.e., emotion] they entreated Mr. C[otton] M[ather] to pray with them. They prayed that God would discover what witchcrafts were among us. They forgave their accusers. They spake without reflection on jury and judges for bringing them in guilty and condemning them. They prayed earnestly for pardon for all other sins and for an interest in the precious blood of our dear Redeemer, and seemed to be very sincere, upright, and sensible of their circumstances on all accounts, especially Procter and Willard, whose whole management of themselves from the jail to the gallows and whilst at the gallows was very affecting and melting to the hearts of some considerable spectators. . . .[3]

Calef says that Procter "pleaded very hard at execution for a little respite of time, saying that he was not fit to die, but it was not granted."[4] That is by no means inconsistent with Brattle's account. A seventeenth-century Christian—particularly one subject to John Procter's violent temper—might very well feel that he had not yet made his peace with his fellow-man or with God. And it is probable that Procter did die inadequately reconciled to his wife, since he left her out of the will which he drew up in prison.

Calef also provides the most complete account of Burroughs' behavior:

Mr. Burroughs was carried in a cart with the others through the streets of Salem to execution. When he was upon the ladder he made a speech for the clearing of his innocency, with such solemn and serious expressions as were to the admiration of all present. His prayer (which he concluded by repeating the Lord's Prayer) was so well worded, and uttered with such composedness, and such (at least seeming) fervency of spirit as was very affecting and drew tears from many (so that it seemed to some that the spectators would hinder the execution).[5]

Ending his prayer by repeating the Lord's Prayer was a brilliant and audacious stroke on Burroughs' part, although it was something of a trick. Popular belief held that a witch could not repeat the Lord's Prayer properly, since it was thought to be said backward at the witches' Sabbaths. If Burroughs had stammered—if he had so much as stopped to clear his throat —the crowd would have concluded he was guilty. But apparently he got through it perfectly, and that created enough of a stir among the crowd so that Cotton Mather thought it necessary to quiet them:

> Mr. Cotton Mather, being mounted upon a horse, addressed himself to the people partly to declare that [Burroughs] was no ordained minister and partly to possess the people of his guilt, saying that the Devil has often been transformed into an angel of light, and this did somewhat appease the people and the execution went on.

Calef adds that the bodies were not properly buried. When Burroughs

> was cut down he was dragged by the halter to a hole, or grave, between the rocks, about two foot deep, his shirt and breeches being pulled off and an old pair of trousers of one executed put on his lower parts. He was so put in, together with Willard and Carrier, one of his hands and his chin and a foot of one [of] them being left uncovered.

This last brutal detail may be false, like some other parts of Calef's work, since excavations on Gallows Hill at the end of the eighteenth century produced evidence only of regular interment there: "upon an examination of the ground the graves were found of the usual depth, and the remains of the bodies, and of the wood in which they were interred."[6] Whether the bodies were properly buried or not, the fact is that the executions of August 19 produced the first public expression of sympathy for persons condemned as witches, and the first evidence of substantial public belief in their innocence. In this Judge Samuel Sewall's diary confirms Calef: "Mr. Burrough[s] by his speech, prayer, protestation of his innocence, did much move unthinking persons, which occasions their speaking hardly concerning his being executed."

Sewall's contempt for "unthinking persons" and Cotton Mather's quieting of the crowd may have had something to do with the fact that the public had been moved by Burroughs' appeal to what most of the learned considered a superstition. Despite the long-standing reservations of the Boston clergy and the newly aroused doubts of the public, Sewall was still firmly convinced of the rightness of his course. So were the other judges, and so were their clerical allies in Essex County, Samuel Parris of Salem Village and Nicholas Noyes of Salem. The minister of Beverly, John Hale, may by this time have had some doubts. At the very least, he took Burroughs' protestations of innocence as grounds for serious inquiry. Burroughs, Hale later wrote,

denied all, yet said he justified the judges and jury in condemning of him because there were so many positive witnesses against him, but said he died by false witnesses. I seriously spake to one that witnessed of his exhorting at the witch-meeting at the Village, saying to her, "You are one that bring[s] this man to death. If you have charged anything upon him that is not true, recall it before it be too late, while he is alive." She answered me, she had nothing to charge herself with upon that account.[7]

But Hale, among the Salem leaders, was a minority of one. The judges were so far from questioning the testimony of the accusers that they were still refusing to accept recantations. They had condemned George Jacobs, Sr., in part on the testimony of his granddaughter, Margaret Jacobs. Before his execution she repudiated her testimony, but the judges' only response was to throw her into the dungeon and indict her for witchcraft. The day following her grandfather's execution she wrote to her father, giving an account of her actions.

From the Dungeon in Salem Prison, August 20, '92

Honored Father,

After my humble duty remembered to you, hoping in the Lord of your good health as—blessed be God—I enjoy, though in abundance of affliction, being close confined here in a loathsome dungeon. The Lord look down in mercy upon me, not knowing how soon I shall be put to death by means of the afflicted persons, my grandfather having suffered already, and all his estate seized for the King. The reason of my confinement is this. I having, through the magistrates' threatenings and my own vile and wretched heart, confessed several things contrary to my conscience and knowledge, though to the wounding of my own soul—the Lord pardon me for it. But oh! the terrors of a wounded conscience, who can bear? But blessed be the Lord; He would not let me go on in my sins, but in mercy I hope so my soul would not suffer me to keep it in any longer, but I was forced to confess the truth of all before the magistrates, who would not believe me, but 'tis their pleasure to put me in here, and God knows how soon I shall be put to death. Dear father, let me beg your prayers to the Lord on my behalf, and send us a joyful and happy meeting in heaven. My mother, poor woman, is very crazy, and remembers her kind love to you and to uncle, *viz.* D[aniel] A[ndrew]. So, leaving you to the protection of the Lord, I rest your dutiful daughter,

Margaret Jacobs[8]

At the time set for Margaret Jacobs' trial she had "an imposthume [an abscess] in her head," and thus she outlived the witch hunt. But others were not so fortunate. The magistrates, far from hesitating, were accelerating the trials. The court sat twice in September, and condemned fifteen people to death. Eight of them—Martha Corey, Mary Easty, Alice Parker, Ann Pudeator, Margaret Scott, Wilmot "Mammy" Redd, Samuel Wardwell, and Mary Parker—were executed on September 22. The other seven lived. Abigail Faulkner pleaded pregnancy. Mary Bradbury's friends contrived her escape from prison. Dorcas Hoar confessed, and Judge Sewall recorded in his diary for September 21 that "an order is sent to the sheriff to forbear her execution, notwithstanding her being in the warrant to die tomorrow. This is the first condemned person who has confessed." Presumably Rebecca Eames, Mary Lacy, Ann Foster, and Abigail Hobbes followed her example. Governor Hutchinson wrote that he had seen the confessions of "several" of those condemned to die on that date, although the confessions themselves, like most of the documents Hutchinson consulted, are no longer in existence. It would, of course, be the second confession for Abigail Hobbes; she must have repudiated the confession she made at her preliminary examination in April, or she would not have been brought to trial.

After the execution Nicholas Noyes, "turning him to the bodies, said, 'What a sad thing it is to see eight firebrands of

Hell hanging there.' "⁹ One of them was a witch, and deserved Noyes' comment—Wilmot "Mammy" Redd, the Marblehead woman who had cursed Mrs. Simms, wishing upon her "the distemper of the dry belly-ache." About several of the others there is too little information to reach an adequate judgment. But one of those who died on September 22 was obviously as innocent as anyone who died at Salem. This was Mary Easty, a sister of Rebecca Nurse. At her preliminary examination on April 22 she had maintained her innocence with such candor and conviction that Hathorne had asked the afflicted girls, "Are you certain this is the woman?"¹⁰ They were certain then. But by May 18 they changed their minds, and Mary Easty was released. No sooner was she out of jail, however, than the fits of Mercy Lewis increased sharply in violence, and the specter most prominent in her hallucinations was that of Mary Easty. So on May 20 a warrant was issued for her rearrest, and she had been in prison ever since. Shortly before her death she had sent the following petition to the magistrates and to the Essex County ministers:

To the honorable judge and bench now sitting in judicature in Salem and the reverend ministers, humbly sheweth that whereas your humble poor petitioner being condemned to die doth humbly beg of you to take it into your judicious and pious consideration that your poor and humble petitioner, knowing my own innocency (blessed be the Lord for it) and seeing plainly the wiles and subtlety of my accusers by myself, cannot but judge charitably of others that are going the same way with myself if the Lord step not mightily in. I was confined a whole month on the same account that I am now condemned for, and then cleared by the afflicted persons, as some of your honors know. And in two days time I was cried out upon by them, and have been confined and now am condemned to die. The Lord above knows my innocency then and likewise doth now, as at the Great Day will be known to men and angels. I petition to your honors not for my own life, for I know I must die, and my appointed time is set. But the Lord He knows it is, if it be possible, that no more innocent blood be shed, which undoubtedly cannot be avoided in the way and course you go in. I question not but your honors do to the utmost of your powers in the discovery and detecting of witchcraft and witches, and would not be guilty of innocent blood for the world. But by my own innocency I know you are in the wrong way. The Lord in his infinite mercy direct you in this great work, if it be His blessed will, that innocent blood be not shed. I would humbly beg of you that your honors would be pleased to examine some of those confessing witches, I being confident there are several of them have belied themselves and others, as will appear, if not in this world, I am sure in the world to come, whither I am going. And I question not but yourselves will see an alteration in these things. They say myself and others have made a league with the Devil; we cannot confess. I know and the Lord He knows (as will shortly appear) they belie me, and so I question not but they do others. The Lord alone, who is the searcher of all hearts, knows that as I shall answer it at the Tribunal Seat that I know not the least thing of witchcraft, therefore I cannot, I durst not belie my own soul. I beg your honors not to deny this my humble petition from a poor dying innocent person, and I question not but the Lord will give a blessing to your endeavors.

Mary Easty[11]

There is no reason why we should not take this petition at face value. Those who died on August 19 had prayed from the gallows that no more innocent blood should be shed. Apparently Mary Easty, too, was pleading not for herself (or for her fellows whose "appointed time" was also set) but for those who would, unless there was a fundamental change, come after her. But the Reverend Mr. Noyes had apparently been completely unimpressed by Mary Easty's petition. He was, in fact, unable to distinguish between Mary Easty and Mammy Redd, since he lumped them together as "firebrands of Hell." The judges seemed likewise unaffected, since they made no plans to change their procedure. They adjourned for the month of October, when the General Court was to meet, but they set the first Tuesday in November as the date for their next session.

That neither Noyes nor the judges should be able to distinguish between Mary Easty and Mammy Redd is an index of what a witch hunt does to otherwise decent, sensible, and even kindly men. The sternest of them all, Chief-Justice Stoughton, still had a reputation for sense, integrity, and decency. And many of them had also a reputation for benevolence, like Noyes, and like Sewall. The latter's good will is immediately apparent to anyone who examines his *Diary* or his pamphlet *The Selling of Joseph,* which was the first antislavery tract published in America. That such men could remain unaffected by a petition like Mary Easty's can be explained only by realizing that they had long since ceased to pay attention to anything said by a suspect. Their minds and hearts were so filled with the hideous torments of the afflicted and the frightful tales of the confessors that they were quite unable to absorb anything else.

The single-mindedness of the judges evoked a variety of protests. The Boston clergy gave them contrary (and sound) advice, but then, because of the special Massachusetts attitude toward consensus, tried to pretend their advice had been taken when it obviously had not. Judge Saltonstall resigned from the court, but made no public issue of his disagreement with it. Magistrate Robert Pike voiced his disagreement in a letter to Judge Corwin. Rebecca Nurse's relatives appealed to Governor Phips. So did John Procter, although he sent his appeal through the Boston clergy. Cotton Mather hinted to a member of the Governor's Council that "a famous divine or two" should be appointed to the court. Mary Easty made her gentle protest directly to the judges and the ministers of Essex County who supported them. But the most dramatic protest of all was made by Giles Corey.

Giles Corey had not been an altogether admirable man. He was quarrelsome, and one long-standing quarrel with John Procter had ended in the courts. He was violent as well, and it was said that he had beaten to death a former hired hand. He had thought his wife a witch, and freely said so, both in and out of court. But when Giles Corey was indicted he did something nobody else had dared to do. He stood mute, refusing to answer to his indictment. And under both English and New English law a man who refused to answer could not be tried. He could, however, be tortured—be subjected to "peinc forte et dure"—until he either answered or died. Accordingly Giles Corey was pressed: placed upon the ground with gradually increased weight piled on him. It took him two days to die. Sewall recorded the event in his diary for September 19:

About noon at Salem, Giles Corey was pressed to death for standing mute. Much pains was used with him two days, one after another, by the court and Captain Gardner of Nantucket who had been of his acquaintance, but all in vain.

Calef adds the brutal detail that "in pressing, his tongue being pressed out of his mouth, the sheriff with his cane forced it in again when he was dying."

Why he chose to undergo so terrible a death has been the subject of much debate among nineteenth-century historians, some of whom guessed that he was trying to preserve his property for his heirs. It is true that the property of capital offenders was subject to sequestration "for the king," and that much property seems to have been seized; it is also true that Giles Corey made a will in prison. But John Procter too, made a will, in spite of his being condemned, so there are difficulties with the theory that Corey was thinking of his heirs and his estate.[12] Besides, Calef, who was Corey's contemporary, has given us a perfectly adequate explanation of his behavior. Answering an indictment consisted of two parts. To the question "How do you plead?" the accused would answer "guilty" or "not guilty." To the question "How will you be tried?" he was supposed to answer, "By God and this court," thus, in effect, agreeing that the court had the right to try him. According to Calef:

Giles Corey pleaded "not guilty" to his indictment, but would not put himself upon trial by the jury (they having cleared none upon trial), and knowing there would be the same witnesses against him rather chose to undergo what death they would put him to.

Giles Corey, then, was pressed to death because he would not agree to be tried by the Special Court of Oyer and Terminer. His death was a protest—the most dramatic protest of all—against the methods of the court.

In retrospect Giles Corey seems a very large figure, and presumably his protest, like the others we have examined, did have some effect at the time. Yet the Special Court of Oyer and Terminer seems to have fallen less because of the protests against it than because, as the summer ended, it became apparent that the court was unable to perform the functions for which it had been created. It was created to clear the jails, so that people would not have to lie in them during the uncomfortable summer. But the more the court sat, the more the prisons were crowded. Surely, also, Massachusetts had expected that the court would succeed in quieting the disturbances in Salem Village. Yet quite the opposite had happened. The afflicted girls had not gotten better, but worse. (If you give hysterics an attentive audience, as the court was doing, you will aggravate their fits, as French psychiatrists were to rediscover in the nineteenth century.) Furthermore, hysterical fits are catching. Not only were the fits increasing in violence, but the longer the court sat, the more people were afflicted. And the afflictions were spreading geographically as well as numerically.

A good part of this geographical spreading came from using the afflicted girls of Salem as witch finders. Because they were supposed to have "spectral sight," they might be called upon by anybody who thought themselves or their relatives bewitched, to see who was afflicting them. A classic instance of this occurred at Andover, a town which had enjoyed the unfortunate reputation that

they were much addicted to sorcery in the said town, and that there were forty men in it that could raise the Devil as well as any astrologer. . . .[10]

One Joseph Ballard of Andover sent "horse and man" to Salem for some of the girls to examine his wife. The visit was a success, and shortly Andover was producing its own afflicted persons, together with a good number of confessors. The accusations came so fast that "more than fifty" Andover citizens were complained of. Justice of the Peace Dudley Bradstreet (the son of the old governor) signed "thirty or forty" warrants and then refused to grant more. Soon he and his wife were

complained of, and had to escape. His brother, John Bradstreet, was accused of afflicting a Salem Village dog. The
brother escaped to New Hampshire and the dog was, according
to Calef, put to death (although Calef does not explain why an
afflicted dog was put to death). Still another dog was killed as a
result of the Andover witchcraft after it appeared in the hallucinations of the afflicted.

One of those accused at Andover was "a worthy gentleman
of Boston," who sent friends to Andover with "a writ to arrest
those accusers in a thousand pound action for defamation."
This was a tactic no other accused person had used, and it
seems to have worked very well. A thousand pounds was an
immense sum in the seventeenth century, and the mention of it
seems to have shocked the accusers back to their senses. The
worthy gentleman's friends made inquiries at Andover to be
certain of their charges, "in doing which their business was
perceived, and from thence forward the accusations at Andover generally ceased."

Beside those at Andover who used the Salem girls as witch
finders there was "a person from Boston, of no small note,"
who carried his sick child to Salem to ask who afflicted her.
Provided with an answer, he returned to Boston to swear out a
complaint. But the Boston magistrates refused to issue one, and
the Reverend Increase Mather "took occasion severely to re-
prove the said man, asking whether there was not a God in
Boston, that he should go to the Devil in Salem for advice."[14]
The girls were also called to Gloucester in October and November, and four persons there were arrested as a result of
their spectral sight. But by this time the witch hunt was ending,
and nothing further came of these trips.

The witch hunt had also spread without the girls' help. The
mere news of what was happening at Salem was enough to
provoke a witchcraft trial in Connecticut, according to the
Reverend Gershom Bulkeley of that state.

In the spring of the year 1692 there was a great noise of witchcraft in the Massachusetts and a report that there were many
witches through the country. It is not long before some in the

county of Fairfield are accused of witchcraft. Thereupon, about the middle of September last past, a Court of Assistants is called and held at Fairfield, wherein they proceed to inquire of it. Some of the persons accused were easily discharged by proclamation (upon what grounds, they know best who did it). But Mercy Disborough was indicted and tried upon her life for witchcraft. . . .[15]

Bulkeley says that nothing was "brought in against her of any great weight to convict a person of witchcraft, yet some of the court were very zealous, others more moderate." And the jury members were just as zealous as the court. All but one thought her guilty. He refused to agree to a guilty verdict, and the court adjourned to ask the advice of the Connecticut General Court, which met in October. At that time the advice of the Connecticut clergy was also asked, and they gave the following opinion:

The Ministers' Advice about the Witches in Fairfield, 1692

As to the evidences left to our consideration respecting the two women [the second, of whose indictment Bulkeley was ignorant, was Elizabeth Clawson of Stamford] suspected of witchcraft at Fairfield, we offer

1. That we cannot but give our concurrence with the generality of divines that the endeavour of conviction of witchcraft by swimming [the water ordeal, to which both women had been subjected] is unlawful and sinful and therefore it cannot afford any evidence.

2. That the unusual excrescences found upon their bodies ought not to be allowed as evidence against them without the approbation of some able physicians.

3. Respecting the evidence of the afflicted maid, we find some things testified carrying a suspicion of her counterfeiting; others that plainly intimate her trouble from the mother [i.e., hysteria], which, improved by craft, may produce the most of those strange and unusual effects affirmed of her, and of those things that by some may be thought to be diabolical, or effects of witchcraft. We apprehend her applying of them to these persons merely from the appearance of their specters to her to be very uncertain and fallible from the easy deception of her senses and subtle devices of the Devil, wherefore [we] cannnot think her a sufficient witness. Yet we think that, her affliction being something strange, it well deserves a farther inquiry.

4. As to the other strange accidents, as the dying of cattle, etc., we apprehend the applying of them to these women as matters of witchcraft to be upon very slender and uncertain grounds.

HARTFORD   *Joseph Eliot*
October 17th, 1692   *Timothy Woodridge*[16]

There is a note to the effect that "the rest of the ministers" approved the substance of this document, although they could not wait while it was being drawn up.

The clergymen's recognition of hysteria in the afflicted girl is, for the seventeenth century, both rare and commendable. And the fact that they did not, like Sir Thomas Browne at Bury St. Edmunds, attribute her hysteria to demons acting on the instigation of witches makes it doubly so. The advice they gave was, of course, excellent. But in Connecticut as in Massachusetts the advice of the clergy was better than the actions of the courts. The General Court ordered the trial court to reassemble on October 28. The jury acquitted Goodwife Clawson but brought Mercy Disborough in guilty. Asked to reconsider, they reaffirmed their verdict. The court accepted it, and the governor signed a death warrant. However, three of the Hartford Assistants issued a reprieve until the next meeting of the General Court, giving as one reason the fact that one of the original jurymen had gone to New York and been replaced, illegally, on the second jury. But their second reason is far more important.

We had a good account of the evidences given against her, that none of them amounted to what Mr. Perkins, Mr. Bernard, and Mr. Mather with others state as sufficiently convictive of witchcraft, namely (1st) confession (this there was none of), (2dly) two good witnesses proving some act or acts done by the person which could not be but by help of the Devil. This is the sum of what they center in, as their books show. As for the common things of spectral evidence, ill events after quarrels or threats, tits, water trials and the like, with suspicious words, they are all discarded and some of them abominated by the most judicious as to be convictive of witchcraft. And the miserable toil they are in [in] the [Massachusetts] Bay for adhering to these last-mentioned litigious things is warning enough. Those that will make witchcraft of such things will make hanging work apace, and we are informed of no other but such as these brought against this woman. . . .

May 12th, 1693

Samuel Willis
William Pitkin
Nathaniel Stanley[17]

There is no record of further proceedings; apparently the reprieve became permanent, because Mercy Disborough was still living in 1707.

Massachusetts' example had started Connecticut's last witchcraft trial, and Massachusetts' example also stopped it. What is most interesting is the Connecticut assistants' appeal to "Mr. Perkins, Mr. Bernard, and Mr. Mather" as authorities on the validity of witchcraft evidence. Perkins and Bernard were English authorities: William Perkins, *Discourse of the Damned Art of Witchcraft* (London, 1608) and Richard Bernard, *Guide to Grand Jurymen . . . in Cases of Witchcraft* (1627). Mather is almost certainly Increase Mather, *Cases of Conscience Concerning Evil Spirits Personating Men; Witchcrafts; Infallible Proofs of Guilt in Such as are Accused with that Crime* (Boston, 1693). It is fitting that this little book should have helped prevent the hanging of Mercy Disborough, because it was also this book that ended the witch hunt in Salem.

As we have seen, there were various reasons for the shift in opinion that took place at the end of the summer of 1692. There was the opinion that those who died on August 19 died so well. There were the various protests against the procedures of the Court of Oyer and Terminer. And there was the fact that the court's procedures seemed to be aggravating the witchcraft troubles rather than allaying them. But most important of all, as the witch hunt spread and the accusations flew, people were accused whom nobody could think guilty.

One such accusation had been made early; at the second session of the court, at the beginning of July, the Reverend Samuel Willard of Boston had been cried out on. Nobody could think him guilty, but a ready explanation occurred to someone. John Willard of Salem Village was then in prison awaiting trial; perhaps the girl had gotten the wrong Willard? The court decided this was so. As the summer wore on several were accused whom many thought innocent. These included Captain John Alden; Hezekiah Usher, a prominent Boston merchant; Nathaniel Saltonstall, the judge who had resigned from the court; Phillip English, a Salem merchant (and like Judge Hathorne an ancestor of Nathaniel Hawthorne) and his wife; Dudley Bradstreet, the Andover Justice of the Peace.

By the end of the summer the accusations were becoming preposterous. They included the Secretary of Connecticut; Mrs. Margaret Thatcher, who was the widow of a Boston clergyman and the mother-in-law of Judge Corwin; and "members of [the governor's] Council."[18] According to rumor there were even more startling accusations, including the wife of Governor Phips and the wife of Increase Mather. But these were probably only rumors. It was Robert Calef (a person given to false insinuations, as we shall see) who suggested Lady Phips had been accused, and Cotton Mather called the suggestion "a putrid slander." And if Mrs. Mather was accused, it was not until after October 3. This was the date Increase Mather read to the Boston clergy, for their approbation, the manuscript of *Cases of Conscience,* the little book which put an end to the witch hunt, and in that book he wrote that "it was never the portion allotted to me nor to any relation of mine" to be falsely represented by the Devil.

Throughout the summer Mather had been moving in the traditional New England pattern, presenting his opinions yet trying to accommodate them to an eventual consensus. But if debate aimed at unanimous consensus had always been the New England way, this did not imply that any man was expected to abandon the truth. The Puritans were radical protestants, with the radical protestant's belief in a free and unforced conscience. Although the very basis of their community was a belief in the possibility of reaching unanimous consensus on all fundamental matters, they also acknowledged that there were some matters in which such a consensus could not easily be reached, and an honest minority might disagree with the course the community was taking; some matters were, as they put it, "cases of conscience." So when Increase Mather called his manuscript *Cases of Conscience Concerning Evil Spirits Personating Men* everyone who heard the title knew immediately that he was issuing a flat and direct challenge to the opinions on spectral evidence held officially—held, that is, by the Special Court of Oyer and Terminer.

He reasserted all the Boston clergy's old doubts, but with a new thoroughness and vigor that virtually amounted to a new argument. To begin with, he made it absolutely clear that anybody can be falsely accused of witchcraft and that all such accusations should be taken skeptically.

How often have I read in books written by Jesuits that Luther was a wizard, and that he did himself confess that he had familiarity with Satan! Most impudent untruths! Nor are these things to be wondered at, since the Holy Son of God himself was reputed a magician, and one that had familiarity with the greatest of Devils. The blaspheming Pharisees said, "He casts out the Devils through the Prince of Devils" (Matthew 9. 34). There is then not the best saint on earth, man or woman, that can asure themselves that the Devil shall not cast such an imputation upon them. . . .

At the time when Luther died all the possessed people in the Netherlands were quiet. The Devils in them said the reason was because Luther had been a great friend of theirs, and they owed him that respect as to go as far as Germany to attend his funeral.

It is hardly surprising to find the Devil bearing such hilariously false witness against Luther. At their most celebrated encounter, Luther had thrown an inkwell at him. Luther's view of the Devil's servants was just as ferocious as that of Innocent VIII. "I would have no compassion on the witches," he said. "I would burn them all." But the Devil, Mather added, had slandered Calvinists as well as Luther.

Another time when there was a talk of some ministers of the Reformed Religion, the Devils in the obsessed laughed and said they were not at all afraid of them, for the Calvinists and they were very good friends. The Jesuits insult [us] with these testimonies as if they were Divine Oracles. But the Father of Lies is never to be believed. He will utter twenty great truths to make way for one lie; he will accuse twenty witches if he can but thereby bring one innocent person into trouble.

Mather had no doubt of what should be done in such a situation. He put forward a principle that has always been inimical to witch hunts: "It were better that ten suspected witches should escape than that one innocent person should be condemned." Furthermore, he cast as much doubt on the testimony of confessors as on spectral evidence. One might, he thought, accept a witch's confession of her own guilt,

but as for the testimony of confessing witches against others, the case is not so clear as against themselves. They are not such credible witnesses as in a case of life and death is to be desired. It is beyond dispute that the Devil makes his witches to dream strange things of themselves and others which are not so.

He strongly condemned some of the tests the magistrates had used at preliminary examinations and trials; they were in themselves, he said, a kind of witchcraft.

For my own part, I should be loath to say to a man that I knew or thought was a witch, "Do you look on such a person, and see if you can witch them into a fit," and "There is such an afflicted person; do you take them by the hand and see if you can witch them well again." If it is by virtue of some contract with the Devil that witches have power to do such things, it is hard to conceive how they can be bid to do them without being too much concerned in that Hellish covenant. . . . We ought not to practice witchcraft to discover witches.

But Mather was by no means ready to recognize that the court had already shed innocent blood. He recognized only that the court must be stopped because, given its mistaken ideas on spectral evidence and its mistaken procedures, and given the accusation of obviously innocent persons, innocent blood might be shed in the future.

The Devils have of late accused some eminent persons. It is an awful thing which the Lord has done [i.e., permitted] to convince some among us of their error. This then I declare and testify, that to take away the life of anyone merely because a specter or Devil in a bewitched or possessed person does accuse them will bring the guilt of innocent blood on the land where such a thing shall be done. Mercy forbid that it should (and I trust that as it has not it never will be so) in New England. What does such an evidence amount unto more than this: either such an one did afflict such an one, or the Devil in his likeness, or his eyes were bewitched.

It is not hard to see why Mather was able to persuade himself that the innocent had not yet suffered. He knew the judges to be sensible and honorable men, and they had assured him there was more than specter evidence against all those who had been condemned.

The Judges affirm that they have not convicted anyone merely on the account of what specters have said or of what has been represented to the eyes or imaginations of the sick, bewitched persons.

But in many cases the judges had, because of their belief in specter evidence, accepted confirmatory evidence so slender that it could not possibly have stood by itself. Still, Mather could not have known that. His personal experience of the trials had been limited to that of George Burroughs, where there *had* been more than specter evidence.

Cases of Conscience was not published until 1693, but it almost certainly circulated in manuscript. The same may well be true of another criticism of the court that has received far more attention than *Cases of Conscience*—Thomas Brattle's *Letter*. Dated October 8, five days after Increase Mather read the manuscript of his book to the Boston clergy, it is addressed to an anonymous "Reverend Sir," presumably in answer to a letter now lost. Brattle, a Boston merchant, makes unmistakably clear the split in opinion between the court and the clergy: "Excepting Mr. Hale, Mr. Noyes, and Mr. Parris, the Reverend Elders almost throughout the whole country are very much dissatisfied."[19] He adds that many of the magistrates and leading citizens are disturbed as well, and names some of them. His central issue is spectral evidence. His arguments against it are essentially those of Increase Mather, and are in most respects less thorough than the latter's. Yet he does make clearer than Mather the distinction between bewitched and possessed persons (who are afflicted by Devils, but without the agency of witches), and he suggests that the majority of the afflicted and the confessors are possessed—an opinion in which the majority of Massachusetts, including both Mathers, was eventually to join him.

In two respects he went beyond Mather. He pointed out that most of the indictments were drawn for very specific acts; for afflicting particular persons on particular dates (although, as a matter of fact, one could be indicted simply for being a witch under either English or New English law). And almost all of the evidence offered to the specific matter of the indictments had been spectral evidence. But since this might have been remedied by drawing up new indictments, this legal point was far less important than the second matter in which he differed. Brattle recognized, as Mather had not, that innocent blood had already been shed, and thus his letter has a dimension as yet completely closed to the latter:

What will be the issue of these troubles God only knows. I am afraid that ages will not wear off that reproach and those stains which these things will leave behind them upon our land.

Whatever the force of Brattle's historical perspective, it is unlikely that his letter had much effect in his own time. It was simply one of many opinions, petitions, and protests that followed on the heels of *Cases of Conscience*. Another came from the chief-justice of New York. He was a New Englander, Joseph Dudley, who had been deputy-governor under Andros. Dudley had found that there was no public office open to him in Massachusetts after the overthrow of the Andros government, but he was still in touch with what was happening there. Therefore on October 5 he submitted to the Dutch and French Calvinist ministers of New York a series of questions on witchcraft, the key ones having to do with spectral evidence. And this same series of questions he gave to the Reverend John

Miller, the Anglican chaplain to the King's Forces at New York.

The reply of the Dutch and French ministers, dated October 11, supported what the Boston clergy had been saying since the beginning. Yes, there were witches, and there had been since the beginning of the world. Their craft was performed with the Devil's assistance. But spectral evidence was a thoroughly undependable means for convicting them. Miller's undated answers confirmed, point for point, the opinions of his Calvinist colleagues.[20] It is uncertain whether his answers ever reached Massachusetts, but those of the Dutch and French did, and Cotton Mather tells us in his life of Phips that they were part of the evidence the governor considered before putting a final end to the witchcraft proceedings.

Yet Phips had begun to act well before he could have received the Dutch and French opinions. On October 12 he wrote to William Blathwayt, Clerk of the Privy Council, briefly outlining the situation and saying that he had "forbidden the committing of any more that shall be accused without unavoidable necessity" and that he intended to shelter "those that have been committed . . . from any proceedings against them wherein there may be the least suspicion of any wrong done to the innocent." He asks the advice of the Throne and adds that

as soon as I came from fighting against their Majesties' enemies and understood what danger some of their innocent subjects might be exposed to, if the evidence of the afflicted persons only did prevail either to the committing or trying any of them, I did before any application was made to me about it put a stop to the proceedings of the court, and they are now stopped till their Majesties' pleasure be known.[21]

Phips was not entirely accurate; the court's proceedings were suspended, but not yet satisfactorily stopped. And asking advice from the Throne was a futile gesture since such advice could not arrive until far too late to be of use; when it did come it was couched in such carefully noncommittal language as to be doubly useless. But it is plain that he began to act before he heard from the New York clergy. What he means by an "application" to himself may well be the petition of October 12 from seven citizens of Andover, asking custody, on bond, of their wives and children. Andover, which had once joined so vigorously in the witch hunt, was now prominent among those who joined to stop it. On October 18 the two ministers of Andover, Francis Dane and Thomas Barnard, with twenty-four others, sent a petition to the governor, the Governor's Council, and the General Court on behalf of those Andover women who had confessed because of "the extreme urgency that was used with some of them by their friends and others who privately examined them, and the fear they were then under." The petition ended with a sharp criticism of the court's methods:

Our troubles, which hitherto have been great, we foresee are like to continue and increase if other methods be not taken than as yet have been, for there are more of our neighbors of good reputation and approved integrity who are still accused, and complaints have been made against them. And we know not who can think himself safe if the accusations of children and others who are under a diabolical influence shall be received against persons of good fame.[22]

Such petitions were now being listened to and investigated. On October 19 Increase Mather went to Salem and interviewed the Andover women in prison. He found that the majority of them were indeed repudiating their confessions.[23]

Although the clergy had now made a stand, and the governor had begun to act, and there was substantial popular opposition to the court, the popular majority still seems to have been on the side of the witch hunt. This would seem to be the only conclusion to be drawn from Judge Sewall's diary entry of October 15:

Went to Cambridge and visited Mr. Danforth, and discoursed with him about the witchcraft. [He] thinks there cannot be a procedure in the court except there be some better consent of ministers and people.

The ministers, as we have seen, and as Brattle had pointed out, were now thoroughly dissatisfied with the court's methods. If the people were on the opposite side, the majority must still have been supporting the court. The same conclusion may be drawn from the vote of the people's representatives on October 26. Sewall tells us what happened in the General Court on that day:

A bill is sent in about calling a fast, and convocation of ministers, that [we] may be led in the right way as to the witchcrafts. The season and manner of doing it is such that the Court of Oyer and Terminer count themselves thereby dismissed. 29 Nos and 33 Yeas to the bill. Capt. Bradstreet and Lieut. True, William Hutchins and several other interested persons there in the affirmative.

The bill called for a fast day and for a convocation of ministers in order that Massachusetts might be "led in the right way as to the witchcrafts." The implication, of course, was that the court had been proceeding in the wrong way, and was therefore dismissed. The vote was extremely close, and Sewall makes it plain that the bill passed only because a number of the representatives were "interested"—that is, had relatives among the accused. Without the presence of these "interested" persons the legislature would have voted for rather than against the court.

Sewall was plainly not satisfied with this vote, and on October 28 he asked, as he "had done several times before . . . the advice of the Governor and Council" about whether the court should sit again next week, as it had intended at its adjournment in September. He added that he would not raise the issue again. The only response was a "great silence," which he correctly took as instructions not to continue. Sewall did not raise the issue again, but the following day someone else put the question to the governor more contentiously: "Mr. Russell asked whether the Court of Oyer and Terminer should sit, expressing some fear of inconvenience by its fall. [The] governor said it must fall." With its fall the witch hunt was over; the clergy's cases of conscience over spectral evidence had prevailed.

11

❖❖❖❖❖❖❖

More Wonders of the
Invisible World

Cases of Conscience was not simply an expression of personal opinion on the part of Increase Mather. Cotton Mather tells us that the book was written at the request of "the ministers of the province,"[1] who were afraid that without such a positive statement of principles their advice on specter evidence would "not be duly followed." We can assume that since the elder Mather was being asked, in effect, for a fuller and more positive exposition of views he had already expressed, he found the task a congenial one. In the fall of 1692 Cotton Mather was also happily accepting the opportunity to write; Governor Phips had asked him to draw up an account of some of the Salem trials.

We should recall at this point how sane and temperate Cotton Mather had been in his previous dealings with witchcraft. His handling of the afflicted Goodwin children in 1688 had been exemplary. He had managed both to cure them and to suppress the accusations they made after they came under his care. He had offered to undertake the cure of half-a-dozen of the Salem girls early in 1692, but unfortunately his offer had been rejected. He had several times warned against accepting specter evidence at face value, and when he found the judges stubbornly maintaining the opposite opinion he wrote to a member of the Governor's Council suggesting that abuse of specter evidence might be prevented by placing an eminent minister or two on the bench. If his suggestion had been followed he would probably have practiced what he preached; he had always discounted specter evidence in 1688. It is necessary to recall his sanity and temperance now because the book he wrote in October of 1692, *The Wonders of the Invisible World*, was anything but temperate, and some of Mather's more excitable enemies among historians have gone so far as to call it insane.

To understand Mather's position we must recognize that our prevailing view of the Salem witchcraft trials has been, to put it bluntly, simple-minded. Both the majority of historians and the majority of imaginative writers who have dealt with the subject have asked us to accept a view of Massachusetts during the witchcraft that divides the community into two parties: on the one hand the ministers and magistrates, a group of wild-eyed fanatics using the trials as a means to bolster their own flagging powers; on the other a little band of stalwart citizens who opposed the witchcraft as nonsense from the beginning; in between these two parties the public. That such a view is grossly in error should by now go without saying.

There was a full spectrum of opinion about witchcraft in Massachusetts, ranging from those who accepted every bit of specter evidence as the revealed truth, through those who discounted spectral evidence but were inclined to believe there had been some witchcraft at Salem, to those who would not believe there had ever been a genuine case of witchcraft in Massachusetts. These last were an extremely small minority, and since they wrote nothing that has survived until the witch hunt was over we have heard nothing of them so far. But they were apparently beginning to talk, at least, and rather loudly, by the end of the summer. And the substance of their talk was apparently a sharp condemnation of the judges.

Although Mather had consistently opposed the judges' methods, he knew and respected them as persons, and thus his immediate instinct was to defend them against criticism.

I saw in most of the judges a most charming instance of prudence and patience, and I knew their exemplary piety and the agony of soul with which they sought the direction of heaven. . . . For this cause, though I could not allow the principles that some of the judges had espoused, yet I could not but speak honorably of their persons on all occasions.[2]

On September 20 he wrote to Stephen Sewall, the clerk of the court, to ask (apparently for the second time) for "a narrative of the evidences given in at the trials of half a dozen, or if you please a dozen, of the principal witches that have been condemned." And he made it plain that he intended to put the trial evidence to partisan use. He was willing, he wrote, "to expose myself to the utmost for the sake of my friends." He urged on Sewall a similarly partisan stance:

I shall be content if you draw up the desired letter by way of a letter to me . . . [and] I am willing that, when you write, you should imagine me as obstinate a Sadducee and witch-advocate as any among us. Address me as one that believed nothing reasonable. . . .[3]

Two days later, according to Judge Sewall's diary, Mather, Stoughton, Hathorne, Captain John Higginson, and Stephen and Samuel Sewall met at the latter's house to discuss "publishing some trials of the witches." Mather put the book together in less than three weeks, because on October 11 Stoughton and Sewall attested that they had read it and found "the matters of fact and evidence truly reported."

In all cases Mather's data squares with the data in the surviving trial documents. But it is also true that Mather, as Calef put it, "wrote more like an advocate than an historian."[4] He reported five trials, and included among them those two which depended least on specter evidence: those of Bridget Bishop and George Burroughs. Two of the remainder were of persons with long and unsavory reputations: Susanna Martin and Martha Carrier. And he gave no attention to persons, like Rebecca Nurse and John Procter, who now seem most obviously innocent.

He still maintains the inadequacy of specter evidence. He thinks that "among the persons represented by the specters which now afflict our neighbors there will be found some that never explicitly contracted with any of the evil angels." But this cautionary advice, which had previously been the main burden of his writings on Salem, is now virtually lost in the process of justifying the court. In his desire to defend his friends he is frequently abusive. He calls Martha Carrier "this rampant hag," and while the phrase is not original with Mather—it occurs in several seventeenth-century English witchcraft narratives, including *Saducismus Triumphatus,* by the Oxford scholar Joseph Glanvill—one still cannot forgive him for it. And when his language is not abusive it is generally overwrought. For in defending his friends Mather accepted the idea that the events at Salem were part of "an horrible plot against the country by witchcraft." The court, then, had been doing battle with "an Army of Devils," a "terrible plague of Evil Angels."

Thus Cotton Mather converted himself from a man who, during the trials, had been one of the most cogent critics of the court's methods to the man who, once the trials were over, became their chief apologist. Neither *The Wonders of the Invisible World* nor *Cases of Conscience* were published until 1693, presumably because of Phips' moratorium on witchcraft publications. But the governor sent a copy of the former along with his letter to the clerk of the Privy Council. And presumably both circulated widely in manuscript. Because by the time they were printed people were already beginning to think of Increase Mather as the man who had criticized the court and of his son as the man who defended it, and the father therefore added the following postscript to his book:

Some I hear have taken up a notion that the book newly published by my son is contradictory to this of mine. 'Tis strange that such imaginations should enter into the minds of men. I perused and approved of that book before it was printed, and nothing but my relation to him hindered me from recommending it to the world [i.e., in a preface]. . . .

Increase Mather was, of course, correct. Father and son agreed in condemning the court's methods—and in refusing to condemn the members of the court.

History has not been fair to Cotton Mather. Indeed the majority of historians have, in complete defiance of the facts, presented him as a man who instigated witchcraft trials to satisfy his own lust for fame and power. This view owes much to Robert Calef, but the historian chiefly responsible for perpetuating it is the Reverend Charles Wentworth Upham, whose *Lectures on Witchcraft* (Boston, 1831) and *Salem Witchcraft* (Boston, 1867) made him the standard authority in the field. Upham, who was a mayor of Salem as well as its minister, was Hawthorne's model for Judge Pyncheon in *The House of the Seven Gables,* and Upham's books display both the malice and the defective moral perceptions of his fictional counterpart. It is Upham who perpetuated the warped image of Cotton Mather which remains his popular image, despite the efforts of more conscientious historians to correct it.[5] And yet it is not all Upham's fault, nor that of later historians who have echoed him. It was, after all, Cotton Mather who chose to write *The Wonders of the Invisible World,* and chose to write it precisely as the witch hunt was ending. With this hasty, ill-considered, overwrought, partisan defense of his friends he was the first to fasten the false image of witch hunter on himself.

If Cotton Mather was never a witch hunter he was always a witchcraft scholar. His scholarship was thoroughly impervious to shifts in popular opinion. When the popular excitement over witchcraft was at its height he retained his skepticism of specter evidence; when popular opinion had begun to turn against the court he retained his interest in witchcraft. Circumstances provided him food to nourish that interest. For more than a year after the fall of the Special Court of Oyer and Terminer he studied a fascinating display of witchcraft symptoms in two girls from his own neighborhood, Mercy Short and Margaret Rule.

Mercy Short had been a captive of the Indians, who had "horribly butchered her father, her mother, her brother, her sister, and others of her kindred."[6] In the early summer of 1692 she was a seventeen-year-old servant girl in Boston, whose mistress sent her on an errand to the prison. There Sarah Good, who was later to curse Nicholas Noyes from the scaffold, threatening him with "blood to drink," asked her for "a little tobacco." Mercy, belying her name, "affronted the hag . . . by throwing an handful of shavings at her and saying, 'That's tobacco good enough for you.'" Sarah Good responded to this insult as she would later respond to Noyes—with a curse. "And poor Mercy was taken with just such, or perhaps much worse, fits as those which held the bewitched people then tormented by invisible furies in the County of Essex."

Mather treated her with prayer, as he had treated the Goodwin children, and he effected a temporary cure. Mercy was free of her afflictions for "diverse months." But on November 22, two months after the last executions at Salem, her fits returned. This time it took nearly four months, until March 16, 1693, to cure her. Thus Mather had considerable acquaintance with her and was able to give a thorough account of her symptoms. These are, as we might expect, hysterical. The most consistent were her hallucinations. Like the Salem girls she was afflicted by a succession of specters, who came not only singly but in groups. On Christmas Day (which the Puritans condemned as a pagan festival) Mercy

said they were going to have a dance, and immediately those that were attending her most plainly heard and felt a dance, as of barefooted people upon the floor, whereof they are ready to make oath before any lawful authority.

That Mercy should see specters having a dance is not particularly surprising since the Salem girls had consistently reported witch meetings and ceremonies. But that nonhysterical bystanders should hear and feel an invisible dance is something else again. Suggestion may account for it, as for so many other witchcraft phenomena. On another occasion Mercy saw the specters preparing her image, to torment her, and spent a "terrible evening" as a consequence. Furthermore, she told Mather "in whose custody that image might be found." But Mather did not pursue the hint. In fact, he suppressed all her accusations, just as he had done with the Goodwin children, and for the same reasons:

As for the specters that visited and afflicted Mercy Short, there were among them several who are doubtless innocent as to the crime of witchcraft. It would be a great iniquity in me to judge them otherwise, and the world, I hope, shall neither by my means nor by hers ever know who they were. But there is cause to fear that some few of the persons thus represented are as dangerous and as damnable witches as ever were in the world. . . .

Even these latter, however, he would not expose without "more cause," preferring, as most of the Massachusetts clergy had done, to rely on prayer and fasting for the cure of witchcraft rather than on accusation.

Among Mercy's hallucinations, as at Salem, was the Devil —a black man who offered her a book to sign. Mather was inclined to doubt that the book, supposed to contain witches' pacts, was real, but he reported that

Mercy herself, she thinks it is and gives this reason for it: that a touch of it (they told her) would have cured her. Besides, they diverse times made her eyes very sore by thrusting it hard [i.e., close] upon them to make her touch it when she should unawares lift up her hands to save her eyes.

In all, Mercy was tempted from three books. The third "she demanded that they let her read before she think of signing it." Mather refused to report much of what was read from this spectral book, but he did say that

in general the book seemed a journal of the chief things acted or designed at their great witch-meetings, not without some circumstances that carried an odd resemblance of the Koran. It had in it the methods to be used in seducing of people unto the service of the Devil, and the names of them that had been seduced, with the terms which they were to serve. It particularly surprised some in the room, on the eve of March 9, 1693, to overhear her, in the book then opened unto her, spelling a word that was too hard for her, but from the best judgment that could be made of the letters that she recited it was "Quadragesima."

In spite of this and other very specific details Mather found it difficult "to believe that there was any corporeal (or any more than a mystical) book in the business." Although Mercy reproached him for his skepticism he continued to look "upon these things as having much of diabolical delusion in them, and as intended partly to make diversion for Devils that love to play upon mankind."

During her hallucinations Mercy frequently lost her normal sight and hearing. She could see the specters, but she was

so little able to see anything else that although we made as if we would strike at her eyes it would not make her wink. . . . Her ears were altogether stopped unto all of our noises, being wholly engrossed by the invisible assailants, insomuch that though we sometimes hallooed extremely loud in her ears yet she heard nothing of it.

She conversed at length with the Demons who visited her, and Mather says the demonic voices were "big, low, thick" as they had been reported to be in European witchcraft accounts.

One symptom that appeared in Mercy Short's case was hysterical loss of appetite. She went virtually without food for periods of seven, nine, twelve, and even fifteen days. During this longest fast

she was permitted scarce to swallow one bit or drop of any victuals. One raw pear she ate, and now and then an apple, and some hard cider she drank, things that would rather set an edge upon the severity of her fast. Sometimes a chestnut might go down into her craving stomach and sometimes a little cold water. If anything else were offered her, her teeth would be set and she thrown into hideous torments, and it must be usually for two or three days together that such poor things as these also must be denied her.

Mather could not understand how life could be supported under such conditions. But he knew, and alluded to, cases of even more severe fasting in European accounts. Thus he concluded that "it seems that long fasting is not only tolerable but strangely agreeable to such as have something more than ordinary to do with the invisible world." At the end of her afflictions, however, Mercy Short was "left under a very ill habit of body, whereof she could not be cured without some time and care," and the fasting may well have been responsible, since hysterics do not usually suffer any lasting physical effects.

She was, like many other afflicted persons, a pathological swallower, and bystanders, with some difficulty, removed pins from her mouth.[7] She also had more than her share of psychosomatic skin lesions, of the sort that can be produced today in hypnotized persons. (For example, if you touch a hypnotized person's arm with a pencil but tell them it is a lighted cigarette, a burn mark or a blister will appear at the point of contact.) Mercy had "the bloody marks" of spectral pins, "which would be, as 'tis the strange property of most witch-wounds to be, cured perhaps in less than a minute." Her worst torments, however, came from spectral fire. Mather says,

We saw not the flames, but once the room smelled of brimstone, and at other, yea, at many times, we saw her made excessively sore by these flames, and we saw blisters thereby raised upon her. To cure the soreness which this fiery trial would give unto her we were forced sometimes to apply the oil commonly used for the cure of scalds. And yet (like other witch-wounds) in a day or two all would be well again. Only the marks of some wounds thus given her she will probably carry to her grave. I may add that once they thrust an hot iron down her throat, which though it were to us invisible, yet we saw the skin fetched off her tongue and lips.

The smell of brimstone is probably, again, a result of suggestion. Aside from that Mather is, as always, a scrupulously accurate observer. As always, he takes care to distinguish between what Mercy sees—the spectral hot iron—and what he does. Skin lesions have been reported in twentieth-century witchcraft cases from the Hawaiian Islands,[8] but Mercy Short's must have been particularly horrible. "We saw the skin fetched off her tongue and lips." One cannot help but be impressed again at the genuinely terrible sufferings of afflicted persons. Indeed, her sufferings were so severe that Mather thought the rapid healing of her wounds was part of a design to keep her in continual torment. She was, he wrote, "wounded with a thousand pains all over, and cured immediately that the pains of those wounds might be repeated."

One of Mercy's symptoms occurred when her hallucinations were peopled by specters bringing her a little cup that had a whitish liquor in it (unto us wholly invisible), which they would pour down her throat, holding her jaws wide open, in spite of all [her] shriekings and strivings. . . . We saw her swallow this poison, though we saw not the poison, and immediately she would swell prodigiously and be just like one poisoned with a dose of rats-bane [arsenic trioxide]. After these potions she was capable ordinarily to beg of us that we would help her to some salad-oil, upon the taking whereof the swelling would in a little while abate.

Gulping followed by a pronounced swelling of the abdomen is a symptom observable in twentieth-century hysterics,[9] and it was often reported in the classical world: oracles would often speak out of swollen bellies. In Mercy's case, the symptom was directly linked to her hallucinations. Mather noted that

sometimes our laying our hands on the mouth of Mercy Short when we perceived the specters forcing their poisons into her mouth did keep her from taking of them in.

Like the Goodwin girl, she was unable to hear prayer or religious instruction directly. But she could hear if the crucial words were given her indirectly—if Mather said "an Old Snake" instead of "Satan" or pointed to heaven instead of naming God, or if, as in the Goodwin case, he spelled the words. As has been mentioned previously, this symptom is precisely parallel to one in a case reported by Breuer and Freud, where a terrified girl was unable to pray in her native German but managed to say an English prayer learned in childhood.

The spectators in this case were clearly subject to suggestion. Not only did they hear the spectral Christmas dance which Mercy saw, but several times they had "their arms cruelly scratched and pins thrust into their flesh by . . . Fiends while they were molesting Mercy Short." And suggestion produced an even more frightening experience:

Several persons did sometimes actually lay their hands upon these Fiends. The wretches were palpable while yet they were not visible, and several of our people though they saw nothing yet felt a substance that seemed like a cat or dog. And though they were not fanciful they died away [i.e., fainted] at the fright.

Mather was convinced that the Fiends were real. The experience of them had been "too sensible" (that is, too much a matter of sense impressions) "and [too] repeated a thing to be pure imagination." We can hardly blame him for failing to realize the extent to which the senses can be affected by the imagination.

All in all, the case of Mercy Short is as remarkable as that of the Goodwin children. It is hardly astonishing that Mather thought it might help him evolve "a system of consistent thoughts about such works of darkness." Yet he never produced such a system. Nor did he try to publish his narrative of Mercy's case, *A Brand Plucked Out of the Burning*. He did not even complete it; the manuscript breaks off in the middle of a sentence. The reason is given us by Mather himself. By the time that Mercy Short was cured, in March of 1693, a vehement public reaction against the Salem trials had set in, and the public mood was now as violent in its hostility to witchcraft investigations as it had once been in support of them. Mather sadly recorded that

such is the forward, flouting, cidered [i.e., soured], and proud humor whereunto the people are now enchanted, no man in his wits would fully expose his thoughts unto them till the charms which enrage the people are a little better dissipated.

We cannot be certain that Mercy Short's case is a full-fledged case of witchcraft, because although Sarah Good was clearly an ill-tempered old woman and much given to the unchristian practice of delivering curses, we do not know enough about her to say whether she was actually a practicing witch. But within six months of Mercy's cure Mather had another case to care for. And this time it began with a curse delivered by a woman known to have practiced white magic, although again it is not absolutely certain that she had practiced malefic witchcraft.

'Twas upon the Lord's Day, the 10th of September, in the year 1693, that Margaret Rule, after some hours of previous disturbance in the Public Assembly [i.e., church], fell into odd fits, which caused her friends to carry her home, where her fits in a few hours grew into a figure that satisfied the spectators of their being preternatural. Some of the neighbors were forward enough to suspect the rise of this mischief in an house hard-by, where lived a miserable woman who had been formerly imprisoned on the suspicion of witchcraft, and who had frequently cured very painful hurts by muttering over them certain charms, which I shall not endanger the poisoning of my reader by repeating. This woman had, the evening before Margaret fell into her calamities, very bitterly treated her and threatened her. But the hazard of hurting a poor woman that might be innocent, notwithstanding surmises that might have been more strongly grounded than those, caused the pious people in the vicinity to try rather whether incessant supplication to God alone might not procure a quicker and safer ease to the afflicted than hasty prosecution of any supposed criminal. And accordingly that unexceptionable course was all that was ever followed. Yea (which I looked on as a token for good), the afflicted family was as averse as any of us all to entertain thoughts of any other course.[10]

Mather's concern for the possible innocence of this "miserable woman" strikes one as rather too unctuous and self-righteous. He himself had pointed out the state of public opinion in 1693. In such a state it would have been impossible to obtain a conviction for witchcraft, and there was therefore rather less cause to congratulate himself on his restraint than he would have us believe. Swearing out a warrant against this woman, in 1693, was not a genuine alternative. And yet his restraint was real enough, and his previous behavior suggests that if going to court had been a real alternative he would still have rejected it. Certainly he took every precaution, as he had in the Goodwin case, to protect the objects of spectral evidence from the consequences even of malicious gossip.

The young woman was assaulted by eight cruel specters, whereof she imagined that she knew three or four, but the rest came still with their faces covered, so that she could never have a distinguishing view of the countenance of those whom she thought she knew. She was very careful of my reiterated charges to forbear blazing the names, lest any good person should come to suffer any blast of reputation through the cunning malice of the great Accuser. Nevertheless, [she] having since privately named them to myself, I will venture to say this of them, that they are a sort of wretches who for these many years have gone under as violent presumptions of witchcraft as perhaps any creatures yet living upon earth, although I am far from thinking that the visions of this young woman were evidence enough to prove them so.

Margaret Rule's hallucinations were somewhat more varied than those of Mercy Short. She saw not only spectral witches and the "Black Man . . . their master" but also a "White Spirit" whom she took to be an angel. Such a figure had also been seen at Salem and in several European witchcraft cases; Mather knew of the appearances at Salem and of those in a Swedish case reported in the 1689 edition of Glanvill's *Saducismus Triumphatus*. The white spirit comforted and advised her during her attacks. Among other things, he told her that Cotton Mather was her spiritual father:

" 'Margaret, you are now to take notice that' (such a man) 'is your father. God has given you to him. Do you from this time look upon him as your father, obey him, regard him as your father, follow his counsel, and you shall do well.' "

Mather was flattered by what the white angel had to say. But by Margaret Rule's final hallucination he could only be appalled.

Her tormentors made *my* image or picture to appear before her, and then made themselves masters of her tongue so far that she began in her fits to complain that I threatened her and molested her, though when she came out of them she owned that they could not so much as make my dead shape do her any harm, and that they put a force upon her tongue in her exclamations. Her greatest outcries when she was herself were for my poor prayers to be concerned on her behalf.

He had always maintained that Devils might appear in the shape of an innocent person, and had even considered the unlikely possibility that they might assume his own shape. Now that the possibility had become a reality, however, he was horrified, particularly since many of his fellow-citizens had come to think of him as the chief apologist for the Salem trials, and he knew what such people would make of his spectral appearances.

Being hereupon extremely sensible how much a malicious town and land would insult over me if such a lying piece of a story should fly abroad that the Devils in my shape tormented the neighborhood, I was put upon some agonies and singular sallies and efforts of soul in the resignation of my name [i.e., reputation] unto the Lord, content that if he had no further service for my name it should be torn to pieces with all the reproaches in the world. But I cried unto the Lord, as for the deliverance of my name from the malice of Hell, so for the deliverance of the young woman whom the powers of Hell had now seized upon. And behold! Without any further noise the possessed person, upon my praying by her, was delivered from her captivity on the very same day that she fell into it, and the whole plot of the Devil to reproach a poor servant of the Lord Jesus Christ was defeated.[11]

Margaret had the common inability of afflicted persons to hear religious words, especially, in her case, "the words pray or prayer." Mather had recourse to the old and successful expedient of spelling them to her. But he could not do it often, because New England had become hypercautious in handling afflicted persons, and some people "were so ridiculous as to count it a sort of spell or charm for any thus to accommodate themselves to the capacity of the sufferer."

She had a full catalog of physical symptoms. She would be "strangely distorted in her joints and thrown into such extravagant convulsions as were astonishing unto the spectators in general." She would be "cruelly pinched with invisible hands very often in a day, and the black and blue marks of the pinches became immediately visible unto the standers by." She was also afflicted with pins, both real ones found about her person and spectral ones. The wounds, as Mather had noted of other psychosomatic skin lesions, "would in a few minutes ordinarily be cured." As with Mercy Short, her specters burnt her with spectral brimstone, and she would be "so bitterly scorched with the unseen sulphur thrown upon her that very sensible blisters would be raised upon her skin, whereto her friends found it necessary to apply the oils proper for common burning. But the most of these hurts would be cured in two or three days at farthest." Mather thought these, among other symptoms, an argument that her afflictions were preternatural rather than natural:

I think I may without vanity pretend to have read not a few of the best systems of physic [i.e., medicine] that have been yet seen in these American regions, but I must confess that I have never yet learned the name of the natural distemper whereto these odd symptoms do belong. However I might suggest perhaps many a natural medicine which would be of singular use against many of them.

This was no idle boast. He had been a medical student, and his success in curing afflicted people was unusual on either side of the Atlantic.

Like Mercy Short, Margaret Rule was forced to swallow spectral poisons. She "would sometimes have her jaws forcibly pulled open, whereupon something invisible would be poured down her throat. We all saw her swallow, and yet we all saw her try all she could . . . that she might not swallow." She would cry out "as of scalding brimstone poured into her" and would be "so monstrously inflamed that it would have broke a heart of stone to have seen her agonies." She also had hysterical fasts, although they were shorter than those of Mercy Short and she showed no visible signs of suffering from them. After one nine-day fast

she was unto all appearance as fresh, as lively, as hearty at the nine days' end as before they began. In all this time, though she had a very eager hunger upon her stomach, yet if any refreshment were brought unto her, her teeth would be set and she would be thrown into many miseries. Indeed, once or twice or so in all this time, her tormentors permitted her to swallow a mouthful of somewhat that might increase her miseries [i.e., by sharpening her appetite], whereof a spoonful of rum was the most considerable.

That spoonful of rum has been a favorite of anti-Puritan historians. One of them went so far as to insist that Margaret Rule was a case of *delirium tremens,* although he did not explain how you achieve *delirium tremens* on a spoonful of rum. But surely there is nothing odd about giving a spoonful of liquor to a sick person?

When she recovered from her fits she was still not entirely well. She was "extremely weak and faint, and overwhelmed with vapors, which would not only cause her sometimes to swoon away but also now and then for a little while discompose the reasonableness of her thoughts." The weakness may have been partly due to the fasts, but her symptoms were so general that it is impossible to be certain.

Suggestion operated on the spectators here as it had in the case of Mercy Short. They thought they smelled the spectral brimstone being poured down her throat; "scores of witnesses" were prepared to testify that the whole house smelled "so hot of brimstone that we were scarce able to endure it." And on one occasion "the standers by plainly saw something of that odd liquor itself on the outside of her neck." There was a spectral powder thrown into her eyes, and "one time some of this powder was fallen actually visible upon her cheek, from whence the people in the room wiped it with their handkerchiefs." And again they thought they felt a tangible but invisible Imp; Mather himself laid his hand upon it:

We once thought we perceived something stir upon her pillow at a little distance from her, whereupon one present [Mather] laying his hand there, he to his horror apprehended that he felt, though none could see it, a living creature not altogether unlike a rat, which nimbly escaped from him. And there were diverse other persons who were thrown into a great consternation by feeling, as they judged, at other times the same invisible animal.

But the most startling phenomenon in Margaret Rule's case was levitation. "Once," said Mather, "her tormentors pulled her up to the ceiling of the chamber and held her there before a very numerous company of spectators, who found it as much as they could all do to pull her down again." Mather obtained signed confirmations of this and other instances of levitation:

I do testify that I have seen Margaret Rule in her afflictions from the invisible world lifted up from her bed, wholly by an invisible force, a great way towards the top of the room where she lay. In her being so lifted she had no assistance from any use of her own arms or hands or any other part of her body, not so much as her heels touching her bed or resting on any support whatsoever. And I have seen her thus lifted when not only a strong person hath thrown his whole weight across her to pull her down, but several other persons have endeavored with all their might to hinder her from being so raised up, which I suppose that several others will testify as well as myself when called unto it. Witness my hand,

Samuel Ames

We can also testify to the substance of what is above written, and have several times seen Margaret Rule so lifted up from her bed as that she had no use of her own limbs to help her up, but it was the declared apprehension of us, as well as others that saw it, impossible for any hands but some of the invisible world to lift her.

Robert Earle
John Wilkins
Daniel Williams

We whose names are underwritten do testify that one evening when we were in the chamber where Margaret Rule then lay in her late affliction, we observed her to be by an invisible force lifted up from the bed whereon she lay, so as to touch the garret floor, while yet neither her feet nor any other part of her body rested either on the bed or any other support, but were also by the same force lifted up from all that was under her, and all this for a considerable while. We judged it several minutes, and it was as much as several of us could do with all our strength to pull her down. All which happened when there was not only we two in the chamber, but we suppose ten or a dozen more whose names we have forgotten.

Thomas Thornton

William Hudson testifies to the substance of Thornton's testimony, to which he also hath set his hand.[12]

These statements might possibly describe an *arc de cercle*, a violently arched position of the body not uncommon in hysterical fits, which would raise the trunk of the body a considerable distance off the bed. Combined with the power of suggestion to affect the bystanders' senses, this might account for their belief that they had witnessed levitation. Yet they were not simply bystanders; they were engaging in violent physical activity, trying to bring her body back to the bed. Such activity would, ordinarily, tend to break the power of suggestion. And levitation has been so frequently reported, from so many times and places (from the twentieth-century Indian fakir to the Medieval or Renaissance saint), that one cannot be at all sure there is a satisfactory explanation for it, particularly since so many witnesses insisted that no part of Margaret Rule's body was touching the bed. In an *arc de cercle* the head and feet do, of course, touch.

But whatever the explanation for this final symptom, Margaret Rule's case was plainly a complex one, and Mather deserves considerable credit for having cured her. He had every right to call his account of her afflictions *Another Brand Plucked Out of the Burning.* As with *A Brand Plucked Out of the Burning,* however, he made no attempt to publish. When, in 1700, Robert Calef published it without his consent, it was under circumstances that turned his accomplishment to gall and wormwood.

12

❖❖❖❖❖

Mauling One Another
in the Dark

"Witchcraft," wrote the Reverend John Higginson, "is one of the most hidden works of darkness."[1] And Massachusetts witchcraft had its full share of obscurity. Men groping their way in the dark are unlikely to be either stable or judicious, and thus it is hardly surprising that much of the writing evoked by the witchcraft should be violent and partisan. Cotton Mather rightly described the temper of much of the debate when he wrote, "The Devil improves the darkness of this affair to push us into a blind man's buffet, and we are even ready to be sinfully, yea, hotly and madly mauling one another in the dark." The quotation, in fact, is an excellent description of the temper of the book from which it comes, *The Wonders of the Invisible World*. What is surprising then is not that much of Massachusetts' writings on witchcraft should be violent and partisan, but that even more of it should consist of serious attempts to find the truth. Yet this was the case with most of what was written in the year 1692.

Deodat Lawson's *Brief and True Narrative* was precisely what the title implies: an attempt to give a short and accurate account of the author's experience of Salem in the early days of her troubles. And his sermon, *Christ's Fidelity the Only Shield Against Satan's Malignity*, was, as we have seen, a serious attempt at advising the community on how to behave during its afflictions. Increase Mather's *Cases of Conscience* retained more than a trace of partisanship in its refusal to condemn the judges, but it was remarkably even-tempered for a document written in the fall of 1692, and it is a lucid explanation of the truths concerning spectral evidence which the Boston clergy had propounded from the beginning. Thomas Brattle's manuscript *Letter* is also remarkably even-tempered. Brattle managed to do what Increase Mather could not—he condemned the judges' actions. But he did it with hardly a trace of personal rancor. Thus he could write of Stoughton:

The chief judge is very zealous in these proceedings, and says he is very clear as to all that hath as yet been acted by this court, and as far as ever I could perceive is very impatient in hearing anything that looks another way. I very highly honor and reverence the wisdom and integrity of the said judge, and hope that this matter shall not diminish my reverence for his honor. However I cannot but say, my great fear is that wisdom and counsel are withheld from his honor as to this matter, which yet I look upon not so much as a judgment to his honor as to this poor land.

The irony is unmistakable, but there is no temper and no impugning of Stoughton's motives or of his integrity.

Even irony is absent from a little pamphlet criticizing the court's use of spectral evidence and of testimony from confessed witches: *Some Miscellany Observations on our Present Debates Respecting Witchcrafts, in a Dialogue between S. and B. By P.E. and J.A. Philadelphia, Printed by William Bradford, for Hezekiah Usher. 1692.* It was not printed by Bradford, because the type is not his, nor was it for Hezekiah Usher nor written by P[hilip] E[nglish] and J[ohn] A[lden]. The author was the Reverend Samuel Willard of Boston; the pamphlet was attributed to him by Calef, and the editors of Willard's *A Complete Body of Divinity* (Boston, 1726) include it in a list of his published works. It is unlikely that Willard's motive in concealing his authorship was fear of reprisal, as Burr has suggested.[2] But it does seem that his pamphlet was published during the fall of 1692 in an attempt to ensure that the methods of the Court of Oyer and Terminer would be rejected. Since Phips had forbidden all publication on witchcraft in his desire to let tempers cool, the only way to circulate the pamphlet openly was to pretend it had been printed outside Massachusetts. English, Alden, and Usher's names were used because they had fled the colony. The latter two were members of Willard's church, and the former had been advised to flee the colony with his wife by Willard and has associate, the Reverend Joshua Moodey.[3] "S." and "B." probably stand for Salem and Boston, since the main parties to the argument over spectral evidence were the magistrates in Salem and the ministers in Boston.[4]

The substance of the dialogue is a setting forth of the conflicting opinions over what constitutes adequate evidence of witchcraft, Willard's views being succinctly stated by "B."

There is to be no examination without grounds of suspicion. Some persons' credit ought to be accounted too good to be undermined so far as to be suspected on so slight a ground [as spectral evidence], and it is an injury done them to bring them upon examination, which renders them openly suspected. I will not deny but for persons already suspected, and of ill fame, it may occasion their being examined, but if nothing else comes in nor a confession be made the use of such a presumption any further ceaseth. But if other things of moment appear, a further legal proceeding may be made.
. . .

As for the confessors' testimony, he says,

the persons confessing are witches by their own confession and have therefore abjured God and Christ, and given themselves up to the Devil, the Father of Lies. And what credit is to be given to the testimony of such against the lives of others?

There is, as we have seen, no irony at the expense of "S.", and there is no rancor either, except for a momentary outburst when "S." calls "B." "an admirable advocate for the witches." The ending of the dialogue is virtually a capsule description of the process of debate as the New England Puritan understood it:

S. I see the difference between us and you is very wide, and I fear the consequence.
B. God is able to clear up these things, and let us herein agree to seek him for it, in the ways of his appointment.[5]

Willard, then, like the other Boston ministers, had clearly recognized the size of the differences between Massachusetts' leaders, but he had by no means abandoned hope of an eventual consensus. That last fact does much to explain the temperate tone of his dialogue.

Cotton Mather's *The Wonders of the Invisible World* was, as we have seen, anything but temperate. But in *A Brand Plucked Out of the Burning* and *Another Brand Plucked Out of the Burning* he returned to his other style, which was baroque and frequently high-pitched, but restrained by the kind of exact observation also to be found in *Memorable Providences*, his narrative of the Goodwin children. Mather, in 1693, was doing more than curing Mercy Short and Margaret Rule and writing narratives of their cases. He was also thinking of writing more about witchcraft at Salem. To this end he visited Salem, where, he wrote, he

endeavored that the complete history of the late witchcrafts and possessions might not be lost. I judged that the preservation of that history might in a while be a singular benefit unto the church and unto the world, which made me solicitous about it.

Obviously Mather believed that although the court's methods had been wrong there had been genuine witchcraft at Salem. And he was, of course, right, although he probably was still overestimating the extent of it. One person he talked to was

one Mrs. Carver, who had been strangely visited with some shining spirits, which were good Angels in her opinion of them. She intimated several things unto me, whereof some were to be kept secret. She also told me that a new storm of witchcraft would fall upon the country to chastise the iniquity that was used in the wilful smothering and covering of the last, and that many fierce opposites to [i.e., opponents of] the discovery of that witchcraft would be thereby convinced.[6]

It was on his return to Boston that he found, to his surprise, that Margaret Rule was afflicted. It must have seemed to him a confirmation of Mrs. Carver's predictions.

In speaking of "the wilful smothering and covering of the last" witchcraft, Mather probably had in mind the fact that Massachusetts had swung from one extreme to the other in its handling of the events at Salem. While the Special Court of Oyer and Terminer had been in session, every person brought before it had been condemned; after its fall, every person accused of witchcraft had gone free. And among the latter there were some thoroughly unsavory wretches, like Dr. Roger Toothaker and his daughter, who had boasted of killing a witch by boiling her victim's urine in a pot. Mather, who was now smarting over the criticism he was getting for having defended the court, had begun to think only of demonstrating that witchcraft was a reality and did exist in Massachusetts; he seems virtually to have forgotten what he had been among the first to recognize—that the court had proceeded on unsafe rules of evidence. But if Mather was now apt to see only one side of the witchcraft problem, he was matched by people who were able to see only the other, people who were so shocked by the court's shedding of innocent blood that they would not acknowledge that Massachusetts had ever had a genuine case of witchcraft, even in such notorious instances as those of Goodwife Glover and Mammy Redd. Such persons would, of course, be horrified at the prospect of Cotton Mather poking about in the embers of Salem witchcraft. They would be the last to reflect that Mather's own procedures for investigating witchcraft had always been cautious and judicious. All they could think of was that in his poking about he might stir those embers into a new blaze.

One such person was Robert Calef. Very little is known about him. He seems to have been a weaver, although he liked to give himself the more dignified title of merchant. He was a frequenter of the Boston coffee houses, and he fancied himself a wit. It may very well have been Mather's trip to Salem which decided him on visiting Margaret Rule, but whatever his motives, he did visit her on September 13, only three days after her afflictions had begun, and he tells us that he took care to choose a night when Cotton Mather would be present. Increase was there as well, along with a number of other people. Calef went home that night and wrote an account of his experiences intended for circulation in manuscript, and in that manuscript he handled the Mathers very roughly. In fact, "roughly" is scarcely the word for it. He handled them viciously and libelously. His basic technique was grotesquely false accusation —the "big lie." And, incredibly, his lies have stuck to the Mathers for more than two hundred and fifty years.

I realize that in calling Calef a liar I differ from virtually every other person who has written about him since his own time. But the charge is not made recklessly. It can be proved, and from Calef's own words.

Calef made essentially two charges against the Mathers. One was to suggest that in treating Margaret Rule they were not ministering to a case of bewitchment or even of possession, but catering to a fraudulent adolescent's sexual desires. Cotton Mather had apparently used laying-on-of-hands as a technique for bringing the girl out of her fits, and out of this fact Calef constructed the following. When the girl was in a fit, Calef said, Mather

rubbed her stomach (her breast not covered with the bed-clothes) and bid others do so too, and said it eased her. Then she revived. . . . [Upon her falling into another fit] he again rubbed her breast, etc. About this time Margaret Perd, an attendant, assisted him in rubbing of her. The afflicted spake angrily to her, saying "Don't you meddle with me," and hastily put away her hand.[7]

I think that anybody reading these statements would assume that Margaret Rule had been naked, at least from the waist up, and that Mather had been rubbing her naked breast and belly, and encouraging others to do so as well. That is what Calef intended his readers to think, but it is not the truth. Nevertheless Calef circulated it, with his other charges, and took care to show it to some of Mather's friends. Mather was outraged. He called Calef a liar in private, in public, from the pulpit, and even in court. He charged him with libel, but then apparently realizing that challenging a lie in court is only apt to give it greater currency, he did not appear to press charges. In the meantime Calef wrote him two insolent letters asking why he was upset. And finally, on January 15, 1694, Mather remembered the Puritan clergyman's obligations to debate, even with the reprobate, and answered Calef's charges in a letter. He said simply it was false "that I rubbed Rule's stomach, her breast not being covered. . . . And to be somewhat plainer, [this charge] carries the face of a lie contrived on purpose . . . to make people believe a smutty thing of me." Calef answered Mather's letter on January 18; he replied he had never said "that her breast was not covered." He had only said it wasn't covered with the bed clothes.

In short, Calef had employed the particularly vicious kind of lie that cannot be proved to be such because it depends on ambiguous construction. He was not content, however, with his smutty insinuations against Cotton Mather. Later in his account he added that Mather "put his hand upon her breast and belly (*viz.* on the clothes over her) and felt a living thing, as he said, which moved the father [Increase] also to feel, and some others." To this assertion Mather replied that the spectral Imp had not been on the girl's body at all but "upon the pillow, at a distance from her body." Witnesses, he said, were ready to swear to it, and vindicate both his father and himself. But witnesses are of no use against the Robert Calefs of this world. Calef answered that his "narrative [does not] say you felt the live thing on her belly. . . . And as to your father's feeling for the live creature after you had felt it, if it were on the bed it was not so very far from her." What can you do in the face of someone who libels you; then maintains he hasn't libeled you at all; and finally, in denying your challenge, renews the original libel in a new form? You can do nothing. And that is precisely what Cotton Mather did.

Calef's second major charge was that the Mathers had encouraged Margaret Rule to make accusations of witchcraft against her neighbors based on her hallucinations—that they were, in fact, accepting the evidence of the specters who appeared to her. He made this charge in a number of ways, but one example will suffice:

[Cotton Mather] Who is it that afflicts you?
[Rule] There is a great many of them.
(About this time the father questioned if she knew the specters. An attendant said if she did she would not tell. . . .)

This reads, of course, as though the Mathers were encouraging the girl to make accusations against her will. Mather replied, correctly, that he had never permitted, much less encouraged, the accusation of anyone through specter evidence. It was true, he said, that he had asked Margaret Rule if she recognized the specters afflicting her. But

the question was but an introduction to the solemn charges that we then largely gave, that she should rather die than tell the names of any whom she might imagine that she knew.

To this Calef replied with studied insolence plus his character-istic evasiveness:

It seems improbable that a question should be put whether she knew [them] (or rather who they were), and at the same time to charge her, and that upon her life, not to tell. And if you had done so, I see but little good you could promise yourself or others by it. . . .

There is much more, but all of it fits the same pattern, so that Mather was quite correct in writing to Calef that "I do scarcely find any one thing in the whole paper, whether respect-ing my father or self, either fairly or truly represented."

In 1700 Calef published Mather's account of Margaret Rule as Part I of his *More Wonders of the Invisible World,* and his own account and the exchange of letters in Part II, thus dem-onstrating that he could not care less about the truth of the matter, but that he wanted the world to know he had been able to tell lies about the Mathers and get away with it. The renewal of the old libels in print freshly enraged Cotton Mather. But on reflection he decided that Calef had, for once, been too clever for his own good. Mather wrote that

He has been so uncivil as to print a composure of mine utterly without and against my consent, but the Good Providence of God has therein overruled his malice. For if that may have impartial readers, he will have his confutation and I my perpetual vindication.[8]

Mather was premature in expecting a "perpetual vindication." Some people in his own time realized the truth of the matter. But from that day to this he has had few impartial readers—and not one capable of realizing what a liar Calef was.[9] The result has been a thoroughly upside-down view of the exchange between Cotton Mather and Robert Calef. Our writers and historians have made Mather a villain on the ground that he "got up" the witchcraft, and they have made a hero out of Calef on the ground that he was an enemy of Mather. One could make a several-volume anthology out of the false representations of these men, but two instances—one from the nineteenth and one from the twentieth century—will suffice.

Whittier, in a tiresome little poem called "Calef in Boston,"[10] presents us with a Calef who is "a tradesman frank and bold," an apostle of progress, goodness, and (of all things) truth, and who says to Mather:

"Of your spectral puppet play
   I have traced the cunning wires;
Come what will, I needs must say,
   God is true, and ye are liars."

Whittier, of course, is notorious for letting his moral indignation fly without bothering to consult the facts. One of his best-known poems, "Skipper Ireson's Ride," is as gross, unfair, and inverted a picture of actual persons and events as "Calef in Boston." An historian pointed out to Whittier that he was wrong, and had done violence to an innocent man's reputation. Whittier replied, acknowledging his error, and saying that he "would not knowingly do injustice to anyone, living or dead." He printed the letter at the head of all his further editions of the poem, but since he went on publishing the poem, he continued to perpetuate the original falsehood.

One expects more accuracy from historians than from a self-righteous enthusiast like Whittier, but in this case one does not get it. For example, Marion L. Starkey, in *The Devil in Massachusetts*, deals with Margaret Rule's case in a chapter called "The Devil and Cotton Mather." She says of her, among other inaccurate things, that "she visibly liked being stroked across face and naked breast and belly by the Mathers, father and son. . . ."[11] In short, Starkey accepts Calef's original false accusations as literal truth, ignoring both Mather's denials and Calef's evasive retractions. I cite Starkey not because her book is more inaccurate than others on Massachusetts witchcraft, but because it is less so. So much for Cotton Mather's "perpetual vindication." It is high time that he had it.

The most grotesque of the figures to enter the war of words over Massachusetts witchcraft was Thomas Maule, a Quaker merchant from Salem. Because Nathaniel Hawthorne borrowed his family name for *The House of the Seven Gables* one's first reaction is to think of him as an innocent victim of the Salem trials. But the historical Maule was neither innocent nor a victim. He was in 1682 a member of that company of distinguished Quakers who met in George Walton's house in New Hampshire, only to find themselves afflicted by a stone-throwing poltergeist. Urine was boiled in a pot, with bent pins in it, in an unsuccessful attempt "to give punishment to the witch or wizard that might be the wicked procurer or contriver of this stone affliction."[12] If the experiment had been successful we should have had a Quaker witchcraft trial in New Hampshire ten years before the Puritan trials in Salem.

Maule, like most seventeenth-century Quakers, was both uneducated and proud of his ignorance, as he showed in a doggerel poem of his own composition:

> Humane learning have I not;
> God doth to me afford,
> His Teaching by his Spirit good,
> To understand his Word.[13]

During the early days of the Salem trials he was, like most of the unlearned, far more rabid in his condemnation of the accused persons than any Massachusetts minister. John Hale spoke with him at the execution of Bridget Bishop, where he told Hale "that he believed she had bewitched to death a child of his."[14] Perhaps she had; she was a practicing witch. But he also told Hale that "he believed most of those in prison were witches." Furthermore, he said he would not pray with such persons, as Hale had been doing, on the ground that in covenanting with the Devil they had committed the unpardonable sin, "that sin [of which] the scripture saith we must not pray for it."

In 1690 Maule had finished the first draft of a book he called *The Truth Held Forth and Maintained*, attacking the beliefs and the practices of Massachusetts Puritans. But he did not print it until 1695. By that time most of Massachusetts had changed its mind about the Salem trials, and so had Thomas Maule. Therefore he revised his book with the current state of public opinion in mind. He still believed there were witches, and that anyone who murdered by witchcraft "ought to die."[15] But he had immensely broadened his definition of a witch to include everybody who was not in a proper covenant with God—everybody, that is, who was not a Quaker. Furthermore, he argued that while the Devil might appear in the shape of the reprobate, he could not "act and do such wickedness in the form, shape, and likeness" of the elect (that is, of Quakers). In other words, Massachusetts men had brought the witchcraft on themselves by being Puritans. If they had been Quakers, the Devil could not have assumed their spectral shapes.

Maule was, in short, a crank. But cranks were still apt to be taken seriously by seventeenth-century judiciaries, and on rather solid grounds. As Perry Miller has pointed out, you never knew what their "inner light" might say to them. It might very well command them to go out and slaughter the reprobate, as the Anabaptists had done at Münster. So Thomas Maule was called before Superior Court in Salem in 1696 to answer charges of having written a book full of unsound doctrine. He has given an account of that trial in an hilarious little book: *New-England Persecutors Mauled with their own Weapons, by Theo. Philathes* [Maule]. *New York, William Bradford. 1697.* Maule's brilliant and scathing defense was to argue that his book, *The Truth Held Forth*, carried no evidence of his authorship but his printed name on the title page, and that this printed name was no better than a specter of himself. He told the jury that he knew of no unsound doctrine in his book. To find it, he suggested,

you may seek to the printer for satisfaction. For of any such like matter in the book I know not, and my hand is only to my copy, which now is in another government [New York] in the hands of the printer. And my name to my book made by the printer does not in law evidence the same to be Thomas Maule, no more than the specter evidence in law is of force or validity to prove the person accused by the said evidence to be the witch. . . .[16]

The jury brought him in not guilty. At this the judges were "much dissatisfied" and asked the jury to explain their verdict. The reply was "that the book was not sufficient evidence, for that Thomas Maule's name was thereunto set by the printer." Besides, they protested, it was beyond the competence of ordinary jurymen to judge the orthodoxy of the book, "they not being a jury of divines." So the verdict was accepted. But Chief-Justice Danforth made a speech to the effect "that though Thomas Maule had escaped the hands of men, yet he had not escaped the hand of God." Maule replied that the judges were trying to persecute him "as their fathers before had done," at which "Danforth called out, 'Take him away, take him away.'"

Although the topic of witchcraft was now explosively controversial in Massachusetts, nobody was to deny that people practiced it until well into the eighteenth century, and there was still some interest in investigating it. There are therefore references to it in many of the sermons of the time. In 1694 Increase Mather sent a circular letter to the clergy proposing the collection of more instances of "remarkable providences" (these would include unusual natural phenomena as well as the preternatural). In that same year he made a few references to witchcraft in his sermon, *Angelographia.* The most interesting of them is a report of murder by witchcraft among the Indians:

Some of the Indian Powows [i.e., priest-magicians] in this country, having received the Gospel and given good evidence of a true conversion to God in Christ, have with much sorrow of heart declared how they had, whilst in their Heathenism, by the hands of Evil Angels murdered their neighbors.[17]

Cotton Mather also gave the matter further thought, and planned a two-part essay "relating both to my belief and my practice in those thorny difficulties which have distracted us in the day of our temptation [i.e., during the Salem trials]."[18] He completed the first section in 1695, and in it he conceeded "that the credulities of mankind have been very much abused with untrue stories and notions of witches." Furthermore, he was now in agreement with the position of Brattle and others

that they who are usually looked upon as enchanted [i.e., bewitched] persons are generally, properly, really possessed persons, and that their minds are so imposed upon as so makes very much against any credible validity in their testimonies or their informations.

Indeed he had gone beyond Brattle and decided that some people accused of witchcraft rendered themselves suspicious through actions that should be attributed to possession rather than to *maleficium.* "And yet," he said,

after these concessions I still find it necessary to believe that there are such witches as I have described. And they are those three great convincers, plain scripture, undoubted history, and personal experience that have necessarily compelled me so to believe.

That there are myriad instances of witchcraft both in history and in the Bible need not detain us, but some of Mather's personal experience is remarkable enough to make us wish he had given a more detailed account of it. In referring to Balaam, the biblical conjurer of familiar spirits, he says "we have seen and known (I say *seen* and *known*) such wizards among the Heathen in our own land." And he lists convincing evidence that his experience of witchcraft extended well beyond what he had committed to writing:

I *know* a young man who had gone so far as to get ready a Covenant with Satan, written all of it in his own blood. But before the signing of it the sinful I was made the happy instrument of his deliverance.

I *know* a woman whose brother was tortured with a cruel, pricking, incurable pain in the crown of his head, which continued until there was found with her a puppet in wax, resembling him, with a pin prick[ed] into the head of it, which being taken out he recovered immediately.

I *know* a person who, missing anything, would use to sit down and mutter a certain charm, and then immediately by an invisible hand be directly led unto the place where the thing was to be found.

I *know* a woman who upon uttering some words over very painful hurts and sores did use instantly [to] cure them, unto the amazement of the spectators. Now, thought I, if this wretch can effectually employ Devils to cure hurts, why mayn't she to cause them also, which is the worst that the witches do?

He ended the first section of his essay with a statement and a question. "I have told you my belief: what it has been and why. Shall I now tell you my practice?" Then he sent the manuscript, presumably through one of the Brattles,[19] to Robert Calef. Probably he intended this as a test. His essay was extremely reasonable, and Mather may have thought it would partially convince Calef. If it would convince Calef, Mather's worst enemy and most unreasonable opponent in the debate over witchcraft, then it would convince anybody. But Calef paid no attention at all to Mather's arguments and examples. Instead he scrawled a series of comments in the margin accusing Mather of trying to inculcate superstition. And so Mather gave up. He never wrote the proposed second part of his essay, and he never again wrote more than a passing comment on witchcraft.

In 1697, when Massachusetts proclaimed a day of fasting in repentance for the innocent blood shed at Salem, and those who had lived through the witchcraft trials thought of reporting what they knew of them to posterity, the minister who produced a book on Salem witchcraft was not the famous Cotton Mather[20] but John Hale of Beverly, who was quite conscious of his own obscurity, yet even more conscious of the need for understanding what had happened at Salem.

I esteemed it necessary for some person to collect a summary of that affair, with some animadversions upon it which might at least give some light to them which come after, to shun those rocks by which we were bruised and narrowly escaped shipwreck upon. And I have waited five years for some other person to undertake it who might do it better than I can, but find none, and judge it better to do what I can than that such a work should be left undone.[21]

He called his book *A Modest Enquiry Into the Nature of Witchcraft.*

Hale did not for a moment doubt that there was such a thing as witchcraft, nor did he doubt that New Englanders were still trafficking in the occult. He even warned against becoming too tolerant of white magic in the general revulsion from the wrongs that had been done at Salem. He had been an eyewitness to the "cruel sufferings" of the afflicted, and could not doubt that they were genuine. But what Hale felt most was a sense of error—error long past redemption.

Such was the darkness of that day, the tortures and lamentations of the afflicted, and the power of former precedents that we walked in the clouds, and could not see our way. And we have most cause to be humbled for error on that hand, which cannot be retrieved.[22]

If one could not retrieve past error one could at least prevent its future repetition, by rejecting the principles in which it was embedded. Not that this was an easy process. But it was, for Hale, the central result of his own experience with witchcraft:

I have been from my youth trained up in the knowledge and belief of most of those principles I here question as unsafe to be used. . . . But observing the events of that sad catastrophe, *Anno* 1692, I was brought to a more strict scanning of the principles I had imbibed, and by scanning to question, and by questioning to reject many of them. . . .[23]

He had, in short, rejected all the traditional means for investigating and proving malicious witchcraft. Further, and even more important, he had arrived at his own explanation for the phenomenon of affliction. He recalled the examination of Candy, the slave who had demonstrated the tools of her trade. The magistrates had taken the rags of cloth which she used as images and subjected them to fire and water, with immediate results in the symptoms of the afflicted. "Here note," said Hale, that it was the manipulation of the images which affected "the persons supposed to be thereby bewitched" rather than the agency of the witch herself. Hale's explanation for this is startling. "Probably the cause may be that Satan . . . may inflict his mischief on the person . . . suiting hereby his design to man's faith about it."[24] That is, the victim suffered not because of anything the witch had done but because of her own belief that she would be injured when her image was mistreated. John Hale had discovered that the sufferings of bewitched people were psychosomatic. Furthermore, he was capable of drawing the final inference. If he was right that man suffered from witchcraft because of "man's faith about it," then "the reason why any suspected person is hereby concerned is not because they are guilty but because they are suspected." And a recognition of that fact, of course, would make any trial for malefic witchcraft impossible.

Hale's insight was brilliant. But he put it badly, and he did not insist enough upon it, and so his discovery was simply lost. His book was published in Boston in 1702, after his death, and earned its author a reputation for fairmindedness. There was a second edition, also in Boston, in the eighteenth century. But its largest circulation has come through the excerpts published by Cotton Mather in his *Magnalia Christi Americana* (London, 1702) and by Burr in his *Narratives of the Witchcraft Cases* (New York, 1914), and neither reprinted Hale's explanation for the sufferings of the afflicted.

For John Hale a central meaning of the Salem trials had been that good men might be hideously mistaken. One of his reasons for writing was to insist upon that central meaning and reject any attempt to reduce what had happened at Salem to a simple-minded contest of heroes and villains. "Better sincerely though weakly done," he wrote, "than not at all, or with such a bias of prejudice as will put false glosses upon that which was managed with uprightness of heart. . . ."[25] But at the very time Hale wrote, Robert Calef was putting together *More Wonders of the Invisible World*. That book, much assisted by Upham and other later historians, has done precisely what Hale feared —reduced the events at Salem to a contest between heroes and villains.

More Wonders might better be called an anthology than a book. It is composed of five parts. Part one, as we have seen, is Cotton Mather's *Another Brand Plucked Out of the Burning* —his account of Margaret Rule. Part two has Calef's libelous account of the Mathers' treatment of Margaret Rule, the exchange of letters between Cotton Mather and himself, and a number of his other letters to Boston clergymen, which display as callous a disregard for the truth as his exchange with the younger Mather. Part three is a documentary account of the troubles between the Reverend Samuel Parris of Salem Village and his parishioners after the trials had ended, which culminated in the dismissal of Parris. Part four is a tiresome exchange of letters between Calef and an unknown person, possibly a Scottish clergyman named Stuart.

Part five is an account of the Salem trials, and it is this part which has made Calef's book live. Not that his prose suddenly becomes dependable when he deals with Salem—it does not. Anyone who cares to compare his account of Bridget Bishop's trial with the trial documents will find that Calef is as much of a liar as ever, and through the same techniques—evasions, omissions, and half-truths more often than easily identifiable falsehoods. What makes part five of Calef's book remarkable is not his own prose but a series of striking documents which he prints in full: Nathaniel Cary's account of his wife's examination; John Alden's account of his examination; Rebecca Nurse's explanation of her silence in court; John Procter's petition to the Boston clergy; Margaret Jacobs' letter to her father, renouncing her confession; Mary Easty's petition to the court that they might shed no more innocent blood. Although Calef freely altered facts in his own writing, he does not seem to have seriously falsified documents, and these documents speak eloquently of the sufferings of the innocent at Salem.

We owe Calef a great deal for his printing these documents. So did the English-speaking world of his own time, since his book seems to have had much to do with the decline of witchcraft trials in that world. Yet along with the documents which reveal to us the sufferings of the Salem innocents he has bequeathed us his malicious lies about the Mathers—not only those we have already examined, but a series of others, chiefly insinuating that the Mathers had been particularly "forward" in carrying on trials in New England. Nothing could be further from the truth. Several of the Mathers' parishioners put together a rebuttal to Calef, pointing out how grossly he had lied about them—*Some Few Remarks upon a Scandalous Book* (Boston, 1701). And Increase Mather ceremonially burned a copy of *More Wonders* in Harvard Yard. But nobody paid much attention. Because as the years went by Massachusetts found almost everything else concerning witchcraft blotted out by the presence of one terrible fact—at Salem she had slaughtered the innocent.

13

❧❧❧❧❧❧

The Guilt of Innocent Blood

By October of 1692 enough of Massachusetts' leaders were aware that something had gone terribly wrong in the investigating and trying of the witches for Governor Phips to stop the sessions of the Special Court of Oyer and Terminer. By November even the specters were giving indications that something had gone wrong.

On November 14 a seventeen-year-old girl named Mary Herrick gave some astonishing testimony to the Reverend John Hale of Beverly and the Reverend Joseph Gerrish of Wenham. She had been afflicted for about two months, and lately one of the specters appearing in her hallucinations was none other than the wife of John Hale:

On the 12th of the 9th [November 12] she [Mrs. Hale] came again, and Goody Easty with her, and then Mrs. Hale did afflict her as formerly. Said Easty made as if she would speak but did not. But on the same night they came again and Mrs. Hale did sorely afflict her and asked her if she thought she was a witch. The girl answered, "No, you be the Devil" [i.e., in Mrs. Hale's shape]. Then said Easty said and spake, she came to tell her she had been put to death wrongfully and was innocent of witchcraft, and she came to vindicate her cause. And she cried, "Vengeance! Vengeance!" and bid her reveal this to Mr. Hale and Gerrish, and then she would rise no more nor should Mrs. Hale afflict her any more.

Memorandum: that just before said Easty was executed she appeared to said girl and said, "I am going upon the ladder to be hanged for a witch, but I am innocent, and before a twelve-month be past you shall believe it." Said girl said she spake not of this before because she believed she was guilty till Mrs. Hale appeared to her and afflicted her, but now she believes it is all a delusion of the Devil.[1]

Not everyone was in agreement that the specters had all been a delusion of the Devil. As late as November 22 Judge Sewall noted in his diary a prayer "that God would . . . save New England as to enemies and witchcrafts, and vindicate the late judges. . . ." But events were running against Sewall's hopes; the judges were not to be vindicated. On the other hand, they were not to be condemned either. As Kenneth Murdock has pointed out, every single judge from the Special Court of Oyer and Terminer was elected to the Governor's Council in 1693,[2] and Sewall got more votes than Nathaniel Saltonstall, who had resigned from the court. Massachusetts politics after 1692 shows no trace of popular resentment against the judges. Indeed, the opposite is true; there is every reason to believe that Massachusetts still had confidence in the judges.

In November and December of 1692 the General Court set special sessions of the Superior Court of Judicature to try the remaining persons indicted for witchcraft. Stoughton was the chief-justice, and three of his four colleagues had also been members of the Special Court of Oyer and Terminer: Sewall, Richards, and Winthrop. The fourth, Thomas Danforth, had presided at the preliminary examinations of the Procters and others on April 11, but at some time since then had changed his mind about spectral evidence, since Brattle lists him as an opponent of the court's methods in October. Phips apparently spoke with all the judges to ensure a change in their procedure. He reported to England that

some of them were convinced and acknowledged that their former proceedings were too violent and not grounded upon a right foundation, but that if they might sit again they would proceed after another method.[3]

When the court sat on January 3, 1693, spectral evidence was no longer given any weight, and without it there was generally not enough evidence to convict. Fifty-two indicted persons were brought before this court, and only three of them convicted, all on their own confession. Two of these appear to have been mentally defective; the third was Sarah, the widow of the executed Samuel Wardwell. Stoughton signed death warrants for all three, and for five persons previously condemned but not yet executed, including Elizabeth Procter. But the King's Attorney General gave as his opinion that there was no more reason to condemn these than some of those who had been cleared, and Governor Phips therefore ordered a reprieve "until Their Majesties' pleasure be signified and declared"—until, that is, he should get an answer to the letter he had written to the Clerk of the Privy Council on October 12. At this, Stoughton was, according to Phips, "enraged and filled with passionate anger." He refused to sit upon the bench for the remainder of the session, and Calef quotes him as speaking to the effect that "We were in a way to have cleared the land of these. . . . Who it is that obstructs the course of justice I know not. The Lord be merciful to the country."

The royal advice for which Phips had asked was slow in coming. The matter was brought up in council on January 26, and the Earl of Nottingham directed to prepare an answering letter for the royal signature. But this letter was not signed until April 15 and must have reached America much later. When it did arrive, with Queen Mary's signature, it was not much help:

Trusty and Wellbeloved, We Greet You Well.

It having been represented unto Us that a most horrible witchcraft or possession of Devils hath invested several towns in Our Province of the Massachusetts Bay under your government, and that divers persons have been convicted of witchcraft, some whereof have confessed their guilt, but that others being of a known and good reputation these proceedings had caused a great dissatisfaction among our good subjects, for which reason you had put a stop thereunto until Our Pleasure should be known concerning the same, We therefore approving of your care and circumspection herein have thought fit to signify Our Will and Pleasure, as We do hereby will and require you to give all necessary directions that in all proceedings against persons accused for witchcraft or being possessed by the Devil the greatest moderation and all due circumspection be used, so far as the same may be without impediment to the ordinary course of justice within Our said Province. And so We bid you very heartily farewell. Given at Our Court at Whitehall the 15th day of April, 1693, in the fifth year of Our Reign.

By Her Majesty's Command.[4]

As Burr remarks, this is what Frederick the Great would have called "a vague answer—in the Austrian style—that should mean nothing."[5] So Phips had to act on his own authority. The court had sat again in April. It was at this session that John Alden returned to Boston, where, no one appearing against him, he was freed by proclamation. Finally Phips issued a general pardon, although Hale tells us that the final clearing of the jails was haphazard at best:

Some brake prison and ran away, and were not strictly searched after, some acquitted, some dismissed, and one way or other all that had been accused were set or left at liberty.[6]

But clearing the jails was only the first step; for twenty years following the trial year of 1692 Massachusetts would do penance and make reparation for her sins. The first formal act of penance was on the part of the entire community, in a fast-day proclaimed as follows:

By the Honorable the Lieutenant-Governor, Council, and Assembly of His Majesty's Province of the Massachusetts Bay, in General Court Assembled.

Whereas the anger of God is not yet turned away, but his hand is still stretched out against his people in manifold judgments, particularly in drawing out to such a length the troubles of Europe by a perplexing war; and more especially respecting ourselves in this province in that God is pleased still to go on in diminishing our substance, cutting short our harvest, blasting our most promising undertakings, more ways than one unsettling of us, and by his more immediate hand snatching away many out of our embraces by sudden and violent deaths even at this time when the sword is devouring so many both at home and abroad, and that after many days of public and solemn addressing of him, and although considering the many sins prevailing in the midst of us we cannot but wonder at the patience and mercy moderating these rebukes, yet we cannot but also fear that there is something still wanting to accompany our supplications. And doubtless there are some particular sins which God is angry with our Israel for, that have not been duly seen and resented by us, about which God expects to be sought if ever he turn again our captivity.

Wherefore it is commanded and appointed that Thursday the fourteenth of January next be observed as a day of prayer with fasting throughout this province, strictly forbidding all servile labor thereon, that so all God's People may offer up fervent supplications unto Him for the preservation and prosperity of His Majesty's Royal Person and Government and success to attend his affairs both at home and abroad; that all iniquity may be put away which hath stirred God's holy jealousy against this land; that He would show us what we know not and help us wherein we have done amiss to do so no more; and especially that whatever mistakes on either hand have been fallen into, either by the body of this people or any orders of men, referring to the late tragedy raised among us by Satan and his instruments through the awful Judgment of God, He would humble us therefor and pardon all the errors of His Servants and People that desire to love His Name and be atoned to His Land; that He would remove the rod of the wicked from off the lot of the righteous; that He would bring the American heathen and cause them to hear and obey His Voice.

Given at Boston, December 17, 1696, in the eighth year of His Majesty's Reign.

Isaac Addington, Secretary[7]

The bill was drafted by Judge Samuel Sewall. An earlier version, refused by the Council because it had not been consulted, had been drawn at the Assembly's request by Cotton Mather; Mather had listed many more public sins than Sewall, but had included this among them:

Wicked sorceries have been practised in the land, and, in the late inexplicable storms from the invisible world thereby brought upon us, we were left by the just hand of Heaven unto those errors whereby great hardships were brought upon innocent persons, and (we fear) guilt incurred which we have all cause to bewail with much confusion of face before the Lord.[8]

New England took its fast days seriously. Mather recorded in his diary on January 15 that he had been

afflicted last night with discouraging thoughts, as if unavoidable marks of the Divine Displeasure must overtake my family for my not appearing with vigor enough to stop the proceedings of the judges when the inextricable storm from the invisible world assaulted the country. . . .[9]

He was being somewhat overscrupulous on this point, since no other minister had dared go so far as he had in his suggestion that placing a minister or two on the court might prevent the abuse of spectral evidence. Yet he never seems to have understood that he might be to blame for his overwrought defense of the judges in his *Wonders of the Invisible World*. Still, Mather had less for which to blame himself than others. He had always opposed both spectral evidence and reckless accusations and his chief share in the communal guilt was precisely what he now realized—that he had not opposed these things vigorously enough.

A considerably heavier weight of guilt lay on Judge Samuel Sewall. On December 24 his son Samuel recited to him in Latin from the twelfth chapter of Matthew, and he recorded in his diary that "the seventh verse [If ye had known what this meaneth, I will have mercy and not sacrifice, ye would not have condemned the guiltless,] did awfully bring to mind the Salem tragedy." On the fast day itself he adopted a common device of Massachusetts Puritans who wished to make public acknowledgment of personal guilt. As the Reverend Samuel Willard passed by his pew Sewall handed him a statement to be read from the pulpit:

Samuel Sewall, sensible of the reiterated strokes of God upon himself and family, and being sensible that as to the guilt contracted upon the opening of the late Commission of Oyer and Terminer at Salem (to which the order for this day relates) he is upon many accounts more concerned than any that he knows of, desires to take the blame and shame of it, asking pardon of men and especially desiring prayers that God, who has an unlimited authority, would pardon that sin and all other his sins, personal and relative, and according to His Infinite Benignity and Sovereignty not visit the sin of him or of any other upon himself or any of his, nor upon the land, but that He would powerfully defend him against all temptations to sin for the future, and vouchsafe him the efficacious saving conduct of his Word and Spirit.[10]

Sewall stood during the reading of it, and bowed to the congregation at the end.

It is said that Stoughton, told of Sewall's action, remarked that he himself felt no personal guilt. He had acted, he said, in accord with his conscience, and his acquiescence in the public fast day was therefore apology enough.

Sewall had by no means done a complete about-face where witchcraft was concerned. On November 19, 1697, he spoke to John Hale about the latter's plans for a book on witchcraft, the *Modest Enquiry,* in which Hale would conclude that since the Devil suited his actions to men's beliefs about witchcraft it was a sin past men's analysis, and thus impossible to try in a court of law. Sewall wrote of Hale in his diary, "I fear lest he go into the other extreme." Sewall still regarded witchcraft as a punishable capital offense, but recognized that the court of which he had been a prominent member had proceeded on unsafe principles and was guilty of shedding innocent blood. The same recognition is at the heart of the apology of twelve jurymen:

We whose names are underwritten, being in the year 1692 called to serve as jurors in court at Salem, on trial of many who were by some suspected guilty of doing acts of witchcraft upon the bodies of sundry persons,

We confess that we ourselves were not capable to understand nor able to withstand the mysterious delusions of the Powers of Darkness and Prince of the Air, but were, for want of knowledge in ourselves and better information from others, prevailed with to take up with such evidence against the accused as on further consideration and better information we justly fear was insufficient for the touching the lives of any (Deuteronomy 17.6), whereby we fear we have been instrumental with others, though ignorantly and unwittingly, to bring upon ourselves and this People of the Lord the guilt of innocent blood, which sin the Lord saith in scripture he would not pardon (2 Kings 24.4), that is, we suppose, in regard of his temporal judgments.

We do therefore hereby signify to all in general (and to the surviving sufferers in especial) our deep sense of and sorrow for our errors in acting on such evidence to the condemning of any person, and do hereby declare that we justly fear that we were sadly deluded and mistaken, for which we are much disquieted and distressed in our minds, and do therefore humbly beg forgiveness, first of God for Christ's sake for this our error, and pray that God would not impute the guilt of it to ourselves nor others. And we also pray that we may be considered candidly and aright by the living sufferers as being then under the power of a strong and general delusion, utterly unacquainted with and not experienced in matters of that nature.

We do heartily ask forgiveness of you all, whom we have justly offended, and do declare according to our present minds, we would none of us do such things again on such grounds for the whole world, praying you to accept of this in way of satisfaction for our offense, and that you would bless the inheritance of the Lord, that He may be entreated for the Land.

FOREMAN,	Thomas Fisk	Thomas Perly, Senior
	William Fisk	John Peabody
	John Batcheler	Thomas Perkins
	Thomas Fisk, Junior	Samuel Sayer
	John Dane	Andrew Eliot
	Joseph Evelith	Henry Herrick, Senior[11]

The jurymen's recognition that they were "under the power of a strong and general delusion" is something we shall return to in the final chapter. Their state of mind is commonly but inaccurately referred to as mass hysteria. Perhaps it would be most accurate to say that while the afflicted girls' behavior was pathological—a genuine instance of epidemic hysteria—the behavior of the jurymen, and of the mass of the community, was neurotic, and directly related to the pathological state of the girls.

Although most of Massachusetts was doing penance in 1697, some persons remembered the witchcraft trials chiefly in order to take personal revenge. Calef was one of these; his *More Wonders of the Invisible World* was motivated first by his animus against the Mathers, and only secondly by his desire to put an end to witchcraft trials. Another was Philip English, Salem's richest merchant. When he and his wife fled to New York, Sheriff George Corwin had seized property worth fifteen hundred pounds for the crown, and since Corwin had acted in accordance with the common legal practice of the times English had been unable to recover in a suit before the Superior Court in 1694. But in 1697 the sheriff died, and English had a peculiarly repulsive revenge. He had a suit for debt, apparently unconnected with the witchcraft trials, against the sheriff's estate, and he made it clear that he would seize the sheriff's body in satisfaction of that debt if the body were removed from the Corwins' premises, where English could not legally set foot. So it had to be temporarily interred on the Corwin land until the debt was settled.

Another long-standing quarrel was finally settled in 1697. There had been serious divisions within the Salem Village church before Samuel Parris arrived; he inherited an explosive situation. The witchcraft trials only aggravated it, and so did Parris' behavior afterward. The other two Essex County ministers most concerned with the trials, John Hale of Beverly and Nicholas Noyes of Salem, saw their error relatively early, frankly and openly acknowledged it, were accordingly reconciled to those in their parish who had been injured, and lived useful and productive lives thereafter. But Parris was slow to acknowledge that he had been at fault. Although the relatives of Rebecca Nurse in particular accused him of behaving uncharitably toward her, he would not admit until 1694 that he had followed mistaken principles. Then, in an attempt to reconcile the dissenting members of his church to his ministry, he read from the pulpit his "Meditations for Peace," which included major revisions of principle:

I should not agree with my former apprehensions in all points, as, for instance, (1) I question not but God sometimes suffers the Devil (as of late) to afflict in the shape of not only innocent but pious persons, or so delude the senses of the afflicted that they strongly conceit their hurt is from such persons, when, indeed, it is not. (2) The improving [i.e., using] of one afflicted to inquire by who afflicts the others, I fear may be, and has been, unlawfully used, to Satan's great advantage.[12]

Parris would not admit to having been mistaken in specific cases, and he hedged his general apology by saying people might "conceive" he had erred, and that he "may" have been wrong:

The matter being so dark and perplexed as that there is no present appearance that all God's servants should be altogether of one mind in all circumstances touching the same, I do most heartily, fervently, and humbly beseech pardon of the merciful God, through the blood of Christ, of all my mistakes and trespasses in so weighty a matter, and also all your forgiveness of every offense in this and other affairs wherein you see or conceive I have erred or offended, professing in the presence of the Almighty God that what I have done has been, as for substance, as I apprehended was duty. However, through weakness, ignorance, etc., I may have been mistaken. . . .

It was not enough for several of his parishioners, who continued to refuse to attend on his ministry or to pay for his support. In 1695 they obtained a Council to judge their quarrel with Parris. It was moderated by Increase Mather and included Cotton Mather, Samuel Willard, and James Allen among its sixteen members. The Council suggested, at considerable length, that it would be nice if all parties to the quarrel might be reconciled to each other, but recognized the unlikelihood of this in their sixth and final article:

If the distempers in Salem Village should be (which God forbid!) so incurable that Mr. Parris, after all, finds that he cannot with any comfort and service continue in his present station, his removal from thence will not expose him unto any hard character with us, nor, we hope, with the rest of the people of God among whom we live. . . .[13]

But the quarrel dragged on another two years until the Inferior Court of Common Pleas, to which Parris had taken his case, put the disposition of it to a panel of three arbitrators. The attorneys for the village, two of them relatives of Rebecca Nurse, made it plain that Parris' beliefs and conduct in 1692 were the major issue between them. The law, they argued, required them to support only an "orthodox and blameless" minister. They complained of Parris that

His believing the Devil's accusations and readily departing from all charity to persons, though of blameless and godly lives, upon such suggestions; his promoting such accusations; as also his partiality therein in stifling the accusations of some and at the same time vigilantly promoting others, as we conceive, are just causes for our refusal, etc.

That Mr. Parris's going to Mary Walcott or Abigail Williams and directing others to them to know who afflicted the people in their illnesses, we understand this to be a dealing with them that have a familiar spirit and a denying the Providence of God, who alone, as we believe, can send afflictions or cause Devils to afflict any. This we also conceive sufficient to justify such refusal.

That Mr. Parris by these practices and principles has been the beginner and procurer of the sorest afflictions, not to this village only but to this whole country, that did ever befall them.[14]

It should be noted in passing that the village attorneys had concluded that the girls' afflictions were due to illness caused by demonic possession.

The arbitrators were Wait Winthrop, Elisha Cook, and Samuel Sewall (the first and last had, of course, been judges of the Special Court of Oyer and Terminer). They recommended that the separation of Parris and the church be settled by a cash payment to Parris for his arrears in salary and his property in the Village, and with this the quarrel ended. Parris' successor, the Reverend Joseph Green, restored the congregation to unity. In 1699 the members of the Nurse family were welcomed back to communion. In 1703 the excommunication of Martha Corey was revoked, although "six or seven"[15] members of the church dissented. That this was a major achievement may be seen by the fact that the church in Salem Town did not revoke its excommunication of Rebecca Nurse and

Giles Corey until nine years later, even though the Town had not been split by dissent.

It was Joseph Green as well who received one of the leading accusers, Anne Putnam, Jr., into communion at Salem Village church in 1706, reading her confession from the pulpit:

I desire to be humbled before God for that sad and humbling Providence that befell my father's family in the year about '92; that I, then being in my childhood, should by such a Providence of God be made an instrument for the accusing of several persons of a grievous crime, whereby their lives were taken away from them, whom now I have just grounds and good reason to believe they were innocent persons; and that it was a great delusion of Satan that deceived me in that sad time, whereby I justly fear I have been instrumental with others, though ignorantly and unwittingly, to bring upon myself and this land the guilt of innocent blood; though what was said or done by me against any person I can truly and uprightly say before God and man, I did it not out of any anger, malice, or ill-will to any person, for I had no such thing against any of them; but what I did was ignorantly, being deluded by Satan.[16]

Like Sewall, she stood while this was read, and at the end acknowledged it was hers. Some of the afflicted girls of Salem became "persons of profligate and vicious conversation"[17] in later life, and this fact has generally been extended to bolster the view that their testimony was nothing but malicious lying. But the facts will not bear such an extension, and the later history of Anne Putnam, Jr., ought to lay it to rest once and for all. The evident sincerity of her apology and the fact that the congregation accepted both it and her are the final evidence that the behavior of the afflicted girls cannot be explained as fraud.

Massachusetts did what she could to heal her wounds in state as well as church. The most serious civic problem was that condemned persons who had been reprieved and pardoned found themselves subject to the contention that as condemned persons they had no legal existence. The first to feel the disadvantage of this and to petition for reversal of attainder was

Elizabeth Procter, whose husband had made a will disinheriting her while he was in prison. She found herself unable to contest this will because, as she said in a petition to the General Court in 1696,

although God hath granted my life yet those that claim my said husband's estate by that which they call a will, will not suffer me to have one penny of the estate, neither upon the account of my husband's contract with me before marriage nor yet upon the account of the dower, which, as I humbly conceive, doth belong or ought to belong to me by the law. For they say that I am dead in the law. . . .[18]

Why the General Court did not act immediately on her petition is not known, but hers was followed by others. In 1703 the speaker of the Assembly ordered a bill drawn up which would disallow spectral evidence, so that "no specter evidence may be hereafter accounted valid or sufficient to take away the life or good name of any person or persons within this province,"[19] and in that year the attainder of Abigail Faulkner, Sarah Wardwell, and Elizabeth Procter was reversed.

But this reversed the attainder only of those persons who had specifically petitioned for it. Besides, there were those who felt that the state should do more than merely reverse the attainder. Among these was the Reverend Michael Wigglesworth, the aging author of New England's most popular book, *The Day of Doom*, who wrote to Increase Mather in 1704 of his fear "that God hath a controversy with us about what was done in the time of the witchcraft. I fear that innocent blood hath been shed, and that many have had their hands defiled therewith." Wigglesworth recommended public acknowledgment of guilt,

and humiliation for it, and the more particularly and personally it is done by all that have been actors, the more pleasing it will be to God and more effectual to turn away his judgments from the land, and to prevent his wrath from falling upon the persons and families of such as have been most concerned. . . .

Moreover, if it be true, as I have often been informed, that the families of such as were condemned for supposed witchcraft have been ruined by taking away and making havoc of their estates and leaving them nothing for their relief, I believe the whole country lies under a curse to this day, and will do till some effectual course be taken by our honored governor and General Court to make them some amends and reparations.[20]

On May 25, 1709, Philip English and twenty-one others, whose relations had been executed or who "themselves or some of their relations were imprisoned, impaired and blasted in their reputations and estates," petitioned the General Court to restore their reputations and make amends "as to what they have been damnified in their estates thereby."[21] On November 2 Cotton Mather supported their position in a sermon preached before the Assembly. He told the legislators that

in two or three too memorable days of temptation that have been upon us there have been errors committed. You are always ready to declare unto all the world that you disapprove these errors. You are willing to inform all mankind with your declarations . . . that persons are not to be judged confederates with evil spirits merely because the evil spirits do make possessed people cry out upon them.

Could anything be proposed further by way of reparation (besides the General Day of Humiliation which was appointed and observed through the province to bewail the errors of our dark time, some years ago) you would be willing to hearken to it.[22]

In May of 1710 the General Court established a committee of four to meet in Salem and investigate, which they did, thoroughly and at length, collecting much testimony from relatives and survivors. One document, a letter from William Good, is worth particular notice. Good's family had suffered more than its share of abuse:

1 My wife, Sarah Good, was in prison about four months and then executed.
2 A sucking child died in prison before the mother's execution.
3 A child of four or five years old [Dorcas Good] was in prison seven or eight months, and being chained in the dungeon was so hardly used and terrified that she hath ever since been very chargable, having little or no reason to govern herself. And I leave it unto

the honorable Court to judge what damage I have sustained by such a destruction of my poor family, and so rest

Your honors' humble servant,

Salem, Sept. 13, 1710[23]   *William Good*

Deodat Lawson had seen Dorcas Good before she was committed to prison and remarked that she "looked hail and well as other children."[24] What happened to her is as brutal as anything that occurred at Salem. But it will not do to waste any sympathy on her father, because he had been eager to testify against his wife and was therefore as responsible for what happened to his family as anyone in Massachusetts. For that matter, his wife may not be deserving of sympathy either. She is the Sarah Good who was so liberal with her curses—who threatened Nicholas Noyes with "blood to drink" and whose cursing of Mercy Short sent that young woman into hysterical fits. But most petitioners had a more legitimate case than William Good.

In October of 1711 the committee submitted its report: a list of those executed and those condemned but not executed, and recommendations for financial compensation.[25] The General Court responded by immediately reversing the attainder of all those listed and authorizing compensation in the amounts recommended by the committee. The majority of the accounts were settled in 1712, but some of them dragged on considerably longer. Members of George Burroughs' family, which was split by particularly violent quarrels, were petitioning for additional compensation as late as 1750.[26]

Although the committee did its investigating conscientiously the members were apparently not aware of the previous reversals of attainder in 1703, since they listed the names of Samuel Wardwell and Abigail Faulkner. These two, then, had their attainder reversed twice. The committee, which was doing its work nearly twenty years after the trials, missed some names completely; the attainder stands to this day on Bridget Bishop, Elizabeth Johnson, Susanna Martin, Alice Parker, Ann Pudeator, Wilmot Redd, and Margaret Scott. Over the years sporadic attempts have been made to have the attainder removed from these names, but the only result has been a resolution by the General Court in 1957, announcing that

Whereas, One Ann Pudeator and certain other persons were indicted, tried, found guilty, sentenced to death and executed in the year sixteen hundred and ninety-two for "Witchcraft"; and

Whereas, said persons may have been illegally tried, convicted and sentenced . . . and

Whereas, The General Court of Massachusetts is informed that certain descendants of said Ann Pudeator and said other persons are still distressed by the record of said proceedings; therefore be it

Resolved, That . . . the General Court of Massachusetts declares its belief that such proceedings, even if lawful under the Province Charter and the law of Massachusetts as it then was, were and are shocking, and . . . further declares that, as all the laws under which said proceedings, even if then legally conducted, have been long since abandoned and superseded by our more civilized laws, no disgrace or cause for distress attaches to the said descendants or any of them by reason of said proceedings. . . .[27]

This is, of course, only a pious resolution. It does not reverse the attainder. But since at least two of the persons still attainted as witches under Massachusetts law—Bridget Bishop and Mammy Redd—actually were witches, presumably one can say that two-sevenths justice had been done.

14

A Matter of Warning

The Reverend John Higginson was happy to write a preface for John Hale's *A Modest Enquiry Into the Nature of Witchcraft* because, he said,

I am persuaded that such a treatise as this is needful and useful, . . . that whatever errors or mistakes we fell into in the dark hour of temptation that was upon us may be (upon more light) so discovered, acknowledged, and disowned by us as that it may be a matter of warning and caution to those that come after us, that they may not fall into the like.[1]

Massachusetts did what she could to discover, acknowledge, and disown her errors, and did it so well and so publicly that there is no question that Salem's experience helped put an end to witchcraft trials in Western civilization.

Yet the Salem trials were by no means the last. A woman was condemned to death for witchcraft in England as late as 1712, twenty years after the Salem trials. In that case, the last in England, the judge obtained a royal pardon, so there was no execution. But there were executions in Scotland as late as 1722, and Sarah Bassett, a Negro slave, was burned at the stake in Bermuda in 1730. Hanging was, as we have seen, the usual English punishment for witchcraft. But burning or boiling to death were prescribed where petty treason was also involved—treason against someone other than the king to whom one owed obedience. The murder of one's husband, or parent, or master was petty treason, and since Sarah Bassett had used her charms and her poisons against her master she died at the stake. She was the last to be executed in an English-speaking country, and in 1736 the English and Scottish laws prescribing death for witchcraft were repealed, to be replaced by laws against fraudulent practice of the occult. On the Continent there were executions throughout the eighteenth century: in France as late as 1745; in Germany in 1775; in Spain in 1781; in Switzerland in 1782; in Poland in 1793. There was a rash of witch-burnings in South America during the nineteenth century, and lynchings have continued into the present century. In 1929, for example, three Pennsylvania-Germans were convicted of murdering a "pow-wow doctor." They were after his copy of *The Long-Lost Friend,* the grimoire still in use among the Pennsylvania-Germans, and believed he had used it to bewitch them.[2]

The Salem trials were, however, the last in which an entire community believed its existence threatened by malefic witchcraft. But they enjoyed that dubious distinction by little more than a decade; it was in 1680 that the court of Louis XIV was shaken by a witchcraft scandal which makes for an instructive comparison with the trials at Salem.

Some of the courtiers of the Sun King apparently thought little more of consulting a practitioner of the occult than of consulting their confessor. According to Visconti's memoirs, the Duchesse de Foix had appealed to the Devil for bigger breasts and Madame de Vassé for more comely thighs. Nobody expected revelations more serious than this when in March of 1679 the Paris police arrested Catherine Deshayes, known as La Voisin, the leader of a fashionable ring of occultists who dealt in magic potions, some of them poisonous, as well as in spells and charms. The investigation was conducted by a special commission of twelve called the *Chambre Ardente* after the black-draped, candle-lit room in which the hearings were held, and some of its findings show little more than a depraved curiosity on the part of La Voisin's noble clients: one courtier had merely wished to be introduced to the Devil. Others, however, had wanted considerably more. The wife of the king's flutist was accused of having poisoned her first husband, and she was executed in May. By the end of the year far more important people were incriminated, including the Comtesse de Soissons, the niece of Cardinal Mazarin, who was also suspected of husband-poisoning. She and several others were allowed to flee the kingdom, although Louis instructed Nicholas de la Reynie, one of the commissioners, that the matter was to be pursued to the finish without regard for rank or sex.

Within another year, however, Louis had reduced the commission to two persons (including La Reynie) working in the utmost secrecy, and had personally removed some of their documents from the files. The commission had obtained testimony incriminating no less a person than Madame de Montespan, the mistress of the king, who had been a client of La Voisin for thirteen years. She had asked for and obtained spells to make the king forget his former mistress and his queen, and she had ordered love potions as well. These she had mixed with the king's food over a number of years. Louis was a generally healthy person, and one of the more interesting aspects of this affair is whether his occasional indispositions during this period may not have been a result of the bats' blood, powdered dessicated mole, and similar ingredients his mistress was incorporating in his diet. (One ingredient of her potions, cantharides, is still in use as an aphrodisiac.)

Up to this point most authorities are agreed: Madame de Montespan had been a client of La Voisin, and she had used both spells and potions to obtain and hold the king's love. Beyond this point, however, there is much controversy, in part because of the sensational nature of the testimony and in part because it was obtained under torture.[3]

What the testimony says is that Louis' affections had become increasingly hard to hold, and Madame de Montespan therefore had recourse to more and more drastic measures. A number of priests were part of La Voisin's ring, and in 1672 she called on the most depraved of these, the Abbé Guibourg, to perform amatory masses, which involved using Madame de Montespan's naked body as an altar on which to place the chalice. It also required the ritual sacrifice of an infant, part of whose blood was mixed with flour in the chalice to make an obscene sacramental wafer. At the conclusion of the mass the wafer and some of the infant's blood were given to the Sun King's mistress; as the strongest of love potions, they were to be mixed with his food, as before. Amatory masses were performed again in 1676. But by 1679 the Montespan concluded that she had lost the king and ordered a mortuary rather than an amatory mass. When that piece of imitative magic did not succeed in killing Louis she planned to poison him, but La Voisin was arrested before the plot could be carried out.

As we have seen, the testimony is sensational, and it was obtained under torture; it is not surprising that many have refused to believe it. But there is reason to think that Louis believed it. La Reynie urged the king to make the testimony public so that the worst of the ring—figures like the Abbé Guibourg—might be brought to trial. The king would agree to their trial, but not to making public any of the accusations against Madame de Montespan, and La Reynie felt he could not proceed without these. Eventually the difficulty was solved with *lettres de cachet*, letters from the king by which any of his subjects could be imprisoned for life without trial. La Voisin had been burned at the stake in 1680 before anyone had mentioned the name of the king's mistress, but the surviving members of her ring ended their lives chained to the walls of French prisons. The last of them died in 1724, thirty-two years after the last witch was hanged in Massachusetts. Louis personally burned the testimony relating to his mistress, so what survives is only La Reynie's summary of it.

The king's affair with Madame de Montespan was, of course, at an end, although he permitted her to remain at court for a few years and even paid her occasional visits. In 1691 he pensioned her off to the country. Saint-Simon's description of her final days suggests that, although her death was quiet, she had an extraordinarily heavy load on her conscience. Little by little she gave almost all she had to the poor. She worked for them several hours a day, making stout shirts and such things for them. Her table, that she had loved to excess, became the most frugal; her fasts multiplied; she would interrupt her meals in order to go and pray. Her mortifications were continued; her chemises and her sheets were of rough linen, of the hardest and thickest kind, but hidden under others of ordinary kind. She unceasingly wore bracelets, garters, and a girdle, all armed with iron points, which often times inflicted wounds upon her; and her tongue, formerly so dangerous, had also its peculiar penance imposed on it. She was, moreover, so tormented with the fear of death, that she employed several women, whose sole occupation was to watch her. She went to sleep with all the curtains of her bed open, many lights in her chamber, and her women around her. Whenever she awoke she wished to find them chatting, playing, or enjoying themselves, so as to reassure herself against their drowsiness.[4]

Salem and Versailles were alike in permitting the escape of the distinguished members of the community implicated in the course of their witchcraft investigations. But in virtually everything else they differed, and all of the differences suggest that the French court was the more brutal and barbaric of the two communities. Torture, secrecy, imprisonment without trial —these were the methods of the Old Regime. During and after the Salem trials witchcraft was a matter of continual debate, and when as a result of that debate it became apparent that the innocent had suffered, both individuals and the state did what they could to make reparations. The French court could hardly make reparations, if reparations were in order (as they must have been in some instances—every witch hunt traps the innocent as well as the guilty), because it had not put more than a minority of suspects to public trial. The *lettres de cachet* had closed off not only all questions of guilt or innocence but all possibility of debating them.

From an historical point of view the behavior of the French court is not particularly blameworthy, but that of the Puritans is certainly praiseworthy. In all the history of witchcraft and of witch hunts there are only two other cases in which the authorities, discovering they had been mistaken, acknowledged their error freely and publicly. In 1611 the Spanish tried fifty-three persons for witchcraft at Navarre and found twenty-nine of them guilty. Five of these died in prison; five were flogged; six were burned at the stake. The rest, apparently, suffered only minor penalties. But accusations continued to mount and an inquisitor was therefore assigned to make an investigation. He spent three years at it, and discovered that sixteen hundred persons had been falsely accused. Acting on his report, the Supreme Court of the Inquisition apologized and made reparations for the trials at Navarre. One other such instance took place in Germany when a Prince-Bishop of Würzburg instituted a memorial mass for innocent victims of witchcraft trials in that city.

A Prince-Bishop of Würzburg, the Spanish Inquisition, and the American Puritans make at first sight a wildly incongruous group. But what they have in common deserves our profound respect: a reverence for the truth so deep that it compelled them to admit before all the world that they had been fatally mistaken.

Western civilization stopped executing witches when the literate and balanced portion of its members stopped believing in their capacity to harm. And since the witch's genuine power was a consequence of her victim's belief, the practice of witchcraft has very nearly vanished along with the penalties for it. But new figures have risen to take the spectral place in popular fears vacated by the witch; the spirit of the witch hunt is still with us. This explains in part the continued fascination of the Salem trials. They epitomize those crises of belief which are the ultimate test both of the leadership and the body politic of a democratic society.

It may also help to explain the persistence of the false popular view of the Salem trials. That false view is founded, as we have seen, on the distortions of Robert Calef and Charles W. Upham. But to trace these distortions to Calef and Upham explains nothing but their origin; it does not explain our continued acceptance of them. That acceptance can be understood only by recognizing that there is something in these distortions very appealing to Americans. If that were not the case we should long ago have recognized them for what they are.

The popular view holds that there was no witchcraft practiced at Salem and thus that there was never any real menace to society; the danger was illusory from start to finish. It is comforting to think this, but as we have seen it is quite wrong. There was witchcraft at Salem, and it worked. It did real harm to its victims and there was every reason to regard it as a criminal offense.

The popular view also holds that all of those executed for witchcraft at Salem were innocent, and as we have seen this is also false, although it is true that the majority of those who died were innocent.

Finally the popular view ascribes the blame for the shedding of innocent blood to a corrupt leadership motivated by their own discreditable lust for power, and particulary to the clerical leadership. At the same time it exonerates the general public, ascribing their state of intense excitement to the sermons of their pastors. This is perhaps the most grotesque distortion of all. As we have seen, accusations of witchcraft were endemic among the seventeenth-century common people and were typically kept in check, rather than aroused, by the leadership. What made the trials at Salem possible was that circumstances combined to make the leadership believe that on this occasion there was substance behind the perennial popular fears of witchcraft. As for the clergy's part, they acted throughout as a restraint upon the proceedings and it was their misgivings which finally brought the trials to an end.

It is not difficult to see what is attractive in the popular view. It permits us to feel comfortable both at having outgrown the superstitions of our ancestors and at the thought that they were never in any real danger. It makes the process of selecting martyrs simple by establishing execution as the sole criterion for martyrdom, thus relieving us of the burden of deciding whether there were moral differences between the death of Rebecca Nurse and that of Bridget Bishop. What makes it most attractive, however, is that it panders to the most pervasive of all democratic sentimentalities—the view that the people are always healthy and that social catastrophes can only occur at the instigation of a corrupt leadership.

As we have seen, it is not that simple. The Salem witch hunt cannot be explained by assigning the responsibility to a Cotton Mather, or even to a William Stoughton. A witch hunt can occur only when the majority of a community feels itself so beset by malice—real or imagined—that it loses the capacity to distinguish between the innocent and the guilty.

Any community so beset might well take Salem's experience as a warning and recognize, with the Reverend John Hale, that in matters of malice the devil suits his actions to man's beliefs about them.

Notes

PREFACE

1. George Lyman Kittredge, *Witchcraft in Old and New England* (Cambridge, Mass.: 1929) p. 338.
2. *Ibid.*, pp. 311–312.
3. John Fiske, *New France and New England* (Boston and New York: 1902), chapter V; Edward Eggleston, *The Transit of Civilization* (New York: 1900), chapter I, sections IX–XVII; W.F. Poole, "Witchcraft in Boston" in *The Memorial History of Boston*, ed. Justin Winsor (Boston: 1881) II; Kenneth B. Murdock, *Increase Mather* (Cambridge, Mass.: 1926) chapter XVII; Samuel Eliot Morison, *The Intellectual Life Of Colonial New England*, 2nd edition (New York: 1956) pp. 255–265; Perry Miller, *The New England Mind: From Colony To Province* (Boston: 1961) chapter XIII.
4. Longfellow, *op. cit.* below, p. vii; Barrett Wendell, *Cotton Mather* (New York: 1891) chapter VI; Morison, *op. cit.*; Marion Starkey, *The Devil In Massachusetts* (New York: 1950) chapter XX.
5. Fiske, op cit.; Winfield S. Nevins, *Witchcraft In Salem Village*, preface to the 5th edition (Salem, 1916); Miller, *op. cit.*; Starkey, op. cit.
6. *Essex Institute Historical Collections*, v. XXIX, pp. 129–147.
7. Miller, *op. cit.*, pp. 180–181.
8. v. CIV, pp. 89–108.

1. WITCHCRAFT

1. Deodat Lawson, *A Brief and True Narrative of Witchcraft at Salem Village* (Boston: 1692), reprinted in *Narratives of the Witchcraft Cases: 1648–1706*, ed. George Lincoln Burr (New York: 1914), p. 162. This excellent and indispensable anthology will hereafter be cited as "Burr."
2. John Hale, *A Modest Enquiry into the Nature of Witchcraft* (Boston: 1702), in Burr, p. 413.
3. The symptoms of hysteria may be found in almost any textbook on abnormal psychology. I have also found the following particularly

helpful in providing parallels to the behavior at Salem: J.-M. Charcot, *Lectures on the Diseases of the Nervous System* (London: 1877); Pierre Janet, *The Major Symptoms of Hysteria* (New York: 1907); Pierre Janet, *Psychological Healing* (New York: 1925); Joseph Breuer and Sigmund Freud, *Studies in Hysteria* (New York: 1950).

4. *A Tryal of Witches at the Assizes Held at Bury St. Edmunds . . .* (London: 1682), p. 41.

5. Margaret Murray, *The God of the Witches* (New York: 1952) is a useful short account of this horned god, by the anthropologist who first discovered his importance. Miss Murray's critics are correct, however, in accusing her of extraordinary credulity in regard to individual witchcraft cases.

6. Pennethorne Hughes, *Witchcraft* (London: 1952), p. 198.

7. Murray, *The God of the Witches*, p. 30.

8. "Atque in eodem fano et altare haberet ad sacrificium Christi, et arulam ad victimas daemoniorum." *Baedae Historia Ecclesiastica Gentis Anglorum*, in *Opera Historica*, ed. J. E. King (Cambridge, Mass.: 1930) p. 292.

9. Murray, *The God of the Witches*, p. 18.

10. Giraldus Cambrensis, *Gemma Ecclesiastica*, ed. J. S. Brewer, *Opera* vol. 2 (London: 1862), p. 137.

11. See Lynn Thorndike, *A History of Magic and Experimental Science* (New York: 1958), VIII, pp. 82, 196. The quotation on witchcraft is from Bacon's *Sylva Sylvarum*.

12. Thorndike, *History*, VIII, pp. 180, 197.

13. Boyle, *The General History of the Air*, in *Works* (London: 1772), V, p. 472. The passage is indexed under "Demons, subterraneous."

14. Locke, *An Essay Concerning Human Understanding*, book II, chapter XXIII, paragraph 31.

15. Locke, *Understanding*, book II, chapter XXIII, paragraph 13, where he also proposed "an extravagant conjecture" of his own that spirits might be able to "form their organs of sensation and perception" to "their present design," thus anticipating science fiction in such matters as X-ray eyes.

16. Hobbes, *Leviathan*, part 4, chapter xlvi.

17. Hobbes, *Leviathan*, part 1, chapter ii.

18. *The Works of George Berkeley, Bishop of Cloyne*, ed. A. A. Luce and T. E. Jessop, VIII (London: 1956) p. 47.

2. WITCHCRAFT IN NEW ENGLAND

1. Thomas Hutchinson, *History of the Province of Massachusetts-Bay*, ed. Lawrence Shaw Mayo (Cambridge, Mass.: 1936) vol. 2, p. 12.

2. Wm. F. Poole, "Witchcraft in Boston" in *The Memorial History of Boston,* ed. Justin Winsor, II (Boston: 1881), p. 141.

3. All quotations concerning this case are from a letter written by the Reverend John Whiting to Increase Mather in 1682, *Massachusetts Historical Society Collections,* 4th series, VIII, pp. 466–69.

4. See R. E. L. Masters, *Eros and Evil* (New York: 1962), chapter 18.

5. Increase Mather, *An Essay for the Recording of Illustrious Providences* (Boston: 1684) in Burr, p. 20.

6. Willard's account is printed in the *Massachusetts Historical Society Collections,* 4th series, VIII, pp. 555–70. It was probably the basis for Increase Mather's account of the case in *Illustrious Providences* (Burr, pp. 21–23). All of my quotations concerning the Knapp case are from Willard.

7. Pierre Janet, *The Major Symptoms of Hysteria* (New York: 1907), pp. 98–99. These initial symptoms were known in the ancient world; see Plato, *Timaeus,* 91c.

8. J.-M. Charcot, *Lectures on the Diseases of the Nervous System,* tr. George Sigerson (London: 1877) vol. 1, pp. 280–81.

9. Janet, *Major Symptoms,* p. 100.

10. 1 *Jacob.* Cap. 12. This statute is very similar to its predecessor in 5 *Eliz.*

11. Willard, *Useful Instructions* (Cambridge, Mass.: 1673), p. 42.

12. D. Wilfred Abse, *Hysteria and Related Mental Disorders* (Bristol, England: 1966) pp. 30–31.

13. Cotton Mather, *Memorable Providences* (Boston: 1689) reprinted in Burr, pp. 93–143, from which all quotations concerning this case are taken unless otherwise noted.

14. This twisted posture of the head may be seen in the "Procession of the Possessed of Molenbeek," an engraving of 1642 after Pieter Brueghel the Elder.

15. Witchcraft deaths are not the result of hysteria, but both death and hysteria are attributable to the victim's belief in the witch's power. The cause of witchcraft deaths is discussed in detail at the end of Chapter 5.

16. Dr. Joseph Breuer and Dr. Sigmund Freud, *Studies in Hysteria,* tr. A. A. Brill (New York: 1950), p. 2.

17. Hutchinson, *History,* vol. 2, p. 16.

18. *New-England Historical and Genealogical Register,* vol. 24 (1870), p. 390.

19. *Massachusetts Historical Society Collections,* 4th series, VIII, p. 368.

20. Printed with his *Memorable Providences.* Burr omits it, but substantial selections are reprinted in *What Happened in Salem?,* ed. David Levin, second edition (New York: 1960) pp. 96–106. This

anthology, the most useful after Burr's, will hereafter be cited as "Levin."

21. John Webster, *The Displaying of Supposed Witchcraft* (London: 1677), table of contents, n. p.
22. Richard Baxter, *The Certainty of the World of Spirits* (London: 1691), p. 80.
23. In three volumes (Boston, 1901, 1904, 1928).
24. Cotton Mather, *Memorable Providences,* Burr, p. 99. The belief that Indians and other "pagans" worshipped the Devil persisted among the learned well into the eighteenth century and continues among the unwashed at the present day.

3. THE RAISING OF THE DEVIL

1. In his church records. See Charles W. Upham, *Salem Witchcraft* (Boston: 1867), II, p. 95. This is the standard history and will be cited hereafter as "Upham."
2. Hale, *Modest Enquiry,* pp. 132–33. Burr does not reprint this passage.
3. The witch cake episode is most fully described in the Danvers church records reprinted by Upham, II, pp. 95–97.
4. The language is that of the warrants for Sarah Good and Tituba, which are printed on pp. 11 and 41 of the first volume of W. Elliot Woodward's *Records of Salem Witchcraft* (Roxbury, Mass.: 1864). This two-volume compilation is the most important printed source for Salem witchcraft documents. It is cited hereafter as "RSW." A more complete and more accurate compilation was made by the Works Progress Administration in 1938. It was never published, but is available in typescript in the Essex County Court House.
5. Examination of Sarah Good, RSW, I, pp. 17–21.
6. Testimony of Sarah Gadge, RSW, I, p. 26.
7. See Thomas Rogers Forbes, *The Midwife and the Witch* (New Haven: 1966), chapter 8.
8. The examination of Sarah Osburn is in RSW, I, pp. 35–38.
9. This transcript of Tituba's examination, written by Ezekiel Cheever, is reprinted (from RSW) in Levin, pp. 6–8. A much more detailed but less coherent account, in Jonathan Corwin's handwriting, is printed in Samuel G. Drake, *The Witchcraft Delusion in New England* (Roxbury, Mass.: 1866) III, pp. 187–92. Pp. 192–95 contain her second examination, on March 2. In succeeding quotations I draw on all three documents.
10. RSW, I, p. 38.
11. Most of the documents concerning Martha Corey are in RSW, I, pp. 50–60. Her examination is not in RSW but is printed in Upham, II, pp. 43–50.

4. HOW TO CATCH A WITCH

1. Quotations from Lawson are from his *Brief and True Narrative* (Boston: 1692), reprinted in Burr, pp. 152–64, and his *Christ's Fidelity the Only Shield Against Satan's Malignity* (Boston: 1692).
2. Janet, *The Major Symptoms of Hysteria*, p. 273.
3. Cotton Mather, *The Wonders of the Invisible World* (Boston: 1693), p. 83. Burr reprints substantial portions of the *Wonders*, but not this passage.
4. Most of the documents concerning Rebecca Nurse are in RSW, I, pp. 76–87. The testimony of Israel and Elizabeth Porter is in Upham, II, pp. 58–59.
5. RSW, I, pp. 63–64.
6. There is no extant transcript of this confession. Not all of the testimony was transcribed, according to Stephen Sewall, the clerk of the courts, some of it being taken *viva voce*. And over the years many documents have disappeared, some of them removed by Governor Hutchinson for use in his *History* but the majority presumably entering the collections of light-fingered antiquarians. But fortunately Lawson gives the substance of this confession in his *Narrative*, Burr, p. 160. Dorcas Good's testimony against her mother is in RSW, I, p. 23.
7. The story is in Lawson, *Narrative*, Burr, p. 161. Robert Calef gives a different interpretation in his *More Wonders of the Invisible World* (London: 1700): "The wind shutting the door forcibly gave occasion to some to suppose she went out in anger" (Burr, p. 346). But there is every reason to believe that here as in some other instances (see Chapter 12) Calef's interpretation of his material is not to be trusted.
8. The examination of Sarah Cloyse is in Hutchinson, *History*, vol. 2, pp. 21–23.
9. Samuel Sewall, *Diary* (3 vols., *Massachusetts Historical Society Collections*, 5th series, V–VIII), vol. 1, p. 358.
10. The documents concerning Mary Warren are in RSW, I, pp. 117–35.
11. RSW, I, pp. 54–55.

5. WITCHCRAFT AT SALEM

1. Giles Corey's examination is printed in the 1823 edition of Calef's *More Wonders* and reprinted as an appendix to Drake's *Witchcraft Delusion*.
2. Abigail Hobbs' records are in RSW, I, pp. 172–80, excepting her examination of April 19. I wish to thank the Massachusetts His-

torical Society, and particularly Malcolm Freiberg, Editor of Publications, for providing me a Xerox copy of the latter.

3. RSW has a ditto mark for Nick, but the word is clear in the original document, in the Essex County Court House.

4. The documents relating to Bridget Bishop are in RSW, I, pp. 135–72.

5. Cotton Mather, *Wonders*, Burr, p. 228.

6. Upham, II, pp. 126, 261.

7. Marion Starkey in "Village Circe," chapter XII of *The Devil in Massachusetts* (New York: 1950), sees this experience and those which follow as sexual in content, and remarks that Coman and the others "virtuously repelled [Bridget Bishop's] advances" (p. 152). I think, to put it mildly, that Starkey's interpretations of the documents are frequently mistaken.

8. Her examination is in Hutchinson, *History*, vol. 2, p. 26. A more detailed account, with perceptive analysis, is in Chapter XI of Hale, *Modest Enquiry*.

9. The records concerning Wilmot Redd are in RSW, II, pp. 97–106. The Latin words were presumably substituted by the court recorder for English words used by the witness.

10. Dorcas Hoar's records are in RSW, I, pp. 235–53.

11. Burroughs' records are in RSW, II, pp. 109–28, but are very incomplete. Therefore I have depended heavily on Cotton Mather's summary of the testimony in his *Wonders*, Burr, pp. 215–22. Although the tone of the latter is overwrought, to say the least, comparison of Mather's accounts to the extant trial documents demonstrates that he was scrupulously accurate in his reporting of facts.

12. Cummings' testimony is in RSW, II, pp. 80–82.

13. RSW, II, p. 85.

14. RSW, II, pp. 158–60.

15. Richard Chamberlain, *Lithobolia: or, the Stone-throwing Devil* (London: 1698), Burr, p. 74.

16. Burr omits this passage, which is on pp. 59–61 of the original edition.

17. RSW, II, p. 27.

18. *American Anthropologist*, new series vol. 44, 2 (April–June, 1942), pp. 169–81.

19. A. G. Leonard, *The Lower Niger and its Tribes* (London: 1906), pp. 257 ff.

20. Herbert Basedow, *The Australian Aboriginal* (Adelaide: 1925), pp. 178–79.

21. *Science Digest*, vol. 60, 3 (September, 1966) pp. 21–22.

22. *Archives of Dermatology*, vol. 90 (1964) p. 530.
23. *Psychosomatic Medicine*, XIX, 3 (May–June, 1957) pp. 191–98.

6. A COUNTRY FULL OF LIES

1. William Hobbes' examination is in RSW, I, pp. 182–87.
2. Abigail Faulkner's two examinations are in RSW, II, pp. 129–31.
3. RSW, II, p. 34.
4. RSW, II, p. 108.
5. RSW, I, pp. 113–14.
6. *More Wonders*, Burr, p. 361.
7. RSW, II, pp. 9–10.
8. *Modest Enquiry*, Burr, p. 421.
9. Massachusetts Archives, vol. 135, no. 39. Another version is in the miscellaneous papers relating to witchcraft in the Essex Institute.
10. *Modest Enquiry*, Burr, pp. 419–20.
11. Brattle, *Letter*, Burr, p. 173.
12. The Samuel Wardwell documents are in RSW, II, pp. 146–53.
13. Cotton Mather, *Diary*, ed. Worthington Chauncey Ford (Boston: 1911–1912), I, pp. 151–52. Mather also mentions this incident in his *Life of Sir William Phips* (Boston: 1697), later incorporated in the *Magnalia*.
14. This letter is printed in the *Massachusetts Historical Society Collections*, 4th series, VIII, pp. 391–97 and reprinted in Levin, pp. 106–10.
15. In his *Speech to the General Court* of 1645. Most anthologies of colonial writing reprint it.

7. THE DOOR IS OPENED

1. RSW, I, p. 84.
2. RSW, I, p. 257.
3. In his introduction to Hale, *Modest Enquiry*, Burr, p. 401.
4. Calef, *More Wonders*, Burr, pp. 350–52.
5. A son of the *Mayflower* John Alden.
6. Calef, *More Wonders*, Burr, pp. 353–54.
7. RSW, II, pp. 200–1.
8. From an anonymous account of the testimony gathered by Increase Mather in Salem on October 19, *Massachusetts Historical Society Collections*, 2nd series, vol. 3, pp. 223–24.
9. Brattle, Letter, Burr, pp. 180–81. Brattle, writing when public opinion was beginning to reverse itself, reported that the husbands had eventually penitently changed their minds. Later the wives repudiated their confessions and maintained that their relatives had urged them to confess only to save their lives. See Calef, *More Wonders*, Burr, pp. 374–75.

10. RSW, II, p. 208.
11. Phillips' testimony and that of his colleague, Mr. Payson, is in RSW, II, pp. 76–78.
12. RSW, I, p. 97.
13. RSW, II, pp. 203–5.
14. RSW, II, p. 22.
15. *More Wonders*, Burr, pp. 357–58.
16. RSW, I, pp. 115–16.
17. RSW, I, pp. 109–10.
18. RSW, II, p. 155.

8. WITCH HUNT

1. Upham is primarily responsible for ascribing the events at Salem to village quarrels, and Starkey for ascribing them to Puritan repressiveness.
2. *Wonders*, p. xiii.
3. 1 *Jacob*. Cap. 12.
4. Reprinted by William Frederick Poole in his edition of Thomas Hutchinson, *The Witchcraft Delusion of 1692* (Boston: 1870), p. 32.
5. Levin, pp. 110–11.
6. *More Wonders*, Burr, p. 304.
7. Brattle, *Letter*, Burr, p. 184.
8. Calef, *More Wonders*, Burr, p. 358.
9. *History*, vol. 2, p. 41, Hutchinson's second footnote. The tradition was still alive when Upham published in 1867. See Upham, II, p. 270.
10. Upham, II, p. 272.
11. Calef, *More Wonders*, Burr, pp. 358–60 is the source for quotations concerning Rebecca Nurse's trial except those otherwise noted.
12. RSW, I, p. 94.
13. Upham, II, p. 290.

9. THE WITCH HUNT DEBATED

1. Calef, *More Wonders*, Burr, pp. 362–64. Who signed this letter beside Procter is not known.
2. Burr, p. 363, note 3.
3. *News from Scotland*, reprinted with James I, *Daemonologie*, ed. G. B. Harrison. The Bodley Head Quartos, vol. 9 (London and New York: 1924), pp. 27–28.
4. Brattle's note, *Letter*, Burr, p. 181.
5. Increase Mather, *Cases of Conscience Concerning Evil Spirits Personating Men* (Boston: 1693), p. 32.
6. *Cases of Conscience*, Postscript, n. p.

7. Pike's letter is in Upham, II, pp. 538–44.
8. *Transactions of the Literary and Historical Society of Quebec,* II (1831), pp. 313–16.

10. CASES OF CONSCIENCE

1. Sewall, *Diary,* August 19, 1692.
2. That reputation was reflected in the testimony against her—several confessors "agreed that the Devil had promised her she should be Queen of Hell." See Cotton Mather, *Wonders,* Burr, p. 244.
3. Brattle, *Letter,* Burr, p. 177.
4. Calef, *More Wonders,* Burr, p. 364.
5. *More Wonders,* Burr, pp. 360–61.
6. The Reverend William Bentley, "A Description and History of Salem," *Massachusetts Historical Society Collections,* 1st series, VI, p. 268.
7. Hale, *Modest Enquiry,* Burr, p. 421.
8. Calef, *More Wonders,* Burr, pp. 365–66.
9. *More Wonders,* Burr, p. 369.
10. The documents relating to Mary Easty are in RSW, II, pp. 27–47.
11. Calef, *More Wonders,* Burr, pp. 368–69.
12. G. H. Moore, in his *Final Notes on Witchcraft in Massachusetts* (New York: 1885), pp. 39–59, argues that no property at all was sequestered. This is flatly wrong, but Moore's is the best exposition of the problem in spite of this major error.
13. The primary accounts of Andover witchcraft are by Brattle (*Letter,* Burr, pp. 180–82) and Calef (*More Wonders,* Burr, pp. 371–73).
14. The story is in Brattle, *Letter,* Burr, pp. 179–80. Mather's advice was not as parochial as it sounds; he was paraphrasing 2 Kings, i, 3.
15. Bulkeley, *Will and Doom, Connecticut Historical Society Collections,* III, pp. 233–34. It is there dated 1692, but the account of the Fairfield witchcraft trial cannot have been written before 1693 because it mentions the reprieve of May 12, 1693.
16. J. M. Taylor, *The Witchcraft Delusion in Colonial Connecticut* (New York: 1908), pp. 75–76.
17. Taylor, *Delusion,* pp. 77–78.
18. *Calendar of State Papers,* Colonial Series, vol. 14, p. 63.
19. Brattle's *Letter* is reprinted in Burr, pp. 169–90.
20. Dudley's questions and the answers of the Dutch and French clergymen are printed in the *Massachusetts Historical Society Proceedings,* 2nd series, I, pp. 348–58. Miller's answers, the first of them summarized, are in the *New York Historical Society Collections* for 1869, pp. 275–76.
21. Phips' two letters to England are in Burr, pp. 196–202.
22. Massachusetts Archives, vol. 135, no. 61.

23. An account of this visit, presumably from Brattle's papers, is printed in the *Massachusetts Historical Society Collections,* 2nd series, III, pp. 221–25.

11. MORE WONDERS OF THE INVISIBLE WORLD

1. In his *Life of Sir William Phips* (Boston: 1697), which later became a chapter in his *Magnalia.* Kenneth B. Murdock includes the life of Phips in his *Selections from Cotton Mather* (New York: 1926).
2. *Diary,* I, p. 151.
3. Upham, II, p. 488.
4. *More Wonders,* Burr, p. 379. Mather, in a conspicuous example of double-think, had written "I report matters not as an advocate but as an historian."
5. I have in mind especially Barrett Wendell, George Lyman Kittredge, Samuel Eliot Morison, Kenneth B. Murdock, and David Levin.
6. Cotton Mather tells Mercy Short's story in *Another Brand Plucked Out of the Burning,* Burr, pp. 259–86.
7. Gregory Zilboorg, in *The Medical Man and the Witch During the Renaissance* (Baltimore: 1935), p. 83, reports that Bloomingdale Hospital has a collection of radiographs of pathological swallowers "who for a long time before they reached the hospital successfully practiced the incorporation of numberless hairpins, teaspoons, thermometers, etc." The worst known case of compulsive swallowing is reported in the *Journal of the American Medical Association* for December, 1960: in the stomach of a single patient were found 258 items, including a 3-pound piece of metal, 26 keys, 3 sets of rosary beads, 16 religious medals, a bracelet, a necklace, 3 pairs of tweezers, 4 nail clippers, 39 nail files, 3 metal chains, and 88 assorted coins. Vomiting pins and other foreign objects was common in both European and American witchcraft cases, and is easily explicable as the result of compulsive swallowing.
8. *Archives of Dermatology,* vol. 90 (1964), p. 530.
9. For this information I am indebted to Dr. Ilse Noach-Hellman.
10. Mather's account of Margaret Rule's case is *Another Brand Plucked Out of the Burning,* printed by Calef in 1700 as the first part of *More Wonders.* It is in Burr, pp. 308–23.
11. These quotations on Mather's spectral appearance are from the *Diary,* I, pp. 178–79 rather than *Another Brand.*
12. *More Wonders,* Burr, pp. 337–38.

12. MAULING ONE ANOTHER IN THE DARK

1. Prefatory epistle to Hale, *Modest Enquiry*, Burr, p. 400.
2. Burr, pp. 186–87, n. 3.
3. See the letter from the Reverend William Bentley in the *Massachusetts Historical Society Collections*, 1st series, X, p. 65.
4. W. F. Poole suggested that "S." and "B." might mean Stoughton and Brattle, in the *North American Review*, CVIII, p. 390. But this is unlikely. Stoughton was the chief advocate of specter evidence, but Brattle was a less important opponent than Increase Mather, Cotton Mather, or Willard himself.
5. Willard's *Miscellany Observations* has been reprinted in the *Jahrbuch für Amerikastudien*, vol. 9, pp. 271–82.
6. *Diary*, I, pp. 171, 172.
7. Calef's account, Mather's letter of protest, and Calef's reply are in part II of *More Wonders*, Burr, pp. 324–41.
8. Obadiah Gill, et al, *Some Few Remarks upon a Scandalous Book* (Boston: 1701), p. 36.
9. There is one partial—but only partial—exception. That is W. F. Poole. In his excellent chapter on witchcraft in the *Memorial History of Boston* he is fully aware of Calef's animus and general lack of truthfulness. But he does not seem to have recognized the substance of Calef's lies, nor their manner, nor the pleasure Calef took in them. See his "Cotton Mather and Salem Witchcraft," *North American Review*, CVIII, pp. 379–81.
10. Whittier, *The Complete Poetical Works* (Boston and New York: 1894), p. 371.
11. *The Devil in Massachusetts* (New York: 1950), p. 254.
12. Richard Chamberlain, *Lithobolia*, Burr, p. 74.
13. In the preface to *The Truth Held Forth and Maintained* (New York: 1695), n. p.
14. Hale, *Modest Enquiry*, p. 156.
15. This and the following quotation are from p. 191 and p. 192 of *The Truth Held Forth*.
16. *New-England Persecutors*, p. 61. The following quotations are from p. 62.
17. Increase Mather, *Angelographia*, preface "To the Reader," n. p.
18. The first section, the only one written, is printed in the *Massachusetts Historical Society Proceedings*, vol. 47, pp. 240–68.
19. Burr, p. 306, n. 1.
20. Cotton Mather did publish his *Life of Phips* in 1697, in which he gives a brief account of the events at Salem. But there is little new in it, and it is far from being the thorough history Mather had once planned.

21. *Modest Enquiry*, Burr, p. 403.
22. *Modest Enquiry*, Burr, p. 427.
23. *Modest Enquiry*, Burr, p. 404.
24. *Modest Enquiry* (Boston: 1702), p. 80. Not in Burr.
25. *Modest Enquiry*, Burr, pp. 403–4.

13. THE GUILT OF INNOCENT BLOOD

1. *New England Historical and Genealogical Register*, XXVII, p. 55.
2. Kenneth B. Murdock, *Increase Mather* (Cambridge: 1926), pp. 315–16.
3. Phips' second letter to the home government (February 21, 1693), reprinted in Burr, pp. 198–202.
4. *Essex Institute Historical Collections*, IX (2nd series vol. I), part II, pp. 89–90.
5. Burr, p. 328, note 4. This note also includes a garbled quotation from the Queen's reply to Phips.
6. *Modest Enquiry*, Burr, p. 422.
7. Calef, *More Wonders*, Burr, pp. 385–86.
8. Mather's bill is in G. H. Moore, "Notes on the History of Witchcraft in Massachusetts," *American Antiquarian Society Proceedings*, new series II, part 1, pp. 174–76.
9. *Diary*, I, p. 216. The version of the rejected bill given in the *Diary* is significantly revised.
10. This often quoted statement is from Sewall's *Diary*. Burr reprints it on pp. 386–87, note 2, and Levin on p. 90.
11. Calef, *More Wonders*, Burr, pp. 387–88.
12. "Meditations for Peace" is in Upham II, pp. 547–49.
13. The Council's advice is in Upham, II, pp. 551–52.
14. Upham, II, pp. 497–98.
15. Upham, II, p. 507.
16. Upham, II, p. 510. Upham, with his characteristic malice and obtuseness, thinks she is wrongly though ignorantly shifting the blame onto Satan. "Satan had no share in it," he announces. "Human responsibility cannot be thus avoided." He forgets that the community in general, including members of the Nurse family, had decided that the girls had been deluded by Satan.
17. Reversal of Attainder, RSW, II, p. 217.
18. George H. Moore, *Final Notes on Witchcraft in Massachusetts* (New York: 1885) prints Goodwife Procter's petition on pp. 47–48.
19. Moore, "Notes . . ." (note 8), p. 183.
20. *Massachusetts Historical Society Collections*, 4th series, VIII, p. 646.
21. Upham, II, p. 478.
22. *Theopolis Americana* (Boston: 1710), pp. 29–30. The printed sermon is dedicated to Judge Sewall.

George Braziller, Inc.

ONE PARK AVENUE • NEW YORK, N.Y. 10016

We take pleasure in sending you for review:

WITCHCRAFT AT SALEM

by Chadwick Hansen

Pub Date: April 28, 1969

Price: $6.95

23. *New England Historical and Genealogical Register*, vol. 35, p. 253.
24. *Brief and True Narrative*, Burr, p. 159.
25. Moore, "Notes . . ." (note 8), pp. 184–85.
26. The most important documents relating to reversal of attainder and compensation are in RSW, II, pp. 216–50 and Moore, "Notes . . . ," pp. 182–92. Documents of the quarrel between Burroughs' widow and some of his children by a previous marriage are in RSW, II, pp. 236–40.
27. Levin, pp. 141–42.

14. A MATTER OF WARNING

1. *Modest Enquiry*, Burr, pp. 401–2.
2. A. Monroe Aurand, Jr., *An Account of the "Witch" Murder Trial* (Harrisburg, Pa.: 1929).
3. Representative opinions may be found in Georges Mongrédien, *Madame de Montespan et l'Affaire des Poisons* (Paris: 1953); Th. de Cauzons, *La Magie et la Sorcellerie en France* (Paris: n. d.), VIII, pp. 276–91; Charles Williams, *Witchcraft* (New York: 1959), pp. 263–75; and E. M. Butler, *Ritual Magic* (Cambridge, England: 1949), pp. 110–18.
4. Saint-Simon, *Memoirs* (New York: 1910), vol. 1, p. 466.

Selected Bibliography

The literature of Salem witchcraft is extensive, and the literature of witchcraft in general so voluminous as to require a bibliographical volume in itself. The following list has been rigorously selected, and it includes only the most important works mentioned in the text and in the notes.

Glanvill, Joseph, *Saducismus Triumphatus* (London, 1689; reprinted 1966 by Scholars' Facsimiles and Reprints).
   The best-known English defense of the orthodox view of witchcraft in the later seventeenth century, and therefore an important influence upon opinion at Salem. It contains many narratives of English cases which make for instructive comparisons with Salem.

Kittredge, George Lyman, *Witchcraft in Old and New England* (Cambridge, Mass., 1929).
   The title is somewhat misleading; only the last chapter deals with New England, and that chiefly to demonstrate that there was nothing very unusual about witchcraft trials in the seventeenth century. But this deserves to be considered the standard work on English witchcraft. Kittredge was a folklorist as well as a literary scholar, and his appreciation of the force of popular belief makes this book far more dependable than Notestein's *History of Witchcraft in England*.

Lea, Henry Charles, *Materials Toward a History of Witchcraft*, ed. Arthur C. Howland (Philadelphia, 1939). 3 volumes.
   A monument of scholarship, it consists of Lea's notes for what he intended to be a definitive history of witchcraft in Western civilization. Unfortunately Lea approached his materials from the point-of-view of a nineteenth-century rationalist; he never understood that there was a time when sane and intelligent men believed in witchcraft, and thus he ignored much of the most interesting evidence he encountered. Therefore the *Materials* is to be used only with extreme caution; so used, however, it is indispensable.

Murray, Margaret Alice, *The God of the Witches* (New York, 1952).
   Miss Murray was the anthropologist who first demonstrated that the Christian devil is a variation upon a pagan fertility god. This major achievement remains in spite of her credulity in regard to individual witchcraft cases.

Narratives of the Witchcraft Cases: 1648–1706, ed. George Lincoln Burr (New York, 1914; reprinted, 1959).

> This basic anthology includes the following works, or substantial excerpts from them: Deodat Lawson, *A Brief and True Narrative of Witchcraft at Salem Village*; John Hale, *A Modest Enquiry into the Nature of Witchcraft*; Cotton Mather, *Memorable Providences*, *The Wonders of the Invisible World*, and *A Brand Pluck'd Out of the Burning*; Robert Calef, *More Wonders of the Invisible World*; Thomas Brattle, "Letter"; and Governor Phips's two letters on witchcraft to the home government. I have not used Burr's texts, for the reasons explained in the preface. But because this anthology is so convenient and because Burr's notes are so very useful, in spite of his anti-Puritan bias, I have keyed my footnotes to this anthology wherever possible.

James Sprenger and Henry Kramer, *Malleus Maleficarum*, tr. Montague Summers (London, 1928).

> This fifteenth-century work by two German Dominicans was very nearly the definitive authority on witchcraft and witch trials for more than two centuries. It was known in seventeenth-century Massachusetts, although its influence there was chiefly indirect.

Records of Salem Witchcraft, printed for W. Elliot Woodward (Roxbury, Mass., 1864). 2 volumes.

> Less complete and less accurate than the WPA transcription. Printed in an edition of less than 300 copies, it is relatively rare. But since it is more readily available than the WPA transcription or the original documents I have keyed my footnotes to it wherever possible.

Summers, Montague, *The Geography of Witchcraft* (London, 1927).

> Summers was a believer in the occult, as credulous as Lea was skeptical. Extreme caution is therefore once more in order, but again the work, properly used, is indispensable.

What Happened in Salem? ed. David Levin (New York: 1960). 2nd edition.

> Includes selections from the trial documents (Woodward's transcription), contemporary narratives (several not included in Burr), and the two best fictional uses of Massachusetts witchcraft—Hawthorne's "Young Goodman Brown" and Esther Forbes's *A Mirror for Witches*. Designed as a research anthology for freshman English classes, this is necessarily far less ambitious than Burr, but within its limits it is extraordinarily well done.

Williams, Charles, *Witchcraft* (London, 1941).

> This is in my view the best single-volume introduction to witchcraft in Western civilization. There are many errors of fact, particularly in the chapter on Salem. But Williams is always imaginative and well balanced, a combination seldom found in the literature of witchcraft.

Works Progress Administration, *Salem Witchcraft 1692* (3 bound typescript volumes, 1938).

This most complete and most accurate transcription of trial documents and related legal documents is in the Essex County Court House at Salem.

Index